All civilisations, ancient and modern
In this fascinating account of one of
of humankind's march from preh
author considers the evidence for the
culture in various parts of the world and presents a balance
based on the archaeology, botany, genetics, ecology and anthropology of domesticates and their wild relatives. The basic agricultural
systems, which emerged from areas yielding traces of the earliest
plant and animal domestication, are described and their drastic
modification in recent times considered. In a concluding chapter
the present situation is reviewed, and the possible risk to a system
that now relies on a relatively small number of species to supply
the majority of our food is discussed.

WITHDRAWN

The living fields

The living fields
our agricultural heritage

JACK R. HARLAN

Professor Emeritus Plant Genetics,
Agronomy Department
University of Illinois

CAMBRIDGE
UNIVERSITY PRESS

PUBLISHED BY THE PRESS SYNDICATE OF THE UNIVERSITY OF CAMBRIDGE
The Pitt Building, Trumpington Street, Cambridge CB2 1RP, United Kingdom

CAMBRIDGE UNIVERSITY PRESS
The Edinburgh Building, Cambridge CB2 2RU, UK http://www/cup.cam.ac.uk
40 West 20th Street, New York, NY 10011-4211, USA http://www.cup.org
10 Stamford Road, Oakleigh, Melbourne 3166, Australia

First published 1995
First paperback edition 1998

Printed in the United Kingdom at the University Press, Cambridge

Typeset in Linotype Meridien 10½/13 [RO]

A catalogue record for this book is available from the British Library

Library of Congress Cataloguing in Publication data

Harlan, Jack R. (Jack Rodney)
 The living fields : our agricultural heritage / Jack R. Harlan.
  p. cm.
 Includes bibliographical references (p.   ) and index.
 ISBN 0 521 40112 7 (hardback)
  1. Agriculture – Origin. 2. Plants, Cultivated – History. 3. Crops – History.
  4. Traditional farming – History. 5. Plant remains (Archaeology) I. Title.
GN799.A4H37 1995
630'.9 – dc20 94-42948-CIP

ISBN 0 521 40112 7 hardback
ISBN 0 521 64992 7 paperback

for Jean, who made it all possible

Contents

Preface

All civilizations, from the earliest we know about down to our own, have evolved from an agricultural base. Producing food by deliberately raising plants and animals, instead of hunting wild animals and gathering plant foods from the local vegetation, brought about profound and fundamental changes in human cultural development and made our modern world possible.

This book deals with these basic changes and attempts to describe what we know, or think we know, about how they came about. It will try to set the scene in the times and places when and where we can detect the earliest traces of plant and animal domestication and the consequences that followed. I shall describe basic agricultural systems as they emerged from these early trials and how these systems have been drastically modified in recent times. Finally, I shall try to describe our existential situation, our utter dependence on a limited number of species for our food and current threats to their genetic resources.

Acknowledgments

I wish to acknowledge a deep debt to all my students. They have been essential in exploring the natural history of domesticated plants, especially cereals, other grasses and sesame. I also wish to express sincere gratitude for all the people around the world who have helped me along the way in my wanderings. They have provided transportation, hospitality and friendship. Doors have been generously opened everywhere in the some 80 countries I have visited. I have not been anywhere that I could not find kindly and helpful people. Thank you all.

CHAPTER ONE

Of pride and prejudice*

Agriculture as divine gift

We find the subject of agricultural origins in the most ancient literatures and the oldest oral traditions. It must have been a subject of
interest and speculation long before writing was developed. In the
classical mythologies of all civilizations, agriculture came as a divine
gift. A god or goddess came not only to instruct the ignorant in the
arts of farming and of agriculture but to enlighten them with respect
to law, religion, household arts and proper ways of living.

In the Mediterranean region, instruction came from a goddess, Isis
in Egypt, Demeter in Greece, Ceres in Rome. According to Diodorus
Siculus, agriculture originated in this way: five gods were born to
Jupiter and Juno, among them Osiris and Isis. Osiris married his sister,
Isis, and

> did many things of service to the social life of man. Osiris was the
> first, they record, to make mankind give up cannibalism; for after Isis
> had discovered the fruit of both wheat and barley which grew wild
> all over the land along with other plants but was still unknown to man,
> and Osiris had also devised the cultivation of these fruits, all men
> were glad to change their food, both because of the pleasing nature of
> the newly-discovered grains and because it seemed to their advantage
> to refrain from their butchery of one another. As proof of the discovery
> of these fruits they offer the following ancient custom which they still
> observe: even yet at harvest time the people make a dedication of the
> first heads of the grain to be cut, and standing beside the sheaf, beat
> themselves and call upon Isis, by this act rendering honor to the goddess
> for the fruits which she discovered at the season when she first did
> this. Moreover in some cities, during the festival of Isis as well, stalks
> of wheat and barley are carried among the other objects in the
> procession, as a memorial of what the goddess so ingeniously discovered
> at the beginning. Isis also established laws, they say, in accordance
> with which the people regularly dispense justice to one another and
> are led to refrain through fear of punishment from illegal violence

* From *Pride and Prejudice* by Jane Austen, 1813

and insolence; and it is for this reason also that the early Greeks gave Demeter the name Thesmophorus, that is lawgiver, acknowledging in this way that she had first established their laws.

Translation by C. H. Oldfather, 1946

It was Demeter who taught Tritolemous

. . . to yoke oxen and to till the soil and gave him the first grains to sow. In the rich plains about Eleusis he reaped the first harvest of grain ever grown, and there, too, he built the earliest threshing floor . . .
In a car given him by Demeter and drawn by winged dragons he flew from land to land scattering seed for the use of men . . . ?

Fox, 1916

Half a world away, we find a myth containing exactly the same elements: (a) people without agriculture are savages who live like animals and eat each other; (b) through some divine instruction they learn not only how to produce food but also to live by laws and to practice religion and those household arts common to civilized life.

From the Royal Commentaries of the Inca Garcilaso de la Vega (1961) we read:

Know then that, at one time, all the land you see about you was nothing but mountains and desolate cliffs. The people lived like wild beasts, with neither order nor religion, neither villages nor houses, neither fields nor clothing, for they had no knowledge of either wool or cotton. Brought together haphazardly in groups of two or three, they lived in grottoes and caves and like wild game, fed upon grass and roots, wild fruits and even human flesh. They covered their nakedness with the bark and leaves of trees, or with the skins of animals. Some even went unclothed. And as for women, they possessed none who were recognized as their very own.

Seeing the condition they were in, our father the Sun was ashamed for them, and he decided to send one of his sons and one of his daughters from heaven to earth, in order that they might teach men to adore him and acknowledge him as their god; to obey his laws and precepts as every reasonable creature must do; to build houses and assemble together in villages; to till the soil, sow the seed, raise animals, and enjoy the fruits of their labors like human beings.

The Inca king and queen arrived from heaven and were given a sign by which they would know where to establish a capital city. The place was located (Cuzco) and they set out to teach the savages 'how to live, how to clothe and feed themselves like men, stead of like animals.' The epic continues:

While peopling the city, our Inca taught the male Indians the tasks that were to be theirs, such as selecting seeds and tilling the soil. He taught them how to make hoes, how to irrigate their fields by means of canals that connected natural streams, and even to make these same shoes that we wear today. The queen, meanwhile, was teaching the women how to spin and weave wool and cotton, how to make clothing as well as other domestic tasks.

In short, our sovereigns, the Inca king, who was master of men, and Queen Coya, who was mistress of the women taught their subjects everything that had to do with human living.

Garcilaso de la Vega, 1961 edition

From cuneiform tablets, we learn that the source of agriculture for the Babylonians, Chaldeans and Phoenicians was a god named Oannes, who appeared to inhabitants of the Persian Gulf coast and instructed them on growing crops and raising animals (Fiore, 1965). According to Maurice (1795), 'He also taught man to associate in cities and to erect temples to the gods, he initiated them in the principles of legislation and the elements of geometry. He showed them how to practice botany and husbandry and he reformed and civilized the first rude and barbarous race of mortals.'

In Chinese mythology, P'an Ku separated the heavens and the earth, created the sun, moon and stars and produced plants and animals. There followed 12 celestial sovereigns, all brothers, who ruled 18 000 years each, then 11 terrestrial sovereigns, all brothers, who also ruled 18 000 years each. After that came nine human rulers, all brothers, who governed a total of 45 600 years. Among them was Shên-nung who taught the people agriculture and developed medicine. In another version, 16 rulers came after the nine and these were then followed by the 'Three Sovereigns', one of whom was Shên-nung. There are many variations of this particular theme (Latourette, 1941; Fitzgerald, 1950; Christie, 1983) including the following description of Shên-nung by the ancient historian Se-ma-Tsien (first century BC) Shên-nung, he said, had the body of a man and the head of an ox and his element was fire. He taught the people to use the hoe and the plow and initiated the sacrifice at the end of the year. He also found drug plants that cured and made a five-stringed lute (Chavannes, 1967).

The mythologies of the American Indians are enormously varied and complex, but here I shall present themes of only the Aztec and

Maya to compare with the Incan myth already cited. In the Aztec creation literature, Quetzalcoatl was described as

> god of the air, a divinity who during his residence on earth instructed the natives in the use of metals, in agriculture and in the arts of government. Under him, the earth teemed with fruits and flowers without the pains of culture. An ear of Indian corn was as much as a single man could carry. Cotton, as it grew, took on of its own accord, the rich dyes of human art. The air was filled with intoxicating perfumes and the sweet melody of birds. In short, these were the halcyon days which find a place in mythic systems of so many nations in the Old World. It was the *Golden Age* of Anahuac.
>
> *Prescot, 1936*

Interestingly enough both the Aztec and the Maya thought that maize was on earth before mortals. In the Aztecan story, Quetzalcoatl disguised himself as a black ant, stole the cereal from Tonacatepel and took it to Tamoachan for the benefit of the people. In the Mayan myth, the flesh of humans was actually formed out of maize meal and snake's blood (Recinos, 1947). It is little wonder that the maize plant is venerated to this day in Mexico and Guatemala. The Mayan epic also contains oblique references to a garden of Eden or Golden Age in which nature yielded abundantly of its own accord.

> In this manner they were filled with pleasure because they had discovered a lovely land full of delights, abundant in yellow ears and white ears (of maize) and also abundant in (two kinds of) cacao and innumerable fruits of mamey, chirimoya, jocote, nance, white zopote and honey. The foods of Paxil y Cayalá were abundant and delicious.
>
> *Popol Vuh pt.* III, *as reported in Recinos, 1947; my translation*

It is also of interest that the Australian Aborigines who did not practice agriculture had their own mythologies and creation stories in which gods taught the people how to gather foods. An elderly Aborigine woman recited this part of the creation legend as reported by Berndt and Berndt (1970):

> Ngalgulerg (a mythical woman) gave us women the digging stick and the basket we hang from our foreheads, and Gulubar Kangaroo gave men the spear-thrower. But that Snake that we call Gagag (Mother's mother) taught us how to dig for food and how to eat it, good foods and bitter foods.

In all the myths and tales about the origin of agriculture, knowledge is gratefully received as a blessing from the gods. There is one outstanding exception found in Genesis where agriculture comes as a curse.

> . . . cursed is the ground for thy sake; in sorrow shalt thou eat of it all the days of thy life; thorns also and thistles shall it bring forth to thee; and thou shalt eat the herb of the field; in the sweat of thy face shalt thou eat bread, till thou return unto the ground; for out of it wast thou taken: for dust thou art, and unto dust shalt thou return. (3: 17–19)
> And the Lord God said, Behold, the man is become as one of us, to know good and evil: and now, lest he put forth his hand, and take also of the tree of life, and eat, and live for ever: therefore the Lord God sent him forth from the garden of Eden, to till the ground from whence he was taken. (3: 22–23)
>
> *King James Version*

The elements of the traditional mythologies are:

1. There was a time before agriculture when people gathered their food from the wild.
2. Not farming is primitive, wild, uncivilized, lawless, graceless and brutish.
3. Nonfarmers did not farm because of ignorance or lack of intelligence.
4. A god or goddess was required to enlighten humans as to agricultural practices as well as laws, arts, religion and civilized behaviour.
5. Agricultural people knew themselves to be superior to hunter–gatherers.

Agriculture as discovery

It may be that the anthropologists, archaeologists, botanists, philosophers and others who deal with agricultural origins no longer believe that it came from divine revelation, but many have had faith in inspiration. A typically Victorian view was expressed by Charles Darwin:

> The savage inhabitants of each land, having found out by many and hard trials what plants were useful, or could be rendered useful by

various cooking processes, would after a time take the first step in cultivation by planting them near their usual abodes . . . The next step in cultivation, and this would require but little forethought, would be to sow the seeds of useful plants; and as the soil near the hovels of natives would often be in some degree manured, improved varieties would sooner or later arise. Or a wild and unusually good variety of a native plant might attract the attention of some wise old savage; and he would transplant it, or sow its seed.

Darwin, 1896

Darwin, among others, was convinced that nomadic people could not develop agriculture:

Nomadic habits, whether over wide plains or through the dense forests of the tropics or along the shores of the sea, have in every case been highly detrimental (to 'progress'). Whilst observing the barbarous inhabitants of Tierra del Fuego, it struck me that the possession of some property, a fixed abode, and the union of many families under a chief, were the indispensable requisites for civilisation. Such habits almost necessitate the cultivation of the ground; and the first steps in cultivation would probably result, as I have shewn elsewhere (above), from some such accident as the seeds of a fruit tree falling on a heap of refuse and producing an unusually fine variety.

Darwin, 1909

Darwin (1909) concluded, however, that 'the problem . . . of the first advance of savages towards civilization is at present much too difficult to be solved.' Genetics was not well developed in Darwin's time and he clearly felt that environment would modify heredity. It does, of course, but through selection of genes favoring fitness to the environment, not in the manner perceived by Darwin. At any rate the mind-set favored the Eureka! or 'lucky accident' school. Agriculture was the result of an idea, a concept that had to be discovered.

A pervasive and pernicious stereotype developed, based, in part, on traditional mythologies but essentially universal among agriculturalists. Europeans applied the term 'civilized tribes' to some eastern North American Indians who cultivated plants and lived in towns. But these same Indians referred to the hunting tribes of the plains as 'wild Indians.' In Africa, farming groups that surround hunter–gatherers 'did not merely assert their political dominance over the hunter–gatherers and ex-hunter–gatherers they encapsulated, they also treated them as inferiors, as people apart, stigmatized and discriminated against them' (Woodburn, 1988, p. 37). Similar attitudes prevail in Asia, Oceania and tropical America. The stereotype that developed includes the idea that hunting–gathering people were always on the verge of starvation and that the pursuit of food took so much of their time and energy that there was not enough of either one left over to build more 'advanced' cultures. Hunters were too nomadic to cultivate plants and too ignorant or unintelligent to understand the life cycles of plants. The idea of sowing and planting had never occurred to them and they lacked the intelligence to conceive of it. Hunters were concerned with animals and they had no interest in plants. In the stereotype that developed it was generally agreed that the life of the hunter–gatherer was 'nasty, brutish and short' and that any study of such people would only reveal that they lived like animals, were of low intelligence and were intellectually insensitive and incapable of 'improvement.'

Aspects of the traditional prejudice still show up in the literature and in current speculations on agricultural origins. One result is the concept that vegetative propagation of crop plants must be earlier than seed agriculture because it is easier to think of. It would not occur to the savage mind that seeds could be sown in order to produce useful plants. The savage had no concept of life cycles of plants and was ignorant of the modes of plant reproduction. Another corollary is the idea that agriculture is so unusual and the conception so difficult that the 'event' could only have occurred once or at most two or three times. Some diffusionists have even argued that the concept of agriculture must have diffused across the Pacific or Atlantic oceans thousands of years ago because the idea was too difficult for the American Indian to conceive. But agriculture is obviously so superior and so appealing that it would be accepted readily and gratefully. The idea would diffuse rapidly around the world even if new suites of cultivated plants had to be developed everywhere from the local flora. It also follows that a crop must have a center of origin because the process of domestication is so complex and difficult that domestication could only have occurred once for each species. Fortunately, these ideas are testable by archaeology, studies of patterns of diversity, genetics and by studies of surviving hunter–gatherers.

An alternative view: suppose we were not descended from tribes of idiots; suppose our ancestors had the same genes we do, the same intelligence and powers of observation; suppose plant-using hunter–gatherers knew all about life cycles of plants, about flowering, fruiting, seed germination and plant growth; suppose they were economic botanists with an extensive knowledge of plant lore; suppose agriculture began on a basis of knowledge and not ignorance; suppose we were willing to admit that hunting and gathering might be a viable alternative to farming, could we look at the problem more objectively? Let us take a closer look at the Victorian 'savage.'

While there have been some perceptive observers in the past, a general turning point in our thinking occurred when, in 1966, Richard B. Lee and Irwin DeVore organized a symposium on 'Man, the Hunter', held at the University of Chicago and published in 1968 (Lee and DeVore, 1968a). Lee reported on his studies of the San !Kung of the Dobe area of Botswana. Over a three week study period, Lee (1968) found that the !Kung Bushmen spent 2.3, 1.9 and 3.2 days of the first, second and third week respectively in subsistence activities. He wrote, 'In all, the adults in the Dobe camp worked about 2½ days a week. Since the average working day was about six hours long, the fact emerges that the !Kung Bushmen of Dobe, despite their harsh environment, devote from 12 to 19 hours a week in getting food.'

Among the Bushmen, neither children nor the aged are pressed into service. Children can help if they wish, but they are not expected to contribute regularly to the work force until they are married. The aged are respected for their knowledge, experience and legendary lore, and are cared for even when blind or lame and unable to contribute to the food gathering activities. Neither nonproductive children nor the aged are considered a burden.

Sahlins (1968) recorded almost identical figures for subsistence activities of the Australian Aborigines he studied and elaborated on his term 'original affluent society.' One can be affluent, he said, either by having a great deal or by not wanting much. If one is constantly on the move and must carry all one's possessions, one does not want much. The Aborigines also appeared to be well fed and healthy and enjoyed a great deal of leisure time.

Other reports at the symposium tended to support these general claims. A picture emerged of leisured, if not of affluent, societies, where the food supply was assured even under difficult environmental conditions and could be obtained from the natural productions with little effort. The picture described did seem to fit some sort of Golden Age or Garden of Eden.

The publication was a surprise to many who had some version of the hunter stereotype. The stimulation was enormous. There have been four international conferences on hunter–gatherers as a direct result, but not all were published. As of this writing, the last one was held in 1986 on the twentieth anniversary of the original symposium and published in 1988 (Ingold, Riches and Woodburn, 1988).

In addition one might cite Dahlburg (1981); Winterhalder and Smith (1981); Koyama and Thomas (1982); Williams and Hunn (1982); Price and Brown (1985); Harris and Hillman (1989) and such regional treatments as Hallam (1975); Silberbauer (1981); Riches (1982); Lee (1984); Akazawa and Aikens (1986); and there are many dozens, if not hundreds, of separate research papers. There is now a vast amount of new material on the subject, but some of the oldest papers are the most useful as observations were made before the hunter–gatherers were so restricted and encapsulated as they are now.

Understanding hunter–gatherers begins with the fact that there is enormous diversity among the many tribes and in their methods of exploiting the environment. To describe this diversity would require volumes. I shall, instead, select a few examples for illustration. Hunter-gatherers can, of course, be classified in various ways. A useful concept of *immediate return* and *delayed return* strategies was introduced by Woodburn (1988 and elsewhere). The Bushmen and Hadza are immediate return foragers. As we have seen, the Bushmen bands forage for a day or two, then stay in camp until the food is consumed, then forage again. The Hadza spend even less time assembling food, in part because they scavenge. They watch the sky for gatherings of vultures in their range, usually a sign of a lion kill. They follow the column of circling birds to the kill site, drive off the lions and help themselves to whatever pieces of freshly killed meat they choose. Needless to say this requires some understanding of lion behaviour. According to studies by O'Connell *et al.* (1988), 15–20% of total animal food obtained by Hadza comes from scavenging and that mostly from lion kills. In immediate return systems people live from hand to mouth, which may appear to be precarious, but they may be perfectly sure the food is always there for the taking.

Delayed return strategies have longer term goals that include: manufacture of boats, weirs, nets, traps and deadfalls; tending bee hives; capture and keeping of animals to be eaten later; managing vegetation with fire; water spreading; irrigation; flooding of forests;

sowing seeds for later harvest; arranged marriages, etc. Delayed return strategists are much closer to agriculturalists than they are to immediate return foragers. There are, as expected, intermediate states and conditions. Many of the Australian Aboriginal tribes were delayed return strategists of great skill.

At the time of European contact, the continent of Australia was inhabited by some 300 000 Aborigines living by hunting, gathering, fishing and shell fishing. They did not exploit any domesticated plants or animals and no true agriculture was practiced. They had however evolved complex delayed return food-procurement systems requiring high levels of skill in managing the flora and fauna and an extensive knowledge of the plants and animals they comprised.

Kangaroo Island lies some 35 km off the coast of southern Australia. It was once inhabited by Aborigines but they either left or died out well before European contact. Presumably it was cut off rather late from the mainland by rising seas. At the time of contact, the woody vegetation had thickened up to form thickets almost impossible to penetrate, while the vegetation on the adjacent mainland, with the same climate and species composition, was covered with an open woodland of well-spaced trees with grasses and other herbaceous vegetation in between. The contrast was quickly noted by Europeans, who could ride horses or drive wagons freely through the mainland countryside, but had to cut their way through Kangaroo Island. It was obvious that the Aborigines had put their stamp on the mainland vegetation. Australians have been entranced and intrigued ever since by the extent of vegetation management by the Aborigines and the skill with which it was practiced. Rhys Jones (1969) has called it 'firestick farming' and Douglas Yen (1989) 'aboriginal agronomy'. The Aborigines had effectively domesticated the landscape but not the plants or animals. Europeans have tended to reduce burning and put out fires once they have started; the results have not always been happy.

The question of burning has recently come up in respect to management of a national park in northern Australia. Should the park rangers burn like Aborigines or prevent fires like Europeans? In a discussion between park rangers and an Aborigine, the subject of a recent (1984) fire in southern Australia, in which 72 people were killed and many millions of dollars of property damage was inflicted, was broached. The Aborigine told the rangers that it was a shame that people lost their lives, but it was a crime to let the country get so 'dirty.' People should look after their country and keep it 'clean.' Such a fire would not have occurred if the Aborigines had been in control. To underline the point, the Aborigine took out a folder of matches, lit the whole lot and casually tossed the fire into some dry grass. He then got into his pickup and drove off leaving the fire to burn. Before the startled rangers could mobilize, the fire had died out of its own accord. Now that is fire control! Fire is the best defense against fire, but it must be used wisely, skillfully and with experience. The rangers are willing to burn but they do not know how (Lewis, 1989).

Over much of Australia if an area is not managed by fire for some years, the woody vegetation thickens up and Aborigines find the area spiritually unsafe (Chase, 1989). To them, it becomes full of evil and malevolent spirits and should be avoided if possible. The concept of safe and malevolent space is prevalent among hunter–gatherers and traditional farmers around the world and shall be discussed in more detail later.

The Aborigines did more than burn. They diverted water to flood forests in the dry season. 'We like to see plenty water in the jungle all the time, for birds of all kinds gather near it and the food plants that we like grow better' (Campbell, 1965). They constructed water spreading devices for the rainy season (Lourandos, 1980) and they ditched to increase the supply of eels and other fish (Walters, 1989). In the course of digging up wild root crops, they churned up huge areas with digging sticks to the point they resembled plowed fields. Sir George Grey wrote (1841): 'In the province of Victoria . . . I have seen tracts of land several square miles in extent so thickly studded with holes where the natives had been digging up yams (*Dioscorea*) that it was difficult to walk across it.'

Native Australians made considerable use of calendar plants. Some common grasses gave them signals, e.g. when grains of *Chrysopogon setifolius* are ripe, it is time to dig yams or when grains of *Heteropogon triticerus* start to shatter, it is time to dig yams, and when all the grains have fallen, it is time to stop. When *Heteropogon contortus* begins to flower, the rainy season will soon be over, and so on. The reason for being particular about timing the yam harvest is as follows: the yams belong to the genus *Dioscorea*. It is a large pantropical genus of 600 species or more and yams are harvested or cultivated on at least five continents and many Pacific islands. Some of the tropical forest yams are perennial and woody and not suitable for food. The ones that are utilized tend to be savanna species adapted to long dry seasons, and the tubers behave as annuals. At the end of the rains, tubers are formed below ground and grow very rapidly. Most of the metabolites in the vine are mobilized and pour down into the tuber. The vine then may go dormant as the vegetation turns brown and they can be subject to both drought and natural or man-set fires. However, the tubers are safe below ground. When the rains begin again, the tubers sprout and vines grow very quickly. The process is reversed and metabolites are rushed upward into the vine, in effect emptying out the tuber. Thus, the time of digging yams is critical. If dug too soon, the tuber is immature and will not recover from damage; if dug too late, there will be loss to vine growth. But the end of the digging season can be determined by the rains and vine growth; digging too soon is the main hazard and calendar plants can be very helpful.

Management of vegetation requires an understanding of local ecology, but did the Aborigines understand life cycles of plants? Did they know that flowers lead to seeds and that seeds can be grown to produce more plants? Is this something that must be learned or discovered in order to commence the domestication of plants or is this a part of the general botanical knowledge of gathering peoples?

An early observation by Sir George Grey (1841) is revealing:

> The natives have, however, a law that no plant bearing seeds is to be dug up after it has flowered; they then call them (for example) the mother of Bohn, the mother of Mud-ja (*Haemadorum* spp.), etc.; and so strict are they in their observance of this rule that I have never seen a native violate it unless requested by an European, and even then they betray a great dislike to do so.

Confirmation of understanding of plant reproduction comes from Gregory (1886):

> The natives on the West Coast of Australia are in the habit amongst other things of digging up yams as a portion of their means of subsistence; the yams are called 'ajuca' in the north and 'wirang' in the south. In digging up these yams they invariably reinsert the head of the yams so as to be sure of a future crop, but beyond this they do absolutely nothing which may be regarded as a tentative in the direction of cultivating plants for their use

The practice of replacing the head of the yam after digging was widespread among hunter–gatherers. Some Aborigines would scold a yam, no matter how large, perhaps even beat it, replace the head and tell it to do better next time.

To the Andamanese, the goddess Puluga symbolizes the southwest monsoon that brings violent winds and rains from April to October. 'Puluga owned all the wild yams and cicada grubs that the people ate, and all the beeswax that they used in hafting, calking, and cordage. Women who dug yams had to replace the tops to fool Puluga . . .' (Coon, 1971). Indeed, if Puluga caught the people misusing her property she would get angry and send bad weather. Here we see the practice of planting reinforced by a religious belief.

There were many similarities between adaptations adopted by the Aborigines and those of the Great Basin Indians of North America. The Indians were faced with a semiarid to arid environment as were many of the Aborigines in their tribal lands. The Paiute of Owens Valley, California, also diverted water. Using small earth dams and ditches, they irrigated fairly extensive tracts. One block covered 5 km^2 and another about 13 km^2. The water spreading was primarily to ensure an increased production of native wild food plants such as *Salvia, Chenopodium, Helianthus, Oryzopsis* and *Eleocharis* as well as a local species of tobacco (*Nicotiana*). But they also sowed seeds to thicken up stands. None of the plants was domesticated (Steward, 1934).

Planting seeds was not uncommon among American Indian hunter–gatherers. Seven of 19 groups studied by Steward in Nevada sowed seeds of wild plants. The most frequently mentioned were *Chenopodium, Oryzopsis, Mentzelia* and *Sophia*. No tillage was practiced. The usual procedure was to burn a patch of vegetation in the fall and sow the seeds in the following spring.

Klimek (1935) recorded 11 tribes of California Indians that grew a local species of tobacco but no other crop. Some tribes in Oregon, Washington and British Columbia followed the same practice (Drucker, 1963). The tobacco was usually either *Nicotiana attenuata* or *Nicotiana bigelovii*. Harrington (1932) made a very detailed study of tobacco among the Karuk and found the extent of botanical knowledge remarkable. The Karuk burned logs in the forest and sowed seeds in the ashes. A tobacco garden was called 'to plant' or more literally 'to put seed.' The Karuk had terms for cultivated tobacco, wild tobacco, roots, stems, bark, leaves, branches, leaf branches, pith, gum, flowers, buds, seed pods, flower stem, clusters of flowers, sepals

and calyx. No standard word was used for petal but descriptive terms
were used: for example, the white-flowered *N. bigelovii* was said to
have 'five white ones sticking out.' The stamens and pistil were
described as 'sticking out in the middle of every flower where the
seeds are going to be.' Stamens are 'flower whiskers,' 'flower threads'
or 'flower hairs.' Pollen is 'flower dust'. Nine stages of flowering to
seed setting were recognized with descriptive terms. There was a classification of seeds, grains, seeds in the midst of a fruit (pit), seeds inside
a shell (nut), etc.

The translation of an informant's description of germinating tobacco
seed is botanically accurate and detailed.

> Its seeds fall to the ground; the dirt gets over them. Then after awhile
> when it gets rained on, the seed sprouts. Sometimes all the seeds do
> not grow up. They say sometimes some of the seeds get rotten. Its
> sprouts are small white ones, pretty near the size of a hair, whenever
> it is just peeping out, its seed is on top of it; then they just have two
> leaves when they first peep out of the ground. They grow quickly when
> they grow; in a little while, they are tall ones.

The Karuk fertilized with ashes, sowed, weeded, harvested, selected
for strength, cured, stored and sold tobacco but grew no other crop.
Clearly the concept of planting seeds was in no way revolutionary
and did not lead to food production.

It should be noted that tobacco is not the easiest crop to grow. The
seeds are very small and the seedlings delicate. The 'rotten' seeds
referred to by the Indian informant is what we call 'damping off'
and is always a serious problem in tobacco culture. Sowing in
ashes provided a sterile medium that probably helped control the
disease.

Tobacco was used by western North American Indians not so much
for recreation as for religious ceremony, and it was smoked in special
pipes on special occasions. It could have simply been harvested from
the wild, but these Indians were afraid of wild tobacco as it might
have sprouted on the grave of someone with malevolent power and
be spiritually dangerous. Death, disease, even injury or bad luck were
perceived as being governed by spirits. They therefore grew their ceremonial tobacco in what was perceived as safe space. It is easy to see
how such perceptions might lead to gardening and could be readily
extended to food crops. The west coast Indians did not follow this
practice and it is obvious that the concept of planting seed does not

necessarily lead to a change in the food procurement system.

With botanical lore of this calibre, it becomes absurd to suggest that the idea of planting seeds had to be taught, discovered or diffused. Hunter–gatherers were, and are, real professional botanists who knew more about plants and plant reproduction than most of our modern urban 'educated' population. There was no need to pass from vegetative propagation to seed agriculture. If the hunter–gatherers chose to grow a plant from seed, they would do so and no new knowledge was required. No information had to be diffused; no god or goddess (instructor) was required. Hunter–gatherers knew all they needed to know to take up agriculture at any time and, within ecologically suitable limits, at any place they chose. The 'wise old savage' was wiser than Darwin thought. A logical outcome would be many and diffuse origins of agriculture, not one or a few centers of origin. If this is the case, archaeological, botanical and anthropological evidence should be found to support it; the concept is testable.

On the Japanese islands, a remarkable hunting–gathering culture evolved called Jomon. The people settled in villages; those near the sea exploited marine resources heavily; those inland depended in part on game animals and fresh water fish. The Jomon people produced some of the earliest known pottery. Traces of it can be found dating to some 10 000 years ago, although it is crude and fragile. With time, however, these crude beginnings evolved into pottery with a flair and great artistic merit. The population became very dense for hunting–gathering societies; the distribution of the villages averaged about 7 km apart on the southern islands. Apparently, natural food resources were rather fully exploited because, in mid-Jomon times, the people began to exploit the horse chestnut, *Aeschylus*, on a large scale and the populations increased noticeably as a result. The horse chestnut is poisonous and must be processed by appropriate leaching techniques before it can be safely consumed. Considerable quantities of horse chestnut shells have shown up in archaeological sites in particular geographic regions. Horse chestnuts are still harvested from wild trees today in precisely the same regions (Akazawa and Aikens, 1986).

Jomon culture flourished and evolved over some eight millennia and became one of the most sophisticated of all known hunting–gathering cultures. The culture collapsed rather quickly when agricultural people, called Yayoi, arrived from the mainland about AD 300.

The Yayoi introduced rice farming to the southern islands and brought other crops as well. There is some indication that Jomon people may have been experimenting with the cultivation of foxtail millet and buckwheat before the arrival of the Yayoi, but there is no evidence of a fully developed agricultural system. It has been suggested that the aboriginal Ainu are survivors of the Jomon people (Aikens and Higuchi, 1982).

Across the Pacific, along the coasts of North America, other advanced hunting–gathering cultures had evolved by the time of European contact. They, too, lived in villages from northern California to southern Alaska and found aquatic resources abundant and easily exploited. The yearly salmon run provided a great source of nourishment in season, and dried fish could be used over much of the year. Some tribes developed such seaworthy canoes that they actually went whaling. Whales not only provided food and oil but figured largely in art, religion and folk lore. These people did not make pottery but developed wood and ivory carving into a high art. Totem poles, masks, wooden bowls, ivory amulets, spirit figures and other ceremonial objects were made with great skill and artistry. They also made elegant baskets, bark boxes and wooden containers prized today by art collectors.

The Pacific 'cedar' (*Thuja plicata*) has such straight grain that it can be rather easily split into planks. A notch is cut with stone axes at an appropriate height and a horizontal incision made to start the process. Ropes are then attached to the upper end of the plank-to-be and as many people as possible pull on the ropes. The wood splits neatly and easily, yielding a plank of near uniform thickness. Planks were used to build houses and buildings for ritual and social uses. The Modoc tribe of the northern California–southern Oregon region foraged in the interior away from the ocean and were not fully sedentary. They maintained a scheduled round of nomadic movements in order to exploit resources in season. They used plank houses in winter camp that were dismantled and carefully stacked each spring when they moved to summer quarters. The houses were reassembled on their return in late fall or early winter (Ray, 1963).

Californian Indians also developed a population density high for hunter–gatherers. Baumhoff (1963) presented some estimates that suggest a density of 0.4 to 2.0 per km² over most of California with local areas over 4.4 per km². This is a greater density than that of agricultural Pueblo Indians of the upper Rio Grande, estimated at about 2.8 per km². Baumhoff concluded that there were about 350 000 people in California living on acorn–fish and acorn–game diets at the time of European contact. Salmon are not the only migratory fish along the west coast; steelhead (*Salmo gairdnerii*) and Dolly Varden trout (*Salvelinus malma*) also go upstream to spawn and can be harvested easily in great quantities. The oak woodlands produced enormous yields of acorns. These contain tannins, which must be leached before consumption, but food was generally abundant and easily obtained.

A number of tribes in the Pacific northwest kept slaves. These were captured from neighboring tribes in raids, purchased, received as gifts in potlatch ceremonies or sometimes generated by voluntary servitude to settle debts. During the extravagant potlatches of the nineteenth century, slaves were sometimes killed as a show of wealth. These tribes in particular were rather sedentary and had such surpluses of goods and commodities that they were distributed freely or simply destroyed. These and the Jomon of Japan appeared to have had the most luxurious of hunter-gatherer economies.

Another class of advanced hunter–gatherers included tribes specialized in particular animal resources. Bison hunters of the North American Great Plains might be taken as one model. This is probably a tradition surviving from late Pleistocene hunters, many of whom died out with the large game animals they preyed on. Castenada, a member of the party led by Francisco Vazquez de Coronado into the Great Plains in 1541 made these observations on a group of bison hunting Indians:

> These Indians subsist . . . entirely on cattle (bison) for they neither plant nor harvest maize. With the skins they build their houses, with the skins they clothe and shoe themselves, from the skins they make ropes and obtain wool. From the sinews they make thread with which to sew their clothing and likewise their tents. From the bones, they shape awls and the dung they use as firewood since there is no other fuel in all that land. The bladders serve as jugs and drinking vessels; they sustain themselves on the flesh of the animals, eating it slightly roasted . . . and sometimes uncooked. Taking it in their teeth, they pull with one hand; with the other they hold a large flint knife and cut off mouthfuls, swallowing it half chewed like birds. They eat raw fat without warming it and drink the blood just as it comes from the cattle . . . they have no other food.
> They dry their meat in the sun, cutting it into thin slices and when

it is dry, they grind it like flour for storage and for making mash to eat. They cook it in a pot which they always manage to have with them; when they put a handful in the pot, the mash soon fills it since it swells to a great size.

Hammond and Rey, 1940, pp. 310–11

They used intestines to carry blood for later drinking and opened the paunch of the bison to squeeze the juice out of the grass and they drank the liquid.

The so-called mammoth hunters of the great Russian plain also might have been specialists. They built houses out of mammoth bones and tusks. One house is recorded as having 95 skulls in the foundation. It may be, however, that they simply found it convenient to gather bones and tusks from animals that died of natural causes. This was the time when mammoths and many other genera of the Pleistocene fauna became extinct. Evidence of actual hunting is very slim.

But if planting seeds does not necessarily lead to agriculture, why do some hunter–gatherers opt to take up farming and others do not? What would induce the first farmers to take it up? Needless to say, these questions have been a subject of long and sometimes lively debate. I shall treat briefly some of the more influential students of the problem.

Agriculture for religious reasons

About the turn of the century, Edouard Hahn (1896, 1909) proposed that domestication might have started for religious reasons. The model he chose was aurochs or wild cattle; they were large, fierce and dangerous. Hahn argued that no one could have predicted the utility of the animal for work and milk until after it had been tamed. It had, of course, been hunted for millennia in Europe, Asia and Africa for meat and hides. The aurochs had crescent-shaped horns and Hahn suggested that the initial steps in domestication were taken to provide animals for sacrifice in lunar cultic rites, there being a symbolic relation between the curved horns and the crescent moon. In his time, most people held the view that human beings developed toward civilization first as a hunter, then as a nomadic herder of animals and then as a plant cultivator. The initial steps towards agriculture therefore began with animal domestication.

Bull painted on the wall of the Lascaux caves, France about
14 000 years ago.

The idea has not received much attention in recent years, but
religious motives can be very strong and the concept deserves fair
consideration. We do know that people in Europe, Asia and Africa
have long held special feelings about cattle. The hall of bulls in Lascaux, the famous caves with Ice Age art, seems clearly to have religious
significance. Çatal Hüyük, in Turkey, an early Neolithic ceremonial
center featured bulls in something like 50 different shrines at different
levels. Most had bucrania, that is racks of horned bull skulls, with
more skulls attached to walls over altars, painted bulls and bulls
molded in clay. In Knossos, Crete, bull vaulting scenes, showing fine
detail and artistic sense, were painted on palace walls.

Cattle were sacred to the ancient Egyptians and sacrificed by the
Hebrews and Romans. To this day there is a 'bull belt' stretching from
Iberia, where bulls are publicly and ceremoniously slaughtered in the
corrida, usually on Sundays, to India, where naked Sadhus lead riots
in support of antislaughter laws to protect cattle. In Assam and Burma,
the mithan (*Bos frontalis*) is raised purely for ceremonial or barter
purposes. The cattle are not penned or herded but allowed to run in

fields and forests. They are individually owned, not used for work or milk, and the meat is consumed only after sacrifice of the animal. Horns of bulls are used to decorate graves and temples. The animals themselves are considered valuable and can be used to pay debts, ransoms, bride prices, etc. Farther east, the sacrificial animal of choice becomes the water buffalo, *Bos indicus,* and the practice is carried on across most of Indonesia.

Other animals are sacrificed, of course, and one could well imagine that sheep, goats, pigs and others were brought into the domestic fold to supply specimens for the purpose. In parts of Asia, chickens are raised, not for eggs and meat, but for divination by examination of entrails and for cockfighting. The fact that some South American Indians also raise chickens but do not eat flesh or eggs led Carter (1971), among others, to speculate on pre-Columbian contacts across the Pacific. But, Nordenskiöld (1922) had pointed out long before that a number of tribes had taken to raising white chickens for their feathers that could be dyed any color they chose. Raising birds for feathers, songs or as pets is widespread; it is not necessary to eat them.

Some plants have been nominated as examples of religiously motivated domestications. A good case can be made for the grain amaranths, especially *Amaranthus hypochondriacus* of Mexico and southwest USA. The blood red inflorescences are themselves suggestive of sacrifice and the plant was used in the rites of human sacrifice by the Aztecs and other Indians. Popped seeds were consumed with human blood by the priests in solemn communion. It was grown as a ceremonial plant from the valley of Mexico to the cliff dwellers of the American southwest. I have seen the brilliant red inflorescences hung over doorways of homes in the Himalayas as spiritual protection. The Mexican marigold (*Tagaetes*) has also become a holy flower in India.

There is a large class of ritual, ceremonial and mind-bending plants used by shamans to communicate with other worlds, but in general there is a preference for gathering these in the wild. Peyote (*Lophophora williamsii*), *Datura, Virola, Banisteriopsis* and many dozens of mushrooms are harvested from local floras. A few have been taken into the domestic fold and cultivated. Among the most familiar are tobacco, coffee, tea, kava kava, chat, opium poppy and coca. As cultigens, they are probably rather late and it seems an unlikely set of plants to lead a charge into agriculture.

Agriculture by crowding

In early decades of this century, V. Gordon Childe came forward with what came to be called 'The Propinquity Theory.' He was a social-minded historian and prehistorian, who was impressed by evidence of desiccation in the Near East during the millennia before agriculture was thought to have begun. He reasoned that both game animals and hunters would have had to retreat to sites near the few permanent oases and rivers remaining. This would have brought animals and humans into closer proximity and eventually resulted in domestication. He was still thinking in terms of the hunter, herder, farmer sequence. The theory did not bring overwhelming support but had the advantage that it was, to a degree, testable by archaeological methods. This will be taken up later. Childe also introduced the concept of a 'Neolithic Revolution.' The change from food gathering to food production was seen as the most revolutionary development since the discovery and use of fire. This was a watershed that led mankind on toward civilization. He thought of it as a sort of 'event' that required only a short time and that spread quickly, a true revolution in human living (Childe, 1925, 1952).

Agriculture by fisherfolk

In 1952, Carl O. Sauer published a very influential book, *Agricultural Origins and Dispersals*. He was a geographer at the University of California, Berkeley, and trained many first class geographers so that his influence was widely felt. Sauer attempted to reason out the most likely region for the beginnings of agriculture. First of all he agreed with Darwin and others that the first farmers had to be sedentary. They not only had to be sedentary but had to be living comfortably, so they would have the leisure and security necessary for the long, slow processes of domestication. Agriculture, he argued, could not have originated under conditions of chronic famine when all time and attention had to be given to food procurement. Second, the region should be biologically diverse with a variety of habitats and a rich assortment of plants and animals. Third, he pointed out that agriculture could not have originated in large river valleys subject to lengthy and uncontrollable floods, where large public works would be needed to dam, dike and somehow control the waters. Fourth, agriculture must have started in wooded lands. Primitive cultivators could easily open new spaces for cultivation by deadening trees, but could not break the heavy sod of grasslands. The sedentary life, he thought, could best be developed by fishing tribes and he sought them in fresh water habitats in a mild climate. Fresh water was selected because, Sauer said, seashore vegetation had contributed relatively little to agriculture.

With these presuppositions in mind, he selected Southeast Asia as the most likely center of agricultural origins. From there it spread northward to China, westward to India and the Near East, Europe and Africa. If agriculture originated independently in the New World, a most likely place would have been under similar conditions in northwest South America. From there it would have spread through Central America to Mexico, down the Andes and east to the Atlantic coast of Brazil and the Caribbean Islands. He left open the possibility of diffusion from the Old World to the New World. He had chosen Southeast Asia as the primary path because anthropologists at the time thought agriculture older in the Old World than in the New.

Edgar Anderson liked the Sauer idea of sedentary fisherfolk and added some genetic threads to the fabric. Anderson was Curator of Useful Plants at the Missouri Botanical Gardens and well known for his theories on genetic introgression among taxa. He espoused the 'Dump-Heap' theory, rather like the Darwinian view but added some ideas about introgression.

> Rivers are weed breeders. So is man. And many of the plants which follow us about have the look of belonging originally on gravel bars or mud banks. If we now reconsider the kitchen middens of our sedentary fisherfolk, it seems that they would be a natural place where some of the aggressive plants might find a home, where seeds and fruits brought back from up the hill or down the river might sometimes sprout and to which more rarely would be brought seeds from across the lake or from another island. Species which have never intermingled might do so there and the open habitat of the rubbish heap would be a more likely niche in which strange new mongrels could survive than any which had been there before man came along.
>
> *Anderson, 1954*

He also thought agriculture was begun in the tropics by sedentary fisherfolk and that most crops were derived from weedy progenitors.

He left open the question of transfer of agriculture from the Old World to the New or vice versa but was convinced of pre-Columbian contacts across the oceans.

Agriculture by stress

Some anthropologists believe that people were forced into agriculture by stress brought on by rising populations and depleted resources in the foraging range. This is a position opposite to that of Sauer (1952). The chief proponent of this view is Mark N. Cohen, who published a book, *Food Crisis in Prehistory* (1977), and has vigorously pursued his argument in many other papers and articles. His research in coastal Peru suggested that, over time, there was a shift from preferred foods to less preferred ones and that the food sources tended to come from progressively greater distances from the sites excavated. He found evidence that this was not unique to coastal Peru and maintained that it was a general phenomenon. The concept is to some degree testable by methods of physical anthropology. Dietary stress leaves marks on the bones and teeth. A study of skeletons, especially long bones, skulls and teeth can reveal much about diet and health. Cohen and G. T. Armelagos organized a symposium on the subject, inviting anthropologists who had studied human remains in various parts of the world at about the time agriculture evolved in each area (Cohen and Armelagos, 1984). The published work gives some fascinating glimpses into the health status of people of the epipalaeolithic and early Neolithic cultures. The results did not indicate a general decline in health before adoption of agriculture, but there was a universal agreement that the diet and health status of early farmers was not as good as that of hunter–gatherers that preceded them.

Surviving hunter–gatherers regulate the population well below the carrying capacity of the foraging range so how could stress evolve that would force people into agriculture? The question does not bother Cohen. Surviving hunter–gatherers, he argues, do not represent the original cultures before agriculture. They are peripheral to the main stream of cultural evolution and are largely found where agriculture is unrewarding as in the Arctic, the deserts of Australia and southern Africa or tropical rain forests where farming is difficult. The hunter–gatherers who could regulate their populations survived, those who could not became farmers. The argument is a good one and difficult to refute.

In 1965 Esther Boserup of Denmark published an influential work entitled *The Conditions of Agricultural Growth*. She assembled data on energy yield per amount of energy expended and showed that, as a general rule, increasing the energy put into a system resulted in low-ered returns of energy per energy input. Her work stimulated many studies along similar lines. The most influential studies in the USA were done by David Pimentel and his coworkers at Cornell University. Much of this work is reviewed by Pimentel and Hall (1989). The most efficient systems use human labor only. For cassava production in Zaire and Tonga, returns in kcal per kcal (1 kcal = 4.184 kJ) invested were 37.5 and 26.9 respectively. For sorghum in Sudan and maize in Mexico returns were 14.1 and 10.1 respectively. Using draft animals, the returns were 3.3 for rice in the Philippines, 3.4 for maize in Mexico, −0.5 for wheat in India and −0.1 for sorghum in Nigeria. For high mechanization, the figures for USA are about 2.5 for maize, 1.4 for rice, 1.8 for wheat and 2.3 for potato (Pimentel, 1974).

Figures for hunter–gatherers are rather sparse but suggest that returns are at least as good as or perhaps better than the most efficient farming systems. I once made a study in Turkey to see how much wild wheat I could harvest, by hand in one hour, using a flint bladed sickle, like those used in the Neolithic, and also a modern steel sickle. The flint blades worked about as well as the steel one, but became dull more quickly. The yields were good, nearly 1 kg of clean grain per hour. Evans (1975) calculated that the returns in kcal per kcal expended was about 50, more efficient than any known agricultural system. This may have been a special case, however, since Ladizinsky (1975) attempted similar harvests in the upper Jordan Valley, where wild wheats are abundant, and got only a quarter of the yields per hour that I obtained. His stands were very patchy compared to the one I harvested near Viranshehir, Turkey. Studies from Australia indicate that gathering is easy and can be efficient, but in any case the time spent is negligible compared to the time required to process the seeds for consumption. Tubers generally yield more kcal per hour of labor than do seeds. On the whole, energy efficiency studies tend to confirm the Biblical version of agriculture as a curse rather than a blessing and something to be avoided if possible. Agriculture is not likely to be welcomed with open arms by hunter–gatherers with a stable, comfortable food-procurement system. Some sort of imbalance would seem to be necessary to induce people to take it up.

Lewis Binford (1968) and Kent Flannery (1986) suggested that such an imbalance might come about after initial post-Pleistocene adjustments had been made. In many parts of the world the first adjustment was towards a watery environment. The glaciers were melting, sea levels rising and drowning coasts and coastal valleys. A substantial percentage of the fauna became extinct and floras were migrating across whole continents. These were very dynamic times and people had to adapt to new conditions. They learned about rafts, canoes and water transport of various kinds; they began to craft smaller, finer and more efficient tools and weapons; they invented harpoons, fishhooks, weirs, nets and fish traps; they were forced to change hunting habits as traditional game animals became extinct. There must have been changes too in plant food resources. As a result of these adaptations, the sedentary fisherfolk cultures imagined by Sauer and Anderson did indeed evolve in many parts of the world. This was a stable, satisfactory adaptation and populations began to increase. In the Binford–Flannery model it was not the fisherfolk who developed agriculture, but groups who budded off from them and moved into foraging ranges already occupied by other hunter–gatherers. The fisherfolk had a stable and adequate food supply. But those who fissioned off faced food procurement crises and it was they who opted to supplement foraging with cultivation. The model has considerable appeal, but Flannery's own research in Mexico did not bear out the proposal very well (Flannery, 1986).

Indigenous perceptions

In fact every model proposed so far has generated evidence against it. One problem I have with all the published models is that they are all conceived by middle class, university-educated, Industrial Age pragmatists, all looking for some golden bottom line that will explain it all. Input–output studies, optimum foraging strategies and a variety of armchair theories are all products of the modern mind-set. Could we not come closer to reality if we consulted some Darwinian 'wise old savage?' Richard Lee once asked a Bushman why he did not farm and received the celebrated reply: 'Why should I farm when there are so many mongongo nuts?' (Lee and DeVore, 1968*b*.) In Australia an Aborigine informant gave a similar reply to Berndt and Berndt:

> You people go to all that trouble working and planting seeds but we don't have to do that. All these things are there for us, the ancestral beings left them for us. In the end, you depend on the sun and the rain just the same as we do but the difference is that we just have to go and collect the food when it is ripe; we don't have all this other trouble.
>
> *Berndt and Berndt, 1970*

Probably more to the point is the view of farming expressed by an Aborigine to A. K. Chase (1989): 'It is not our way. It is alright for other people. We get our food from the bush.' It is a question of perception of what is fitting and proper.

In addition to the major sacred texts with their creation stories, there are hundreds of origin tales concerning individual crops or groups of crops. Essentially all of them involve a death and resurrection theme. A full accounting would take volumes but the stories are so similar in their fundamental messages that a select few will suffice. A basic archetypal story comes from Mexican mythology (De Jonghe, 1905), but I quote Joseph Campbell's translation (1988):

> She was knowing, the goddess Tialteutli, walking on the primordial waters, a great and wonderful maiden with eyes and jaws at every joint that could see and bite like animals. She was absorbed by the two great gods, Quetzalcoatl, the plumed serpent and Tezcatlipoca, the smoking mirror. Deciding to fashion the world of her, they transformed themselves into serpents and came to her from either side. One seized her from the right hand to the left foot, the other from the left hand to the right foot and together they ripped her asunder. From the parts, they fashioned not only earth and heavens but also all the gods. And then to comfort the maiden for what had happened to her, all those gods came down and, paying her obeisance, commanded that there should come from her all the fruits that men require for life. From her hair, they made trees, flowers and grass; from her eyes, springs, fountains and little caves; from her mouth, rivers and great caves and from her nose, valleys and from her shoulders, mountains. But the goddess wept all night for she had a craving to consume human hearts. And she would not be quiet until they were brought to her nor would she bear fruit until she had been drenched in human blood.

Another tale of lesser scope comes from Japan (Kajiki, 'Record of Ancient Matters', AD 712):

A heavenly god asked an earthly goddess for a meal. Having seen her cooking various kinds of food taken out of her mouth, nose and anus, the heavenly god killed her in anger. Shortly afterwards, there appeared seeds of various crops from her corpse; from her eyes, rice; from her ears, the millet; from her nose, the red bean; from her anus, the soya bean; from her vagina, barley . . . while a silkworm came out of her head.

Mabuchi, 1964

From the Maring in New Guinea, I received the following myth:

A group of women lived alone in the grasslands. They had no gardens but ate game which they flushed from the grass by fire. One day a grass fire spread to the forest and burned a *menjawai* forest demon in his lair in an epiphytic fern. After the fire had died down, the women saw a column of smoke rising from the burnt forest. They went to investigate and found a smoking corpse of the demon. In fear, they hurried back to their grasslands but some months later, they returned to find all manner of crops sprouting from the body of the demon. They took and planted cuttings of the crops and experimented with various ways of preparing them before they discovered the proper ways to cook them.

Healey, 1988

Similarities in tales about the origin of drug plants are of interest. Here is one about the origin of tobacco in Japan: A mother who lost her only daughter spent her days weeping at her grave. One day a strange plant sprouted from the grave and grew taller and taller before her eyes. It was not good to eat after boiling it, roasting it or steaming it. She tried smoking it and it comforted her. (Mayer, 1986).

From China we learn:

Opium appeared on the grave of a wife who had been mistreated by her husband. When the husband was near death, she appeared to him in a dream and told him how to gather the latex and smoke it. He did and was comforted and cured of his illness . . . temporarily. If he did not smoke every day, he fell ill again to the point of near death.

Eberhard, 1965

This story not only explains the origin of opium but also the origin of opium addiction.

In the forest region of West Africa, there is a plant, îboga (*Tabernanthe iboga*) belonging to the Apocynaceae. An alkaloid, ibogaine, is extracted mostly from the bark of the root. During initiation rites, it may be used in toxic doses and occasionally to the point of fatality.

The Fang tribe is especially addicted to its use. It can help a person to visit dead ancestors and its origin is as follows: a creator god killed a pygmy, cut off his toes and fingers and planted them and from the digits came this drug plant.

In the Gran Chaco of South America, we are told: 'A cannibal woman is killed by a culture hero and from the ashes, the first tobacco grows.' (Wilbert, 1987). A similar story is told about coca in South America and about the betel palm and the betel leaf in Southeast Asia and south Pacific. From Indonesia, there is a story where someone is dragged to death over plowed land and various crops come up. From the brain comes rice; from the fingers, bananas; from the teeth, maize; from the head, coconut; from the muscles, the yam; hair of the skin gave rise to palms and hair of the head to taro. It seems that someone or something must die for plants to grow. As Mabuchi put it:

> From the one who died the primordial death, there originated food plants while human beings became mortal by this event. By repeating ritually such a primordial act, the fertility of both plants and human beings is to be secured. With this view are closely interrelated the human sacrifice, head hunting, cannibalism, the ritual death in initiation ceremony and so on . . . death, killing, procreation and reproduction forming an inseparable unit.
>
> *Mabuchi, 1964, p. 85*

The widespread folk view of death and resurrection seems somewhat in contradiction to the free gifts of Isis, Oannes, Shên-nung and the Inca and his sister, Children of the Sun. Most modern people would feel uncomfortable with the idea that our food came from corpses, but we are out of touch with the sense of magic and awe experienced by former generations. Even with this view our food is still of divine origins, but a dimension of death has been added. Death before life is almost routinely expressed as in John 12: 24, for example: 'I tell you truly, unless a kernel of wheat falls to the ground and dies, it remains only a single seed. But if it dies it produces many seeds.'

The two themes are confounded. Those who benefited from divine gift also sacrificed to appease the gods. The crops of the Aztec were irrigated by human blood; thousands of human victims were sacrificed yearly to satisfy the gods who controlled the weather and crop growth. The Phoenicians sacrificed their own children to Baal. This horrified the Hebrews who at some time substituted animals for humans, but the number of animals slaughtered is rather remarkable. From

Leviticus 23 and Numbers 28–29 one can calculate a yearly require-
ment of 113 bulls, 37 rams, 1093 lambs, and 30 goats by the priests
alone. This does not include free-will offerings, sin offerings or guilt
offerings volunteered by the people. By the time of Flavius Josephus
(Jewish chronicler and historian of the first century AD), the number
of rams required had increased to 118. Agriculture was born in blood,
some human, some animal, and ritual sacrifice continues to this day.

One may imagine that the death and resurrection theme may have
come, in part, from observing the life cycles of plants. A seed looks
dead and inert, but can, like John Barleycorn, spring to life again
when properly handled. People in temperate climates are accustomed
to seeing trees lose their leaves in the fall and passing the winter in
apparently lifeless condition. The mistletoe, a wondrous exception,
retains its green color (and life) on barren branches throughout the
winter, and was sacred to Druids and other sects of Europe. Pines and
other evergreens are still featured in midwinter festivals. People of
tropical savannas are accustomed to seeing vegetation turn brown
and take on a lifeless appearance in the dry season, and then witness
its resurrection with the monsoon rains. 'Death' precedes 'life' in
nature.

But, why must death be enforced by sacrifice? Why must blood be
spilled, animal or human? The answers may be too varied and obscure
for comprehensive resolution, but one theme is evident. Sacrifice is
designed, at least in part, to get the attention of supreme beings or
higher powers that control climate, weather, disease or other factors
influencing crop yields, and human health and welfare. Human sacrifice may be the ultimate in getting attention, and some gods and
goddesses were thought to have a nearly insatiable thirst for human
blood. Other gods could be satisfied with much less. Central to Christian theology is the sacrificial nature of Christ's death as the Lamb of
God with atonement for the sins of mankind.

CHAPTER TWO

Evolution and revolution: the processes of domestication

The processes of domestication

The words, 'domesticated', 'domestication' and similar ones were derived from the Latin, *domus*, household. A domestic is a servant who lives in the house of the master. For domesticated plants and animals, the *domus* can literally mean the house or dwelling as in pet cats, dogs, canaries, etc. and house plants. More likely it means the kitchen or flower garden, the field, orchard, vineyard, plantation, farm, ranch or forest where the domestics are reared to serve the master. There is a perception that humans are in charge and their domesticated plants and animals are there to serve them. As we shall see, there are some problems with this perception.

The processes of domestication are evolutionary in nature, and consequently there are all degrees and stages of intermediate conditions. Domestication involves genetic changes in populations tending to confer increased fitness for human-made habitats and away from fitness for wild habitats. Most of our fully domesticated plants and animals are completely dependent on human activities for survival. Cereals and pulses that have lost seed dispersal mechanisms (nonshattering) are examples as well as sterile bananas, seedless grapes, etc. Sheep, in general, and white chickens are very vulnerable to predation and many breeds of pet animals would not survive without human assistance.

Australian scientists, recognizing that the Aborigines had effectively domesticated many of their environments, if not the species within them, have searched for words based on *domus* to describe such activities. The term domesticatory was coined and the word domiculture, that is household economy, was revived. A family, clan or tribe ranges over a domain, this word derived from *dominus*, lord . . . not *domus*.

The group is master or lord over this territory within which are at least several 'domuses' or hearths where the people are 'at home.' These sites are thoroughly familiar and spiritually safe. Other parts of the domain may not be so secure (Chase, 1989). In Aborigine mythology, the earth and its features were formed in a 'dream time.' There were then giants who hurled huge rocks about, leaving the enormous rock outcrops characteristic of the Australian outback. Other physical features were shaped by the giants during the dreaming. The landscape is perceived to have been shaped spiritually in the dream time, and the use of certain plants and animals may be prohibited in specific places and times as a result. These perceptions have played a part in the Aboriginal mastery of the domains in which they live. The harvesting or nonharvesting of certain plants can affect their abundance and distribution (Berndt and Berndt, 1970).

The Aboriginal stamp on the landscape is in no way unique. Africans and American Indians did the same. People across Eurasia must have put their imprint on the fauna and flora as well, but the changes have been so radical that traces are hard to find. But altering the fauna and flora to benefit the hunter–gatherer does not necessarily result in outright domestication. Aborigines have been doing this for perhaps 35 000 years and no true domesticates have emerged. The domestication of races of individual species is of a different order.

Cereal crops

The wild progenitors of domesticated cereals are annuals adapted to strongly seasonal climates (long dry seasons). They often produce grain in abundance as wild plants, but the primary problem in optimizing harvest is uneven ripening. Grain is produced over a prolonged period of time and repeated harvests would be required to reap most of the crop. This feature is probably more important than the shattering feature that has been so often the focus of attention in the processes of domestication. The routine of harvesting and planting has automatically developed plant architecture with more even ripening. Species with branching habits like sorghum, pearl millet and maize have evolved forms with single stalks and one or two seed-bearing inflorescences. Species that tiller profusely, like wheat, barley, oats, rye and rice, have evolved races that tiller quickly and the tillers mature more or less at the same time. Whole plant maturity is basic to cereal domestication. Suppression of shattering is also a major feature of domestication (Harlan, deWet and Price, 1973).

In cereals, abscission layers are laid down at special points of articulation in the inflorescence that dry up and break at maturity, letting the seed units fall. When abscission layers function, a smooth scar is left at the point of articulation. In domesticated cereals, abscission layers are suppressed or the abscission is delayed until after harvest. When natural abscission is suppressed, threshing usually leaves a ragged scar and this character has been used by archaeobotanists as a criterion of domestication. The suppression of shattering is usually under the control of one or two genes and is easy to develop in most species. But suppression is often not complete, and shattering is still something of a problem in some crops and in some cultivars of other crops. Most cereals will shatter eventually if left unharvested long enough.

On shattering, the naked grain (caryopsis) alone falls in a few cases, but usually there are appendages of at least lemma and palea, and quite often glumes, bristles and other associated structures are included in the seed unit. The appendages usually have a function. In some cases they serve as a seed planting device. The seed units of the wheats, barley and oats are armed with thorn cells and rough barbs, all pointing upward, and have a sharp callus at the lower end making an arrow-like unit. When falling from the parent plants most are pointing downward; the spikelets work their way into the soil, often aided by rough awns that vibrate in the wind. The mechanism is so effective that after shattering one may observe dense stands of awns rising above the soil surface while the grains are buried in the soil. The system works best on rocky or gravelly talus slopes but can be effective on flat land where the parent stands are dense and if the soil is cracked to permit initial entry. Wild oats have twisted awns that wind and unwind with changes in moisture permitting the spikelets to 'crawl' across the soil until they fall into a crack. There the barbed arrows take over and work the spikelet into the ground. In the goat grasses, related to the wheats, some species have barrel-shaped dispersal units suited for transport by surface water and by birds. In wild pearl millet the small seeds are borne in fluffy fascicles easily dispersed by wind.

Another function of appendages is often the production of germination inhibitors. Dormancy is important for wild species. In general, our cereals are derived from annuals adapted to climates with long dry seasons where the rains are likely to be erratic. If all the seeds sprouted with the first rains and there followed a long dry period before the next rains, the species would then become extinct. Some dormancy is required to build up a seed bank in the soil. Seeds of many species are able to remain dormant for many years and still sprout when conditions are right. When dormancy is governed by germination inhibitors, the inhibitors may degrade over time or be leached out by rain water. In most wild grasses naked caryopses extracted from their appendages germinate readily. This is not true for all species, for some have inhibitors in the caryopsis itself. Some seeds require a cold treatment for germination and others respond to heat shock. One of the features of cereal domestication is regulation of dormancy toward the ideal of either no dormancy at all, or a very short one, to prevent sprouting in the field, but which breaks down before the next planting season. This often involves reduction of the appendages or development of free threshing grains.

From an evolutionary point of view, one of the most interesting features of cereal domestication is the recovery of fertility in reduced or vestigial flower structures. There is a dogma in evolutionary theory that states that evolution is irreversible and cannot retrace its steps. A part once lost cannot be recovered. The dogma can be put into question on several counts in cereal domestication:

> The spikes of wild barley bear three spikelets at each node: the center ones are female fertile; the lateral ones are reduced in size, neuter and bear no seeds. Under domestication, six-rowed types appeared in which all three spikelets are perfect and female fertile. The earliest archaeological finds of barley are all two-rowed like the wild progenitor. In the panicoid tribes, spikelets have two florets: the upper one is perfect and female fertile; the lower one reduced to a vestigial scale. Under domestication, the scale has become a complete fertile flower in some cultivars of sorghum, proso and maize. In the Andropogoneae, spikelets are borne in pairs, one sessile and one pedicellate. In most genera the lower spikelet is fertile, the upper one reduced, male or neuter, or even wanting in some cases, although the pedicel persists. In some small groups, the upper spikelet is the fertile one and the lower one is sterile, and, in the Saccharineae, the sugar cane tribe, both members of the spikelet pair are female fertile. Recovery of fertility in the reduced spikelet has occurred in maize and sorghum. In common bread wheat, certain genotypes produce grains

in the basal glumes that are 'always' sterile throughout the whole grass family. Other genotypes may produce more sterile basal glumes than the normal two (Harlan, 1982*b*).

Pennisetum glaucum has gone even farther in reversing evolution. The involucre in *Pennisetum* is considered to be a reduced and modified branch of the inflorescence with the setae and bristles representing reduced and barren branchlets. The true wild races of pearl millet have only one fertile spikelet per fascicle. Domesticated races may have up to nine. The additional spikelets did not come from reduced remnants but arose *de novo*. The reduced branch is partially restored to its ancestral condition as an inflorescence branch with several spikelets.

Harlan, deWet and Price, 1973

Some of these apparently aberrant types are rare and have little to do with evolution of the crop, but six-rowed barley and maize are major crops with spikelet fertility restored, and pearl millet with more than one spikelet per fascicle is the norm.

With a few exceptions (p. 93) the seeds of domesticated races are larger than those of their wild progenitors. This can evolve easily through cultural practices. The seeds that germinate first and produce the most vigorous seedlings in the seedbed are likely to produce plants that will contribute most to the next generation. Within species, larger seeds produce more vigorous seedlings than smaller ones. Larger seeds also have an advantage when deep-planted as they can emerge from greater depths than smaller seeds. All of the selection pressures push domesticates in the same direction: reduced dormancy, reduced appendages, larger seed, more synchronous ripening, nonshattering, recovery of fertility in reduced or rudimentary flowers, greater fitness for the environments provided, including adaptation to climate, soils, pests and diseases, cultural practices and selection by the growers.

Other seed crops

Pulses (i.e. beans, peas, lentils, chickpeas, pigeon pea, soybean, etc.) are dry seeded legumes. A legume is a pod with two sutures, which open at maturity to release the seeds that are each attached by a short stalk to one of the sutures. Legumes are the characteristic fruits of the Leguminosae. In wild races, the pods usually open explosively, flinging the seeds away from the plant and, in some leguminous trees with large pods, the explosions sound like small firecrackers. The explosive mechanism derives from an inner tissue in the pod lying at an angle to the outer wall of the pod. At maturity, the inner tissue dries first, shrinks, developing pressure and finally ruptures the sutures. The two halves of the pod usually twist under the contraction of the inner layer. Nonshattering is achieved by a reduction or suppression of the shrinking tissue. Archaeobotanists have used this character to monitor domestication of pulses when suitable material is recovered. Inheritance of nonshattering is usually rather simple.

Other seed plants with pods, capsules, siliques or composite heads follow similar paths toward nonshattering under domestication. The case of sesame is interesting in that the capsules are partially dehiscent. This derives from the traditional method of harvest. The stiff, rather shrubby plants produce capsules in the axils of leaves along a considerable length of stem. The capsules are borne in an erect position. At maturity they dehisce at the top end and the segments flare out. Traditionally, harvest is done by cutting the plant off at the base or by uprooting as the early capsules start to split. Bundles are carefully brought to the threshing floor and inverted. As the capsules open they spill clean sesame seeds down onto the floor. A completely nondehiscent capsule would not be desirable because they would have to be broken open and the seeds would contain much more trash. It was only when mechanized harvesting was attempted that a search for indehiscence was initiated, as it is desirable to hold all the seed for machine harvesting until all of it is ripe. This is not necessary with traditional harvesting methods. It is of interest that the capsules of wild sesame also do not dehisce completely and retain some seeds in the base until the plant dries completely and breaks down. These seeds act as a second sowing or backup planting and provide some insurance against erratic rainfall.

What does planting and reaping, planting and reaping, that is farming, do to the genetic architecture of annual seed crops? Most of our answers to this and similar questions have been intuitive or simple guesswork. Some fascinating insights have been coming out in recent years based on experimental populations, mostly in barley but in other crops also. The most studied population to date is composite cross II (CCII). It was created by my father, H. V. Harlan in 1928. After much agonizing, he chose 28 cultivars out of some 6000 in his collection to represent the barley crop, and crossed them in all possible combinations, a total of 378 crosses. F_2 seed was mixed as evenly as possible, grown in an increase block and this population was sent to several experimental stations to be grown year after year without any deliberate selection. The longest and most complete studies were conducted at Davis, California. At this writing, CCII has been grown over 60 generations in large populations to reduce genetic drift and without any deliberate selection. Yields in the early years increased rapidly, then the increase leveled off but continued at a slow but steady rate (Allard, 1990).

After 60 generations, the population is still highly variable, still increasing in fitness, still evolving toward an adapted California land-race. Yields have kept pace with about 95% of the best that barley breeders could obtain over the same period of time. Morphologically the population is moving toward an idiotype with dense, heavy spikes. Increase in yield has been largely in more seeds per plant rather than larger seeds.

With the development of biochemical techniques, genetic architecture could be monitored over the generations. Seeds were saved from each harvest so that gene frequencies and arrangements could be studied in different generations. In the 1960s, isozyme markers were introduced into the study and in the late 1970s, DNA restriction fragments were added. The marker loci were located on the seven chromosomes to establish genetic linkages.

All discreetly inherited marker loci, whether governing morphological traits, disease resistance, isozyme alleles or DNA restriction fragments had large effects on reproductive capacity. Changes over generations in allelic frequencies at all marker loci were also strongly correlated with reproductive capacity. Multilocus analyses showed a rapid buildup of allelic associations in early generations and a clustering of associations in mid- to late generations, characteristic of adaptation to the Mediterranean environment of Davis, California. CCII grown in the continental climate of Bozeman, Montana, developed a very different clustering. The frequency and arrangement of alleles is adaptive and a definite pattern develops regardless of gene linkage.

The number of species studied by such techniques is small but results so far indicate that self fertilizing species are more structured in terms of allelic frequencies and associations than cross fertilizing species, and that structures are reached more rapidly. There is much more to be said about these studies but the overall conclusion seems obvious: farming *is* plant breeding. The landraces still in use around the world are still adjusting in fitness. The environment changes from year to year and the populations respond. The fluctuation in any given region operates around some sort of norm and so do the landrace populations. Self-fertilizing crops apparently are as labile as cross-fertilizing ones but in a more structured way. Despite 60 generations of selfing, the barley population maintained a substantial amount of heterozygosity. Allelic associations are maintained in a dynamic framework appropriate for each region. If a landrace is taken to a different area with a different environment and grown for some generations, the genetic architecture will change. It should be understood that environment includes not only such parameters as rainfall, temperature, day length, soil types and the like but also diseases and pests, human preferences, planting, harvesting and cleaning techniques.

In North America we managed to plant a carpet of wheat from northern Mexico well into the prairie provinces of Canada. The wheat belt is interrupted here and there with patches of sorghum, cotton, flax, barley, oats, rye and alfalfa, but these interruptions are no barrier to the yearly migration of rust disease. Rusts do not grow on agar plates but the simile is apt; we have, in effect, provided a substrate like an agar plate 4000 km in diameter ready to receive and propagate the several kinds of rust. Infection begins each year in northern Mexico and along the Rio Grande valley and spores are blown northward. The spores alight on congenial hosts, germinate, infect, grow mycelia through the plant tissues and the mycelia produce great numbers of spores that again move northward, infecting and increasing with each cycle, feeding on stems and leaves as they go. The rusts cannot overwinter in the northern end of the wheat belt and must arrive each year from the south if wheat is to be rusted. In fact, rusts cannot oversummer in the southern part of the belt so spores must be blown southward to infect winter wheat and renew the spring migration. We have created a gigantic epidemiological system, in which several species of *Puccinia* migrate yearly over 4000 km from a land where they cannot oversummer to a land where they cannot overwinter. The system must be included among the marvels of the biological world; it has been called the '*Puccinia* path.'

Our management of this remarkable ecosystem has reflected a remarkable lack of understanding of its nature. The cultivar 'Marquis,' bred in Canada, was introduced to the northern plains in 1912 and soon became the dominant wheat partly because of its rust resistance. The rust epidemic of 1916 took it out. Farmers turned to durum wheats. Race 11 of rust caused severe damage in them. Ceres, a derivative of Marquis, gave an excellent performance from 1926 to 1934 when race 56 became the dominant race of rust. Severe epidemics in 1935 and 1937 took out Ceres. The epidemic of 1935 is estimated to have cost 160 000 000 bushels in the USA alone. Thatcher was resistant to race 56 and it, together with Hope and hybrid derivatives of both, managed to contain rust outbreaks for a few years. Then race 15B and an array of biotypes of it swept over North America in 1953 and 1954. A gene-for-gene system became evident; for every gene for resistance in the host, a gene for virulence was available in the parasite. The 'agar plate' we established by growing one cultivar over large areas simply selected for the virulent genotype (Harlan, 1981a).

In the winter wheat belt to the south a similar pattern emerged. In 1919 when the first varietal survey was made, well over 90% of the hard red winter wheat area was planted to 'Turkey Red.' This was introduced to Kansas in the latter part of the nineteenth century by Mennonite refugees from Russia, although the word 'Turkey' probably has some meaning. 'Turkey Red' was a landrace and highly variable. Wheat breeders in different parts of the belt could easily select out pure lines that yielded better than the population as a whole. As soon as a pure line was grown on any scale, it acted as a filter to propagate strains of rust that would attack it. Pure lines were crossed with pure lines but resistance was always countered by virulence. It would have been better to have grown Turkey Red as a landrace year after year; it would have evolved increased fitness to each environment and would have resisted the epidemics suffered by pure lines. A noted plant pathologist commented, 'Plant breeders and pathologists are busy patching their mistakes and bragging about how big the patches are.' (Vanderplank, 1968).

In recent years some plant breeders and pathologists have been studying the defenses of wild wheat, barley and oats in the Near East, notably in Israel. Wild populations also have rusts, often the very same races as found in the USA or Europe, but these rusts do little damage. Detailed analyses show that the defenses deployed by wild cereals are remarkably complex. There are indeed gene-for-gene systems, but there are also slow rusting effects, where rust development is delayed until it is too late to do much damage, and systems that delay or reduce spore formation, as well as partial resistance and no doubt other systems as well. It was found that if 30% of the population cannot be infected by a given race of rust, the whole population, including the most susceptible components, is protected. That race cannot build up enough inoculum to damage the whole population. These studies, long overdue, have told us a lot about how we might manage our wheat belts. Landrace populations tend to mimic wild ones in their genetic defenses against disease. The goal of modern plant breeding is to develop defenses similar in complexity to those of wild and landrace populations.

Weed races

A consistent and conspicuous feature of plant domestication is the formation of weed races. Domesticated plants are adapted to human-made habitats, but these habitats also provide a medium congenial for the growth of weeds. With few exceptions nearly all annual crops and many perennial ones have weed races. There are weedy forms of wheat, barley, rice, oats, maize, sorghum, carrots, radish, cabbage, beet, cotton, sunflower, rape, potato, asparagus and just about everything else. There are some exceptions, e.g. tetraploid and hexaploid wheats are not weedy but the exceptions are few. Weedy perennials include sour orange, guava, pomegranate, grape, pear, alfalfa and many others.

A common definition of a weed as 'a plant out of place' is rather naive and ignores some of the main features of what makes a weed, a weed. In the first place, who is to judge if a plant is out of place? This is a matter of opinion or prejudice; as a matter of fact, many weeds are so much in place that they cost us dearly in control measures. How can a plant so well-adapted to human-made habitats be out of place? These habitats are its place. Weeds are organisms adapted to human disturbance and the definition need not be confined to plants. There are weedy animals too. Consider the house sparrow, starling, pigeon, house mouse, sewer rat, *Drosophila*, house fly, etc. And while we are about it, what about *Homo sapiens*? The more they disturb the world, the more they thrive, at least up to a point of total disaster. Weeds can choke themselves (Harlan and deWet, 1965).

Crop weeds can evolve in several different ways. Sorghum provides a convenient model because it is prone to weediness and because it has been rather carefully studied. I shall use some examples from my own experience with the crop for illustration. In parts of Sudan there are vast seas of truly wild sorghum in a tall grass, thorn bush savanna formation: here it is a climax grass. When the Aswan Dam was built to back up Lake Nasser in Egypt, people had to be moved out of the flood basin. Some were relocated near Kassala close to the Ethiopian border where an irrigation project could be developed using water from the Atbara. The project was put down on a sea of wild sorghum: land was leveled, ditched and drains were put in; access roads were built and all the other features of an irrigation project were installed. Wild sorghum, although a climax grass in this area, proved to be at least mildly weedy and has persisted along irrigation ditches, roadways and so on. The farmers relocated from northern Sudan preferred wheat to sorghum. Wheat could grow in the winter with irrigation, and so there was no interaction between wild and cultivated sorghum on the project. The weed sorghum of Kassala is local, original.

Some 170 km to the south at Gedaref another project was established for resettlement, but here rainfall was sufficient for dry-land farming provided summer crops were grown. Of course one of the major crops was sorghum. Within two years a formidable sorghum weed appeared, derived from hybridization of cultivated and wild sorghum. It does not look like the wild sorghum at all; it mimics the cultivated sorghum so well that farmers have great difficulty in weeding their fields. It is not until maturity that the true identity comes clear and by then it is too late to prevent infestation of the soil with the seeds of weed sorghum. This kind of mimicry is common among cultivated plants. It is found in wheat, barley, rice, pearl millet, cowpeas and others. At Gedaref the sorghum grown is a dura type with a thick stalk, compact inflorescence and crooked neck. The weed also has a thick stalk, compact inflorescence and at least a partially crooked neck. On the high plateau of Ethiopia the most common sorghum grown is a dura–bicolor, with a thinner stalk and open, lacy panicle. The weed sorghum there also has a relatively thin stalk and open, lacy panicle. The weeds were derived initially from hybridization between wild and cultivated races but the mimicry is due to selection at weeding time. If the weed can escape detection until maturity it will persist. Wild sorghum does not occur on the high plateau of Ethiopia; it is a low or mid-elevation plant. The highland weeds must trace back to ancient hybrids.

In the USA another sorghum weed evolved by a different route. As described above, shattering is suppressed by genes that prevent production of abscission layers. In sorghum there are two independent genes, either one of which will confer nonshattering, and all cultivated sorghums have either one or the other, or both. A race of sorghum, with a secondary seed dispersal mechanism, has evolved from cultivated sorghum. Here, the abscission layers remain suppressed but the pedicel that supports spikelet pairs becomes very thin and breaks at maturity. The seed unit that falls then has a short piece of panicle branch attached. This race is commonly called 'shatter cane' and is a serious pest in sorghum growing regions both in the midwest and in California (deWet, Harlan and Price, 1976).

I have not seen this kind of weed in Africa but I have seen shattering forms of several of the cultivated races. These did not appear to be due to crossing with wild races because often wild races were not present and the morphology was strictly of the cultivated type. I have not checked them out genetically, but suspect that they arose from natural hybridization between genotypes with different genes for abscission layer suppression. Both genes suppress shattering in the homozygous recessive condition and hybrids between the two classes would shatter.

In sorghum, then, weeds can evolve from wild races that are mildly weedy, from hybrids between wild and cultivated races that are serious threats to production, from cultivated races by way of secondary seed dispersal mechanisms and by hybridization between cultivated genotypes. But sorghum has a penchant for weediness and seems to produce them wherever it is grown. The race of wild sorghum at Kassala and in the tall grass savanna of much of Africa is the verticilliflorum race. There is another in West Africa adapted to openings in the rain forest. Wherever the forest is opened to let in a little light, this race, called arundinaceum, thrives. It grows along logging trails, the banks of streams, and every vacant lot in the towns and cities of the region. The verticilliflorum and arundinaceum races are easily distinguished at a glance by their morphology. Somehow both races have made their way to congenial climates in the New World and

Weed mimicry in sorghum. (*a*) Wild sorghum growing in Sudan.
(*b*) Inflorescence of wild sorghum, verticilliflorum race, the apparent
progenitor of domestic races. (*c*) Stand of weed sorghum near Gedaref,
Sudan. The domestic sorghum has been harvested and the weed race
allowed to go to seed and infest the soil. (*d*) Inflorescence of weed
sorghum imitating the local race of cultivated durra sorghum,
Gedaref, Sudan. (*e*) Highland sorghum of the Ethiopian plateau,
durra–bicolor race. (*f*) Weed sorghum of the Ethiopian plateau
mimicking the highland durra–bicolor race of cultivated sorghum.
Called *sipo* by the local farmers and sometimes harvested to make
beer.

Australia. They are not serious pests but weedy enough to get around (Harlan and deWet, 1974).

Weed sorghum can have its moments. We grew a number in a nursery on the experimental farm at Champaign, Illinois, to study morphology, make crosses, analyze chromosomes, do some chemical studies and so on. In conformity to a master rotation plan for the farm, we moved to another area the next year and the field we had used was planted to maize. Some of our weeds were perennial with rhizomes that even Illinois winters would not kill and others had infested the soil with seeds. By midsummer there were weed sorghums twice as tall as the maize, and in the fall the sorghum wrapped up the corn picker and broke it. We were not very popular with the farm crew but that was trivial. We were terrified that something might get loose in the corn belt; this 'stuff' was gigantic. For several years after, I personally patrolled that field with a spade to dig up anything that might emerge. We discontinued our studies of weed sorghum and nothing did escape. The weeds might better be studied where they are.

We once obtained a grant from the Rockefeller Foundation to analyze their world collection of sorghum, and to point out deficiencies and recommend regions in need of collection to round it out. We found, not surprisingly, some groups overcollected, some 'junk' that really meant nothing and some serious gaps that needed to be filled; but we were surprised at the small collection of 'wild' sorghum. Not a single accession of the wild kinds was correctly labeled. In fact, there were no wild sorghums at all in the collection; every accession had been replaced by weed sorghums. Unfortunately, some people had conducted studies on the collection and accepted the labels at face value. As far as wild sorghum was concerned these studies were not only useless but misleading. How do you know what the real wild sorghums look like? First you go to the appropriate herbaria and see the types; then you go to the field and study them in their natural habitats. There is no substitute for these procedures.

Weed mimicry of plant types seems to have originated primarily by selection at weeding time. If the weed cannot be distinguished from the crop it survives to maturity and sheds its seed. Mimicry does not have to be in the same species although that is the most common (see also pp. 124 and 180). There are races of barnyard grass, *Echinochloa crus-galli*, that mimic cultures of rice so perfectly that they may not be detected until flowering time. *Camelina* mimics flax even to specific cultivars (Harlan, 1982*a*).

There are other points of selection pressure. One is in the cleaning process. In traditional farming, cleaning was done primarily by threshing and winnowing and sometimes by screening. A weed with a seed unit of about the size and weight of the crop it infests is likely to be selected favorably and be included in the seed harvest.

The biblical tare is probably *Lolium temulentum* and it produces spikelets of a size and weight difficult to separate from wheat by traditional methods. It also can be infected by ergot-like sclerocia that contain alkaloids and can cause a sort of intoxication or 'madness.' Some of the weed vetches produce seeds difficult or impossible to separate from the grains they infest, whether wheat or barley. Vavilov (1926) found a strain of *Avena strigosa* in Portugal that had evolved a seed unit that could not be separated from the tetraploid wheat grown there. This bit of evolutionary foot-work required the loss of a floret to develop a grain as long and broad as the durum wheat in which it grew. The Ethiopian oat is difficult to separate from the emmer and/ or barley it infests and the seeds are planted along with the crop next season. Baloon vine has recently become a serious pest of soybean in the southeast USA because its seeds are the same size and shape as those of the soybean.

It should be no surprise to learn that modern mimetic weeds are developing in response to the herbicides used. These chemicals are powerful selective screens and plants with the same response are grouped together. Weeds resistant to herbicides that killed their ancestors are flourishing. All of this is predictable. At every selection point, a screen is set up and whatever flows through is shaped to match the crop that is infested.

Vegetatively propagated plants

It has often been stated that cultivation of vegetatively propagated plants preceded seed agriculture although real evidence is lacking. This is a sort of armchair theory based in part on the stereotype of the ignorant hunter–gatherer. In either case, one puts planting material into the ground and, considering the extensive botanical lore of hunter–gatherers, I can find no reason to suppose one came before the other. Archaeology has not been of much help so far. It is true that the earliest traces of domesticated plants we can find are of seed crops, but roots and tubers do not preserve well and lack of archaeological documentation is simply no evidence.

We have seen that hunter–gatherers in various parts of the world regularly replace the head of a yam after digging it to ensure a harvest the next season. They also protected plants in flower so they could harvest the seed, and some hunter–gatherers regularly planted seed of wild plants. Dependence on vegetatively propagated plants is called vegeculture and is said to be typical of indigenous tropical agricultural systems, while seed agriculture is typical of temperate climates. Still, more cereals were domesticated in the tropics than in temperate zones. The whole issue is moot and probably not worth pursuing very far because we are not likely to obtain evidence to resolve it.

It is true that for manioc, for example, all we need to do to propagate a clone is to cut some stakes (stems) and stick them in the ground during the rainy season, and they grow. For potatoes we plant the tubers: if the potatoes are small, the whole potato; if they are large, they can be cut into pieces so that each piece has at least one eye. Sweet potatoes are commonly reproduced by 'slips,' that is a piece of the end of a vine. Bananas send up shoots from short rhizomes, better used for planting stock. In pineapple, the tops of the fruits can be used and the plant may have other buds as well. In sugarcane, a bud is borne in the axil of each leaf; pieces of cane, two–three nodes in length, are usually planted in a shallow trench or slanted into the ground so that at least one bud has a chance to grow. For yams the head is replanted as hunter–gatherers do; one saves whole yams through the dry season to be used as planting stock when the rainy season begins. All this sounds easy but why is it easier than planting seeds?

As far as actual domestication is concerned, however, vegetatively propagated plants have an advantage. Any clone selected for replication becomes instantly domesticated. It is domesticated in the sense that it cannot reproduce itself (exactly) without the aid of humans. Some crops, for example seedless bananas, pineapples, grapes, some clones of yams, etc., lose the ability to reproduce sexually after being exploited.

Vegetative reproduction becomes sophisticated with the development of grafting. We do not know where or when this was first developed, but it is presumed to be in Eurasia and before classical times. There are several advantages in the technique. Root stocks may be selected for disease and/or pest resistance, for root growth, for dwarfing so the scion does not become too large, etc. A desired clone may be maintained and propagated indefinitely (provided the stock does not become infected with virus). More than one clone may be grafted onto a single root stock. In commercial rubber it is not uncommon to graft a high latex yielding clone on a suitable root stock and then top graft to genotypes resistant to leaf diseases. The tapping panel is the only part of the triple genotypic plant to produce the latex but the yield is not much affected by either the upper photosynthetic portion or the lower root stock. Grafting is the only way to maintain many selected cultivars. Seeds from a 'Golden Delicious' apple will produce trees that bear apples but not 'Golden Delicious' apples. Of course an occasional tree might produce apples better in some way and this could be propagated by grafting.

Some grafts are partially to completely incompatible. The most striking cases I have seen were in pistachio. On some wild pistachio (*Pistacea*) root stocks the cultivated race of *Pistacea vera* provided strange unions. The diameter of the root stock trunk may in some cases be about half the diameter of the scion above the graft. This makes for a remarkable trunk conformation. Nevertheless, the desirable dwarfing effect is achieved. Dwarfing of fruit and nut trees is desirable from the point of view of harvest. The less one must climb up and down a ladder, the more efficient the process.

Animal domestication

Most mammals can be tamed easily by capturing young animals and raising them in the *domus*. If milking animals are already available, the captives can be very young, even newborn. Without a source of milk, the captives must be near weaning age, although there are records of women nursing pigs, dogs, lambs and probably others. The younger the captive the more easily it adapts to the *domus*, but animals of weaning age can be tamed easily by feeding and tender care. In general, the taming is not difficult.

In my youth, I spent seven summers in and around the Sawtooth Valley, Idaho. One summer a young orphaned sandhill crane was found in one of the hay meadows and brought to the ranchstead where it was released among chickens, geese and ducks that ranged freely around the ranch yard. They were fed ad lib by scattering mixed grain on the ground twice a day. The crane adapted easily and grew rapidly, soon reaching one and a half meters in height. It seemed to enjoy the company of people, amused itself by untying shoelaces and, when we played catch with a baseball, it would often position itself between two throwers and easily dodge the balls no matter how hard we threw them. When fall came and the wild sandhill cranes flew south to their wintering grounds, this one stayed on through the bone-chilling winter. The elevation of the ranch was about 2200 m and the winter temperatures would fall to some -35 °C. The normal wintering grounds of the cranes have mild climates. This bird made one adaptive concession to the cold: as evening came on it flew to the Salmon River, about 3 km distant. The river was too large and too swift to freeze except along the edges and shallow pools, and the crane returned each morning with a small ring of ice around one leg.

The bird survived the winter, stayed through the following summer and then left in the fall, not to be seen again. Whether it joined other sandhill cranes or was shot by some 'sportsman' because of its unusual tameness, we never knew. This illustration shows how easy it is to tame an animal by raising it in a *domus*, and that such taming can disrupt strongly established instinctive behavior.

But taming is only a step. True domestication depends on rearing animals over generations and altering the genetic structure of populations. Some fascinating reports have come from the distinguished Soviet geneticist, D. K. Belyaev, who has spent a lifetime domesticating black (silver) foxes and mink for the fur trade. The wild fox in captivity tends to be scrappy, aggressively defensive and likely to bite the hand that feeds it. Belyaev's initial selections were simply for more docility and he continued selection for several generations using no other criteria, at least to his knowledge. When one mates like with like in a population, however, some inbreeding is inevitable. This, no doubt, contributed to the rather startling results. Soon pied coats appeared, tails began to curl, ears flopped like puppy dogs, in fact his silver foxes were turning into domesticated dog-like creatures before his eyes.

Belyaev and his team examined the effect of domestication on hormonal balance and time of production. The testosterone production from testes in the first month after birth was lower in domesticated animals than in the wild population, but domesticated males had an earlier rise in production in prepuberty. There were other differences in hormone production patterns and domestication, clearly, had genetic effects controlling behavior as well as morphology (Logvinenko *et al.*, 1978).

It is almost a cliché that the dog was the first domesticated animal and it is probably true. The earliest archaeological evidence we have now are *c.* 12 000 BC in Iran and *c.* 11 000 BC in Idaho. Wolf-like dogs are indistinguishable from wolves, but captivity or cohabitation with humans eventually leads to telltale morphological changes – a shortening of the muzzle is one of the surest and most diagnostic. Fully domesticated breeds often have morphologies radically different from lupine progenitors.

Early domestication saw a decrease in the body size of sheep, goats, cattle and pigs. This could well have been due to selection for greater tractability and ease of herding. Other features soon appeared, such as reduction in size or complete loss of horns in female sheep, corkscrew twisting of horns in male sheep and mutations for wool, fat tails, long thin tails, etc. In goats, twisted horns appeared and eventually long hair, the mohair used by black-tent people to make their tents. Breeds of cattle appeared; long horn, short horn, crumpled horn, humped backed and so on.

In animals, as with plants, one can usually get what one selects for within biological limits. Large, heavy breeds of dogs have been selected to pull sleds, carts, travois or to be used as pack animals. Slim, swift, running breeds have been selected to hunt gazelle, deer, elk, etc. Active, wiry, agile breeds were selected to hunt or bait bears. Hounds were bred to follow the scent of game and hold the prey for humans to kill. There were short-legged breeds to dig out badgers or hares; sheep dogs were developed to herd and protect the flocks and others were used for working cattle. Many American Indian tribes were fond of dog for food and the Mexican Indians developed a breed with little hair and no bark that could be fattened for the table.

To a degree, animal domestication resembles the plant process in producing feral populations. Under the right conditions, animals can escape the domestic fold and return to breeding in the wild. Feral horses have flourished in western USA since some escaped from

Coronado's army in the sixteenth century. Mariners have introduced goats to many islands around the world to serve as provender on return voyages. In the absence of predators, they often built populations that did severe damage to the island fauna and flora. Pigs escape easily and thrive especially in oak woodland and marshes. Feral cattle have done very well in some cases. Sheep are too susceptible to predation to succeed except where predators are completely eliminated. In Southeast Asia local breeds of chickens resemble, or are, game cocks and may interbreed with jungle fowl. These breeds can escape but the heavy breeds of chickens are helpless.

Feral dogs and cats are common in cities of both Europe and North America and probably elsewhere. Cats especially can become very secretive and their number underestimated because they are not conspicuous. The weediest of domestic animals is probably the rock dove. I am not familiar with either the historic or genetic relationships between the flocks in Trafalgar and San Marcos Squares and truly wild rock doves. Pigeon breeders have developed many specialized strains that could not possibly survive in even such weedy environments, let alone the craggy rocks of wild habitats. City buildings have provided artificial cliffs and rocks and the doves have made them into a sort of domus for themselves.

Geography of plant domestication

Modern studies on geographic origins of crop plants may be said to have begun with the classic work of Alphonse De Candolle, the distinguished Swiss botanist and geographer. His primary work on the subject, *L'Origine des Plantes Cultivées*, was published in 1882 and has been reprinted and translated several times since (see Candolle, 1959). It was scholarly and eclectic in the sense that he used all sources of information available to him. Distribution of near relatives and wild races of the crops, names in various languages, uses, customs, traditions and the limited amount of archaeological information available were all studied to draw up a list of the most likely origins of the cultivated plants in question. Over a century later the work is still a useful reference because of the scholarship involved. There was little field work, and distributions came from herbarium sheets, published floras and correspondence with botanists and explorers. Origins were not precise and were assigned to whole continents and there were some errors, but on the whole the work was a major contribution and is still useful.

Nikolai Ivanovich Vavilov

One of the most influential scientists in the twentieth century, with respect to origins of cultivated plants, has been Nikolai Ivanovich Vavilov. He proposed a very simple and logical method for determining the area of origin of a crop. One samples the diversity of the crop, classifies it and wherever the greatest diversity occurs is the 'center of origin.' It seems only reasonable; a crop must originate somewhere and spread out from there. Vavilov pointed out that the variation in the centers should have more dominant genes than in the periphery, as recessives accumulate during the spread while the center remains closer to wild type. The presence of wild progenitors was also a logical feature of centers of origins. By this method of analysis, he felt he could show many crops had common centers of origin. The proposal was outlined in 1926 in a classic essay dedicated to De Candolle and titled *Studies on the Origin of Cultivated Plants*. He proposed eight primary centers with some subcenters (Fig. 2.1). The essay, in fact, was largely a literature review and lacked documentation of genetic diversity of most of the crops. It was widely accepted however and echoes still persist despite much negative evidence now at hand.

The idea was simple, logical and intellectually satisfying, but was widely accepted primarily because of N. I. Vavilov. He was a most remarkable person and some personal impressions may explain the influence he had on biologists all over the world. Vavilov had charisma. He was not a large man but seemed to fill a room when he entered, and instantly became the center of attention. He had a dark, swarthy complexion, brilliant piercing eyes, quick movements and his body was always tense with some sort of inexhaustible internal energy. One could sense the tension across a room. His powers of concentration and facility with languages were legendary. His whole life style was intense; I have never known anyone else so driven by his work. There was no time for trivia, for fun and games. Time was always too short, and must be filled completely with efforts towards his objectives and goals. He slept very little; time was too short. Vavilov

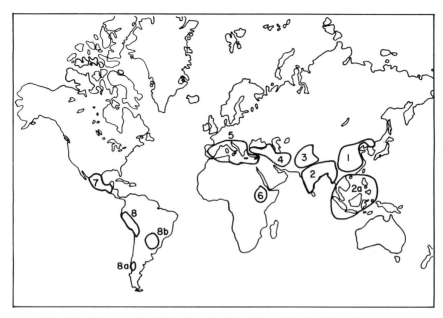

Fig. 2.1. Centers of origin after Vasilov. From Harlan (1971):
copyright by the Americian Association for the Advancement of
Science.

and my father were good friends and when Vavilov came to Washington, as he did twice, in 1930 and 1932, he stayed in the guest room
of our home. I would see him at breakfast and again in the evening
when he and my father sat in our living room and regaled each other
with the adventures and mishaps of plant collecting. Vavilov never
missed an opportunity to learn; my mother chased him out of the
kitchen because he was asking so many questions, she could not keep
her mind on her cooking. His facility with languages came out in
the casual conversation. We knew he published in English, French,
German and Russian. My father asked him about interpreters in
Afghanistan; 'Afghanistan?' Vavilov replied, 'You don't need an
interpreter in Afghanistan. In every village you can find someone
who speaks Farsi.' My father had collected in Ethiopia a few years
before Vavilov. On advice, he had hired two interpreters, one Christian and one Muslim, because each would tattle on the other if the
interpretation was not reasonably correct. He asked Vavilov how he
handled the situation. It turned out that Vavilov had only one

interpreter who told him lies, so halfway through the expedition, he fired him. By then Vavilov knew enough Amharic that he no longer needed an interpreter. Vavilov was held up at the Mexican border for three days because of visa problems; he used the time to take 26 lessons in Spanish and entered Mexico speaking Spanish. To be sure, if one knows six or eight languages another becomes very easy, and his knowledge of French was a great asset. But his powers of concentration were the key. He was a very intense person.

One evening my father came home from work and said that he and Vavilov were going to make a field trip next day and would I like to go along. Of course the answer was an enthusiastic 'Yes.' It seems Vavilov wanted a sample of American wild rice, *Zizania aquatica*, to take back to USSR. We drove down to the Patuxent river wetlands, one of the best on the east coast and now protected by the Patuxent Wildlife Refuge. We were going to collect in American Indian style. My father rented a rowboat, instead of a canoe, and had a canvas shock cover, which we spread over the bow. Vavilov insisted on rowing; his intense energy would not permit him to be passive. He rolled up his sleeves and propelled the boat with vigor into the massive stands of wild rice; I would bend stalks over the canvas sheet with one stick and beat the panicles with another, following the American Indians' method of harvesting the wild rice. We soon had a goodly collection, but Vavilov was curious about everything. There were large flocks of birds in the marsh and, as he had noted I had an interest in birds, he asked me what they were. 'They are bobolinks,' I told him. 'You have a bird book. Let me see,' he said. True, I had a little pocket paper book; this was long before Petersen's guides were available. I showed him the picture and description. He looked at the Latin name, *Dolichonyx oryzivorus*. 'Do you know what that means?' he asked. I had had some Latin but had to confess I did not. '*Oryzivorus* means rice-eater,' he explained. I thought 'Wow! those funny names mean something!' I have been dealing with those funny names ever since, but Vavilov was the first to open my eyes. We did not know then, and it was many years before we found out, that the seed of *Zizania aquatica* has a very high moisture content and if it dries out it dies. Vavilov took home a couple of kilos of dead seed.

My father and Vavilov corresponded over the years. Sometimes the letters were just feelers. They had a crude but simple code. If Vavilov responded, 'My dear Dr Harlan,' it meant that things were not going well; the gulag was ever at work. If he responded simply, 'Dear Dr Harlan,' things were at least more or less normal. I was so impressed by Vavilov that I took two years of Russian at the university in case I could go to Leningrad and study under him. As graduation was approaching and I was casting about for advanced study, my father wrote to Vavilov asking if this would be possible. The answer came back rather promptly:

> My dear Dr Harlan,
> What you said about Chinese barley is very interesting . . .

Since my father had said nothing about Chinese barley, the meaning was clear. The dark, malevolent cloud of Lysenko was looming on the horizon. I went to the University of California at Berkeley.

Vavilov was eventually declared an enemy of the people and hauled off to prison where he was finally executed by starvation. There was really little ideology involved; it was more a Byzantine–Rasputin-like intrigue: 'If I can get rid of this person, I can take his place.' Personal ambition on the part of Lysenko was at the root, and Lysenko caught the ear of Stalin. At any rate, after Khrushchev, Vavilov was rehabilitated and became an icon in the Soviet pantheon. What he said and wrote is gospel and cannot be altered. I was invited to deliver a plenary address at the closing ceremony of the International Genetics Congress held in Moscow in 1978; the ceremony was dedicated to Vavilov. In 1987, I was also invited by the organizing committee to attend the celebration of the one hundredth anniversary of the birth of Vavilov. I was one of only two Americans invited. Paul Fryxel represented the United States Department of Agriculture and I, as far as I know, represented my father. The main celebration was in Moscow, but many of us went on to Leningrad (St Petersburg) and visited the offices of the Vavilov Institute of Plant Industry (VIR). They had made a small museum of Vavilov's office and study; here were the books he read, and some of his correspondence with Bateson and other geneticists of his time was on display. I was pleased to recognize a sheet of yellow paper with my father's scrawl all over it. He seldom had his letters typed, but messages were scribbled on a yellow writing pad. Few people on earth could decipher his scrawl.

The concepts of centers of origin captivated the scientific world. Everyone was brain-washed. Well, not my father. I do not think there was anyone who admired and respected Vavilov more than my father, but he did not buy the theory. I heard him once comment to a colleague, 'If what Vavilov says is true, then barley originated in eastern Tennessee.' My father knew barley. In fact, a recent study by Peeters (1988) based on the Cambridge barley collection and more than 100 000 observations over a three-year period, indicated that the country with the greatest diversity of barley is the USA, followed by Turkey, Japan, the former USSR and China, but that Germany and France had about as much diversity as China. Centers fingered by Vavilov such as Ethiopia and Afghanistan were sixteenth and seventeenth respectively.

For the Vavilov centennial, I prepared a paper on studies of genetic diversity since his time. It was not published and never will be, because not a single modern study has agreed with Vavilovian theory. I was captivated, along with everyone else, for a while, but when I began to get more field experience and became familiar with the real situation, I could see that the centric concept was not always very useful. My paper in *Science* (1971) was a sort of halfway house on my way out of the center-of-origin addiction. I reduced his eight centers to three (Fig. 2.2), and since then my three centers have been eroding by mosaics of flanking activities.

For all its faults, the concept of centers and noncenters has some merit, especially for the Near East and Africa, which was my original model. In the light of more recent evidence, the North Chinese 'center' appears to be more a part of a mosaic than a center, and Andean Peru has taken on the characteristics of a center apart from the lowland noncenter in South America. Because of the ambiguity of geographic patterns, it is best to treat each crop separately and consider origins on an ecological basis. This is the strategy adopted in this book.

Crop origins and evolution

The Crop Evolution Laboratory at the University of Illinois was in operation for 20 years and studied the origin and evolution of a number of crops, mostly cereals and pulses but sesame, *Xanthosoma* and others were included. Our laboratory attracted students from many parts of the world and some of them, on returning to their homelands, undertook investigations of local materials. One of our

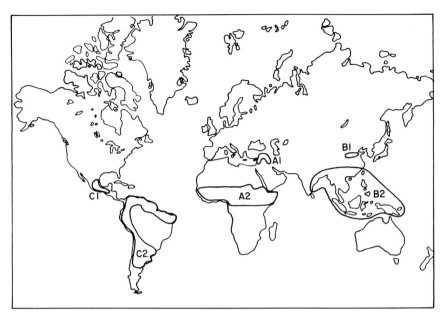

Fig. 2.2. Centers and noncenters of agricultural origin. A1, Near East center; A2, African noncenter; B1, north Chinese center; B2, Southeast Asian and South Pacific noncenter; C1, Mesoamerican center; C2, South American noncenter. From Harlan (1971): copyright by the American Association for the Advancement of Science.

students, Kanti, obtained employment in Nigeria and did a very fine study on the origin and distribution of cowpeas. It was a great help to have students who could speak and read other languages. There was a time, in fact, when our laboratory had facility in 19 different languages; this permitted us to survey literature that otherwise would have been out of reach, and gave us very interesting perspectives into agricultural origins and evolution of cultivated plants. It may be appropriate here to describe the methods used to study the origin and evolution of a crop, especially where archaeological information is scant or lacking.

A study such as this begins in the library. One can learn a great deal from what has already been published on the more important crops, and the published works of the Vavilov Institute of Plant Industry (VIR) in St Petersburg provide a good starting point. The Institute is a venerable one and was doing excellent research in the days of the tsars before the revolution. Vavilov was in charge of it from 1920 to 1940, and pursued a vigorous program of germplasm collection and its evaluation and utilization in breeding programs. During his tenure many volumes were published, containing papers by a distinguished staff studying many crops of value or potential value to the USSR. Many of the studies seem old fashioned now, but they are still a good place to start because they were undertaken at a time when patterns of diversity were more authentic than now. Most of these studies cannot be repeated; the world of Vavilov has all but disappeared.

The VIR staff was competent and thorough, and one could find at least one short article on almost any plant domesticate of interest. For the most part, the articles are in Russian with English, French and German summaries. Having been introduced to background information about a crop from the Russian work, we pursue other sources. Local floras are often very helpful; taxonomic studies indicating relationships among species within a genus; agronomic studies related to production and adaptation are useful, and there may be references to herbarium collections that should be studied.

With some grasp of the situation in hand, the next step is a study of herbarium material. This can be most enjoyable as well as instructive. A considerable amount of research in our laboratory was devoted to African crops. This required repeated visits to the herbaria of: the Royal Botanical Gardens at Kew, near London, where huge collections are available; Paris for specimens from former French African colonies; Brussels for Zaïre; Florence for former Italian colonies; Berlin for the pre-World War I collections from the former German possessions; and Portugal for material from Angola and Mozambique. To do a professional piece of work, these visits are mandatory.

From herbarium specimens, one learns what wild and weedy races look like. Almost every specimen is dated, so that one can find out when the material is in bloom or when it is likely to be ripe for collection, and the locations are given with various degrees of precision. From this information, one can plot the distribution of wild relatives, and prepare an itinerary for a collecting trip that could bring you to the right places at the right time and with some information on what you really want to collect. Herbarium studies are basic homework for the collector, but they also lead to fascinating insights of both collectors and taxonomists via the notes to each other on the annotation slips. One must get thoroughly acquainted with the materials to be on safe ground, and the herbaria of the world are essential to this degree of understanding.

Type specimens are critical. One does not really know what an epithet means until the type is examined. Unfortunately, some types are mere scraps or even pencil sketches on a sheet of paper and some species are named without a type specimen. In these circumstances, one can only follow the lead of the botanist most familiar with the group. At the Crop Evolution Laboratory we generally followed the work of the botanists at Kew.

The different phases of an investigation are not mutually exclusive. One can always read and one should visit as many herbaria as possible, but these visits do not all have to be made before field work commences. Field work is an essential phase of any study of cultivated plants: one must go in person to collect, to see what is going on, to observe natural hybridization in the field among wild, weed and domesticated races; and one must observe differences in adaptation, ranges of habitat, variation in time of blooming and cultural practices of the cultivators. In the course of field work, one has the opportunity to visit small herbaria along the way and add information from these sources. The living material, of course, is returned, if possible, to home base for further studies.

Introduction of foreign materials into the USA requires an introduction permit, a quarantine examination and some advance arrangements for handling the material. In my career, I have introduced over 15 000 accessions, mostly for the United State Department of Agriculture, but some for my own studies. Most of them have simply added to our germplasm inventory without much merit, but a few, collectively, have provided increases in income of some hundreds of millions of dollars annually. These are, of course, a source of satisfaction, but a collector in the field has no idea whatsoever of which accession will be important and which ones will be just additional accession numbers.

Field work – some personal experiences

When one actually gets out into the field, transportation is almost always the primary problem. Bureaucratic interference or political antagonism occasionally override the transportation matters, but these are either resolved or you go on to another country. Today the long range section of a collecting trip is usually by plane. When my father and his colleagues explored for plants, the long range sections were by steamship and train. Actual collecting was by foot, mule or horseback, or automobile and local means of travel. This latter has not changed much. I have collected on foot, horseback, bicycle, dugout canoe, motor launch, horse cart, ox cart, four-wheel-drive vehicle and car; any means to get where one must get is fair play.

The ideal, of course, is to have personal control of transportation. A jeep, Land Rover or other 4-wheel-drive vehicle, which you drive yourself, will do wonders. Sometimes it is necessary to accept a local driver and this can work out well if the driver is responsive. I have collected by public transportation but this is never very satisfactory. Local buses can get you to some remote villages from whence you can forage by foot, cart or bicycle. In most developing countries there is a class of transport used by the less affluent. Various kinds of vehicles follow a somewhat established route but not a time schedule. When the vehicle is loaded, or more likely overloaded, the driver takes off, losing and gaining passengers along the route. They go by various names: *publico*, service, *servicio*, Rift Valley Peugeot Service, etc. In Turkey they are called *dolmush*; *dolma* means stuffed. I have used them in several countries to get from village to village but they are no good for actual collecting.

Sometimes one gets lucky. On my first visit to Sénégal, I arrived in Dakar. The city was full and I had to share a room with a sailor from a tuna fishing boat in order to get a bed. I needed to contact the Agricultural Research Station operated by the French at Bambey and tried to call by telephone, but I could not get through. So I hired a car, for an exorbitant rate, to get me to the Station some 100 km to the east. The car was a 'wreck,' in general disrepair and with bald tires. Fortunately for me the radiator did not compute; it kept boiling every 10 to 15 km and the driver would stop at some village to get water for it. The roadside was lined with a marvelous swarm of wild and weedy pearl millet, and there were many fields of cultivated pearl millet to examine as well. I took samples at every watering stop and some photographs. By the time I got to Bambey, I had the whole interaction system worked out. I now knew what those specimens at Kew, Paris and elsewhere really meant. If the car had been in good repair, the driver would have whizzed me by all those fascinating populations and I would have had to learn about the system elsewhere.

Almost all of my field work has been done on a shoestring budget. I could not buy a jeep and have real control over my transportation; I could seldom afford to rent a jeep. In general, I was in a 'beggar' position. Part of my homework was, of course, to learn about agricultural research stations and institutions that might be of help, and I am enormously grateful for the help I have received. At the Bambey Station just mentioned, I was provided with excellent transportation and traveled over most of Sénégal in company with agricultural scientists who knew the country and the crops. They were excellent traveling companions and very informative. I later had similar experiences in Mali, Niger and other former French colonies. I doubt, however, if they would have been so generous in their assistance if I had not spoken French. A working knowledge of French has opened many doors for me in French-speaking Africa, Polynesia and the Antilles, to say nothing of France itself.

But the French are not the only ones who have helped me along the way. For example, I contacted the Western Circle of the Botanical Survey of India at Puna. They had jeep transportation and regularly sent out collectors to gather and press specimens of the local flora. At the time I was collecting some highly endemic grasses of the Western Ghats. Some species were known only from a single location. The botanists arranged their field work so that I could ride along to the target locations. They collected what they wanted and I collected my endemic grasses. The international institutes have been very helpful; they are well equipped with vehicles and have often provided a seat for me to go along on their field trips. As our Crop Evolution Laboratory developed over the years, I found I had former students scattered around the world and they were often of great help in securing local transportation.

My interests in the archaeological aspects of crop evolution and plant domestication led to invitations to do field work in Iran, Turkey and Jordan. In the Iranian Prehistoric Project of 1960, three German DKV jeeps were driven out from Germany. I was allowed to take one of them eastward for my work in Afghanistan, Pakistan and India, on the understanding that when I had finished with it I would sell it, and turn the proceeds over to the Oriental Institute of the University of Chicago.

I wanted to take an excursion through the central Asian region of the USSR, Bokhara, Samarkand, Tashkent, etc. So friends drove the jeep to Kabul where we had a rendezvous. The jeep was enormously valuable as I drove it myself and could stop at any time to collect. A good collection of some valuable material was obtained in both Afghanistan and Pakistan, but I was unable to drive it into India because the international carnet had expired. The Indians demanded an import duty in cash, equivalent to the cost of a new jeep. It was left in storage in Lahore, Pakistan, and I went on to collect in India for three months, then to Ethiopia for another two months and finally back to my home base at Oklahoma State University. The jeep was still in store in Lahore. I was willing to sell it to myself and write a check for $1000 to the Oriental Institute, but I found that since I had left Oklahoma State, ten months previous, the University had developed a contract with Pakistan for technical assistance and was in desperate need of transportation. So I walked across the campus and sold the jeep in Lahore and sent the proceeds to Chicago.

In 1964, after an archaeological expedition to Turkey, I was permitted to take a Land Rover to collect wild wheat in the Balkans, on the understanding that when I was finished the trip I would send the Land Rover to Egypt, where the Oriental Institute had another project that needed transportation. Again, I had control of my transportation. However, the shipping of the Land Rover proved to be a contest with bureaucracy. During the process of negotiation I met a Yugoslavian lawyer who spoke French; he advised me to take the Land Rover to Greece, take it to Trieste, take it anywhere, but not to try and send it from Yugoslavia. It was good advice, but negotiations had gone too far. With the communist regime then in place there was only one shipping company and only one insurance company. They knew each other only too well and the insurance was enormous. The Land Rover did eventually arrive, however, but I had long left Yugoslavia before it was shipped.

But, of course, jeeps, Land Rovers, cars do not take you everywhere.

If there is no road, one goes by foot, horseback, dugout canoe and so on. One does whatever one has to do to get the targeted material and one picks up whatever else seems interesting along the way. I might add that the ox cart used in India was excellent for my purpose. It went so slowly I could jump off, collect a plant and catch up with it and continue the ride.

Experimental studies

Many tropical accessions either do not flower at the latitude of Champaign, Illinois, or flower so late that seed cannot be produced before frost. For these, it is necessary to arrange a nursery in the tropics or in a frost-free zone in the subtropics. For our sorghum studies, we worked with programs in Puerto Rico involving the Universities of Puerto Rico and Texas. For our *Tripsacum* (maize) work, we collaborated with the Fairchild Tropical Gardens south of Miami. There are for-profit companies that will plant and tend winter nurseries in both the tropics and subtropics, and we engaged one of them to provide maize in bloom at the right time for crossing with *Tripsacum*. Service companies of this kind have become extremely important for breeding programs around the world.

The materials brought back from abroad were studied in various ways. Many measurements were taken and we used the methods of numerical taxonomy to study morphological differences and similarities. We crossed wild and weedy accession with domesticated ones, examined fertility of the hybrids, chromosome pairing and segregation in later generations. Particular chemical products were studied by chromatography, electrophoresis or other techniques. In a few cases, we studied enzyme digested DNA fragments, but the technique was too expensive for us to use generally in studies of crop evolution. We documented accessions and hybrids with herbarium specimens, and entered living material into the United States Department of Agriculture inventory.

Throughout our studies we had the privilege of interaction with bright, young enthusiastic graduate students. Those whose schedule permitted met with us for coffee in midmorning and midafternoon, and on Fridays at 4 p.m., we all adjourned to a local pub. The professors bought the beer. The conversations were seldom trivial; we talked over our work, what we had read, our chromosome squashing, our isozyme work, etc. The ambiance was both relaxed and heady. We were all learning together, and these were among the most enjoyable times in my life. Bright inquisitive minds can be a great stimulus and I am grateful to all of them.

CHAPTER THREE

Stones and bones

Nature of archaeology

Since most of our agriculture evolved before written history, evidence from the prehistoric times is critical to our studies of domestication. History is not without interest or relevance but it tells us little about our beginnings. In general, evidence from prehistory is generated by archaeologists and the science they practice. Archaeology as a science is comparatively new. Grave robbers and tomb looters have been with us since people started putting valuable goods in tombs, and we must admit that much of the early archaeological work was not much more than grave robbing. There has long been a market for ancient art. Collectors, including museums as well as private individuals, have paid high prices for art pieces from ancient civilizations, which, of course, has promoted grave robbing and looting. I have seen whole hillsides in Iran torn up by people looking for Luristan bronze items in ancient cemeteries. This kind of looting is widespread and profitable despite international efforts to curb the trade in artifacts. Discovery of pieces of fine art is still the hope, if not the goal, of many archaeologists.

Another thread in the fabric of archaeology is the verification of history. Extensive investigations have been made in Rome, Athens, Jerusalem, Troy, Masada, Ebla, Ephesus and Pharaonic Egypt and many other sites of historical interest to confirm or dispute the stories about them that have come down to us. Many biblical sites have been excavated mostly to prove that such sites did exist and that the Bible has historical merit. Some sites are excavated to develop a history as in cases of Maya, Inca and pre-Inca civilizations where written material is sparse and/or difficult to decipher.

Gradually the focus of archaeology shifted from fine art and history to a search for knowledge of how a people lived and died at a given place and time. What did they eat? What plants and animals were exploited? What did they wear? What kind of living space did the rich and poor have? What items were traded and where did exotic artifacts come from? What might have been the religious practices? How good was the diet? How long did they live? What was the mortality rate of different age classes? What chronic diseases did they suffer? What kinds of trauma were common? What was the status of medicine? These and dozens of similar questions came to be asked and became the basis of modern archaeological excavation.

Such questions are not easily answered. It is not just a matter of picking up arrowheads or digging for gold bowls. A battery of experts is required: zoologists to identify the bones; botanists to identify the plants; stone knappers to mimic ancient techniques; chemists to analyze stains and traces of organic material in bowls, jugs and on mortars, etc.; geologists and climatologists to assess the climate of the time range of interest and changes in topography that have taken place since (geologists may also locate sources of stones found in the site or sources of clay for ceramic objects); palynologists to assess changes in vegetation; physical anthropologists to study human skeletal material, to assess health status, morbidity and other demographic parameters; surveyors are needed to establish precise locations, elevations, etc.; and photographers are needed to document progress of the dig and artifacts recovered. The list goes on. Carbon-14 laboratory analyses are needed in almost all cases and other laboratory tests are required for other methods of dating. Even agronomists can be of help in assessing resources available at a site under conditions of the time of occupation. The excavation of even a simple site can be very expensive. A lot of volunteer time, and assays at no charge, are donated simply because of the interest of participants. Archaeology can be fascinating and a lot of fun, and the people involved tend to be congenial and interesting. I have never pretended to be an archaeologist but have worked with some for over 30 years and have enjoyed the contacts enormously.

For studies of agricultural origins, the critical information that can be supplied by archaeology concerns times and places. Place of excavation poses no real problem today although some errors have occurred in the past. Maps, charts, landsite photographs, aerial photos and ground survey accurately place the site on coordinates of latitude and longitude and establish the elevation. Time, however, is another matter.

Dating history

There are problems with dating even within the historical time range. The ancients usually counted years by the reign of the local monarch, for example the sixth year of Pepi II, the tenth year of Rameses III, etc. If one has a complete list of the kings, their correct order and year of death the system works quite well although some small error might creep in because of date of death and date of accession to the throne. When does one start counting if the king or queen dies in March or October, etc? Unfortunately, king lists are not always complete and there are gaps with no information at all. Cross-checking different literatures of different peoples may establish firm dates that cannot be moved and times in between can be adjusted according to the best information available. However the division between BC and AD, 25 December AD 0 or AD 1, was not the date of Christ's birth. We managed to miss it by a few years but how many is not certain. Still, dating over the last 2000 years has been reasonably satisfactory; dating before that has more problems and the older the dates, the greater the problems

Dendrochronology

Time is measured by some stochastic regularity. In climates with marked seasons, trees lay down annual rings in the wood. Tree ring dating – dendrochronology – can be very accurate on a local or regional basis. It may happen that there is little or no growth some years and occasionally, under unusual conditions, some trees may lay down two rings in one year. The error over time is usually small, however, probably less than 2%. A series of dry years produces a sequence of narrow rings while favorable years produce wide rings. This sets up patterns of ring growth that can be identified. Trees of a given locality will have matching patterns. One can start with a core taken from the oldest tree of a region and extend patterns backward in time using dead trees, beams from old houses, etc. Each sample must overlap matching patterns with older and younger patterns. When dendrochronology began, this was a very tedious process. Today the patterns are computerized and readily assessed for matching.

The oldest living trees we know of are bristle cone pines, *Pinus aristada* (or *Pinus longaevia*), in the White Mountains of California. Specimens can exceed 4000 years of age and ring sequences have been built up to some 8000 years. While tree ring dating is one of the most accurate methods, it can be used only over a limited geographic range because it depends on change of local climates. Furthermore, one may not always find archaeological wood suitable for matching.

Radiocarbon

The most common method of dating archaeological sites today is by radiocarbon (^{14}C). The most common isotope of carbon is ^{12}C. Carbon-14 is generated by the interaction of neutrons from cosmic rays and ^{14}N. It is taken up by plants as CO_2 and incorporated into plant tissues. The plants may be eaten by animals and ^{14}C becomes incorporated into bones, horns, shells or other parts than can survive over archaeological time. Carbon-14 slowly decays to nitrogen and the ratio of ^{14}C to ^{12}C drops. The halflife of ^{14}C is usually taken as 5730 ± 30 years. Carbon incorporated into an organism 5700 years ago should have about one half the background percentage of ^{14}C remaining.

In the initial testing of the method controls of known historical age were used, such as wood from Egyptian tombs of known date. The correlation was excellent for materials some 3000 years of age or younger but older objects showed some discrepancies. A radiocarbon date of some 3000 BC was up to eight centuries younger than the historical date. At first some people blamed history, thinking the method infallible and history at fault.

Three assumptions were made in developing the method, all of which must be correct for the system to work:

assumption 1: decay of ^{14}C is constant and not affected by time or environment;
assumption 2: the halflife is correct; and
assumption 3: background concentration of ^{14}C is uniform over the earth and constant through time.

As far as we can detect, the first assumption is correct. There has been some discussion over the halflife and some scientists have proposed another, but this does not correct the calendar year–radiocarbon year discrepancy. Then Professor Hans E. Suess started a calibration using cores from the bristle cone pine. He took segments of known age and tested for ^{14}C and found assumption 3 to be wrong. The flux of ^{14}C varies with time. There were times when ^{14}C concentration was much higher than now and this makes old dates too young. He developed curves for his calibration, but unfortunately they are neither a straight line nor a curve with a function – they are sinuous, difficult to use and a precise calibration seems out of the question. At the order of 8000 BC, radiocarbon years and calendar years differ by about 1000 years and radiocarbon years seem to be misleading.

Most dates given in archaeological reports are in radiocarbon years and not corrected. A convention has been adopted to report dates in radiocarbon years as ad–bc and corrected or historical dates as AD–BC. To further complicate the picture the notation bp–BP (i.e. before present) is also common. I shall try to follow the convention in this book but one must read the dates very carefully; even the authors can be confused.

The bristle cone pine calibration caused a great stir in Europe in many fields (Renfrew, 1975). It had been established as dogma that many cultural traits originated in the Near East and flowed from there across Europe. With the correction of radiocarbon years it now appeared that Megalithic dolmens, minares and Stonehenge were older than the pyramids, which were dated in calendar years. Europe could now claim innovations of a number of elements thought to have been borrowed from the Near East. The Near East was not such a center after all. The effect on New World archaeologists was of less significance, since there was little history to base calendar years on and many archaeologists thought radiocarbon dates were too young anyway.

Some other methods

Thermoluminescence is another method based on change with time. In theory heat, such as firing a pot, will drive electrons from unstable sites in the clay matrix, and these electrons will return slowly and at a steady rate. Reheating will drive them off again and the electromagnetic energy can be measured as photons. The difference between electron-saturated clay and the treated potsherd should indicate when the pot was last fired. The method is not as accurate as radiocarbon but can supply useful information where ^{14}C cannot be used.

Obsidian hydration has been used with some success. When a blade is struck from a core, the edges are exposed to the atmosphere for the first time since the volcanic glass solidified. The silica hydrates at a rather steady rate and measurement of the hydrolyzed zone can give some estimation of time since the blade was struck.

Fission track dating has been used on obsidian and even man-made glass. The tracks are about 20 μm in length and are due to spontaneous fission of large unstable atoms of ^{238}U. The tracks can be observed directly on thin sections with an electron microscope or with a light microscope, after enlarging the tracks by etching with hydrofluoric acid. The method seems to be reliable but is limited to glass.

The potassium–argon method of dating depends on the decay of ^{40}K in relation to argon which does not decay. The halflife of ^{40}K is some 1 300 000 000 years however, which is too long for dating later than about 250 000 years. The method has been used to date the oldest rocks on earth and the oldest humanoids in east Africa. Radiocarbon dating has a limit of some 50 000 to 70 000 years, leaving a substantial gap in dating methodology. A potential bridge of the gap is by amino acid racemization. Amino acids have the property of rotating polarized light either to the left or the right. This can be easily and accurately measured with a microscope with polarized light. The two modes are noted as L- (*laevo*) and D- (*dextro*). All amino acids produced by living organisms are of the L- kind but slowly shift to the D- mode. This change is called racemization and occurs to some degree even in living organisms. It has been suggested that the method could be used to verify the age of people who claim to be exceptionally old by extracting amino acids from the teeth.

The protein most likely to survive archaeological time is collagen in bones, hooves, horns, etc. It is so durable that traces have been found in fossils 300 000 000 years old. The protein is digested and the amino acids isolated. Aspartic acid is the most labile amino acid but its halflife is about 15 000 years at 20 °C. Other acids are even slower to racemize. The process is temperature-dependent and it is not always 20 °C when the bones are baking in the desert sun or buried in Arctic permafrost. The time range of the method is from one to one million years, but temperature is a problem and results can be misleading.

Ceramics

Pottery changes over time as well. Paste, slip, temper, decorations, shape, size, style, method of manufacture and other features are all remarkably time-dependent. Sherd reading was initiated in 1890 by Sir Flinders Petrie when he started excavations at Tell-el-Hesi near Gaza. The system was amplified and refined by biblical archaeologist, W. F. Allbright. It is now a language required of all archaeology students working in the Near East and many other parts of the world as well. Pottery reading takes a lot of practice but can be mastered with time and application.

Dating by pottery is especially useful in surface surveys. Many surveys have been made, but as an example let us examine a Wadi-el-Hasa archaeological survey (1979–83) by Burton MacDonald (1988), because I know something about it and had a small part to play. The Wadi-el-Hasa is an impressive picturesque canyon in west central Jordan, carved by erosion from the eastern desert of Jordan down to the south end of the Dead Sea. The stream itself is the biblical Zered and separates Moab from Edom. Only the southern side was surveyed, and since that covered some 600 km² it was quite impossible to cover it all in three field seasons, 1979, 1981 and 1982, with revisitation to some sites in 1983. Work was therefore concentrated on the western portion of the region. Some of the areas were surveyed by Land Rover as terrain permitted, but more intensive surveys were made by systematic transects covered on foot. The area is extremely rugged and crossed by deep tributary canyons.

A total of 1074 sites was recorded; some were of prepottery age, a few going back to lower Palaeolithic *c.* 500 000 years ago, roughly dated by lithic artifacts. The pottery time range was *c.* 4750 BC to AD 1918. The last date was the end of Ottoman domination and any later sites were not recorded. Pottery was divided into 45 classes, including one 'undetermined.' These have conventional names such as Pottery Neolithic (PN), Chalcolithic, Early Bronze (EB I, II, III and IV), Middle Bronze (MB), Late Bronze (LB), Iron Age (IA with six subdivisions), Hellenistic Nabatean, Roman, Parthian, Byzantine and some 12 classes of Arabic and Ottoman domination. Approximate calendar years can be assigned to these classes based on known chronology of the region.

The number of sites dating to a particular style presented interesting patterns. Neolithic and Chalcolithic were represented by only a few sites but there were 38 of Early Bronze I. The rest of Early Bronze was very sparsely represented, but Iron Age I had 24 and Iron Age II, 35. Hellenistic Age was rather sparse but there was a peaking in Nabatean with 195. This time showed the greatest density of human occupation although Roman presence was conspicuous, not only in pottery style but by roads, road markers, steles, etc. At the time of the Byzantine occupation settlement of the Wadi collapsed, but people returned in late Islamic and Ottoman times.

Calendar year dates for peak occupations are Early Bronze I (3300 to 2900 BC), Iron Age I (1200 to 918 BC), Iron Age II (918 to 539 BC), Nabatean (63 BC to AD 304), late Byzantine (AD 491 to 640), late Islamic (AD 1174 to 1918), Ottoman (AD 1516 to 1918.) There are subdivisions in each class with more precise dating, but a surface scatter of sherds usually represents a considerable time range and sites may be occupied more than once.

The Wadi-el-Hasa is marginal for dryland agriculture. It would not be occupied by farmers unless the better watered and more fertile sites were already occupied. The occupation pattern in the Wadi is one of 'filling up' and 'emptying out.' It appears to be due to events elsewhere and is not correlated with any changes in climate so far reported. Politics and economies are more likely to be the cause of extreme fluctuation in occupation. The Nabateans were masters of desert agriculture and devised a number of ingenious methods of water management and conservation. Roman pressure may have sent some of them into the Wadi-el-Hasa where they could survive until more attractive lands became available elsewhere. At least interpretations of this kind can be generated by surface surveys and pottery reading without the cost in time and money of excavation.

Lithics

Lithic industries change with time also and sites can be assigned a rough date according to the stone tools and debitage recovered from them. In the Wadi-el-Hasa survey, stone artifacts were classed in nine categories ranging from 'Lower Palaeolithic' to 'Pottery Neolithic' and covered a time range of half a million years. The classes were conventional, e.g. Lower, Middle, Upper and Epipalaeolithic, prepottery Neolithic (PPN), etc. and when pottery appeared it was preferred for dating. The time ranges for each class varied enormously. There were some 55 Lower Palaeolithic sites and this seems like a lot, but there were a few hundred thousand years to accumulate these artifacts compared to a few thousand for later time ranges. People ranged freely over the canyon and sometimes camped repeatedly at some favored location so that lithics of different time periods were mixed. Middle Palaeolithic materials were the most frequent of the 'early sites' – early was defined as anything before PPN. Middle Palaeolithic includes Mousterian–Lavalloisian artifacts.

Mousterian flake technique was an important advance over the older core tools but was rather primitive in terms of what was to come later. The Neanderthalers prepared a flint nodule by breaking it at one end and roughing out the flake to be knapped off; then with some skill, the desired flake was removed. Some of the characteristic flakes are called Lavalloisian. In addition to preformed flakes, angular and pointed slivers were also knapped off the core and used for a variety of purposes including spear points. Gradually the flake technique evolved toward the production of blades.

In blade knapping, the flint nodule or piece of obsidian is prepared by breaking one end, much as in the Mousterian procedure, to make a striking platform. With good material, skill, and probably bloody knuckles, it is possible to strike off long, narrow, parallel-sided blades by hitting the edge of the platform with another stone. Force can be applied more accurately by using a punch of antler, bone or stone and striking the punch with a hammerstone. Blade after blade can be struck from a nodule, more or less like peeling leaves from an onion. By careful overlapping, each blade has a sort of spine or midrib and razor-sharp edges on both sides. The process continues until a flaw in the nodule or small size of the core indicates there is no more to be knapped and the core is discarded. The cores can be aesthetically very attractive and small ones, especially of obsidian, are beautiful faceted jewels. A simple vise can be devised by pinching the stone under a flat stick and either sitting or standing on the stick.

The early blades tended to be rather large and coarse. But over time there was a trend toward smaller and smaller blades and bladelets. In some vocabularies, a blade is defined as a flake at least twice as long as wide, and a bladelet as a blade less than 30 mm long. Blade knapping was widespread around the world and probably evolved independently several times. It is an efficient way to use stone. Perhaps the most elegant and sophisticated blades were knapped in and around the Valley of Mexico where obsidian was abundant. Beautiful slender blades were struck, perhaps 15 or even 20 cm long and 1 cm wide. They were so delicate (after all, obsidian is glass) that they may never have been used except for ceremonial purposes.

But blades can be blanks from which other tools can be made. They can be rounded off at one end to make an 'end scraper.' What they were used for we do not really know, but they are abundant in the Near East and perhaps they were used to scrape hides or smooth wood, etc. One can knock the corners off an end, leaving a central point that is a boring tool called a burin. Blades can be 'backed,' i.e. dulled on one edge so the user does not cut himself when using it as a knife. One can break up a blade into small slivers, trapezoids, rhomboids, triangles, etc. These slivers are razor-sharp and can be used for a variety of cutting and penetration purposes including mounting on spears and tipping arrows. Neolithic blades were mounted on hafts of antler or wood and used for sickles.

The stone of choice is obsidian; it produces the sharpest edges. Glass

Neolithic bladelets and small core. Trapezoid and lunate above left flint. The coin is approximately 18 mm in diameter.

still produces the sharpest knives. When we found it necessary to make ultra-thin sections of tissues for viewing with an electron microscope, we found the sharpest blade we could devise was a piece of broken glass. Our Stone Age ancestors knew this thousands of years ago. But obsidian can be found only in very local deposits associated with volcanic activity. Because of its value for tool making it was one of the first items of long distance trade. Obsidian from different sources can be identified by chemical fingerprinting; the proportions of different elements, often occurring in minute quantities, are highly diagnostic. It is possible, therefore, to trace early trade routes from obsidian sources to areas of usage in both the Old and New Worlds.

Flint is more widely available, but good flint can be scarce too and considerable effort may be expended to obtain it. Flint freshly dug from the earth and well hydrated knaps much better than nodules that have been baking in the desert sun. In England, Neolithic people actually dug mines, more or less like coal mines, to get flints for tool making. Good flint can yield incredibly beautiful artifacts in the hands of a skilled knapper. One may find examples illustrated in art books. The lovely Salutrian laurel leaf blades, sacrificial knives of Egypt and Mexico and ceremonial arrowheads of several American Indian tribes are examples.

Blades are still being struck by the truckload in Turkey. The source is a blue-gray flint in western Anatolia and the rather large crude blades are shipped all over Turkey in gunnysacks. They are not for knives or sickles; they are destined for people who manufacture threshing sledges. The use of the sledge is rapidly declining because mobile threshing machines are taking over the threshing process. Traditionally, one of the major methods of threshing was to distribute the grain and straw over a threshing floor and drive a threshing sledge, pulled by draft animals of one sort or another, over the material. The thresher usually rode on the sledge, sometimes sitting on a chair. The sledge was composed of several boards fastened together at the edges and armed below with bits of flint firmly lodged in holes in the boards. The flints break up the heads of grain or whatever crop is being threshed, which could be lentil, vetch, chickpeas, etc.; then the grain is separated from the light chaff by winnowing. The flints in the sledge all come from the one source. While the blades are rather crude, this blue flint has a clear musical ring when one strikes one blade with another. Each blade is broken into about three pieces for mounting on the bottom of the sledge. The sledge is the *tribulum* of ancient Rome and its recent distribution is more or less confined to the former empire. The device is mentioned in Homer as well.

Flint blades keep their edge better than steel. They come out of Neolithic sites in enormous numbers and people sorting blades even 9000 years old must be very careful lest they cut their fingers. However, they do become dull with use and can be resharpened by striking off tiny flakes. Retouched blades often have a sort of 'nibbled' look, and ethnographic reports from Australia indicate the Aborigines do indeed sharpen a stone knife by crushing off bits with their teeth.

Blades, and sometimes flakes, may take on a recognizable gloss or sheen especially on ridges and edges. It has been suggested that this gloss is due to polish from silica cells in grass epidermis tissue. The silica cells are filled with a plant opal which is very durable, and prairie soils contain vast amounts of this material. The gloss may indicate grass seed harvesting or even cereal production. I once tried to test this out by mounting some freshly knapped blades on a wooden haft and harvesting some wild cereal on Karacadağ in Turkey. I got what looked like sheen in minutes but it was mixed with chlorophyll. Wild cereals, at least wheat and barley, are green and succulent at the base while the grain is maturing at the top of the plant. One must always harvest wild cereals a little green because it shatters at maturity. To remove the chlorophyll I wiped the flints with alcohol; the chlorophyll came off but so did the sheen. Later, I tried an experiment in Oklahoma using blades, some 9000 years old, but that had no sheen, from the famous site of Jarmo. Some students and I cut about a half hectare of modern bread wheat. The blades became rounded and dull but no sheen. I now believe the sheen is laid down in solution from juicy stalks and that sheen on sickle blades indicates harvesting grasses with green, juicy lower stems. Modern domesticated cereals are too dry to make sheen although they are heavily loaded with silica cells. Since my crude experiments a number of people have experimented with flint sickle harvesting and have studied wear and abrasion patterns on flint blades under various conditions. Wear patterns can often be identified on archaeological blades, and we are learning a lot about the usage and conditions under which they were used.

In prepottery times, the lithics are the most diagnostic artifacts for defining 'cultures.' The total assemblage from a site, including debitage (waste), often has a style and cohesion that can be classed by culture name, e.g. Kebaran, Ahmarian, Natufian, etc. The names are usually taken from the site where the assemblage was first studied, and other assemblages with characteristics of the type may be found distributed over a considerable area. One culture may follow another in time, producing sequences that can sometimes be dated fairly accurately. Pottery is usually a more sensitive indicator of time than the stone industries. Both are used where available and correlated with radiocarbon dates when possible.

Cultural sequences

Cultural sequences can be read rather easily by specialists of specific regions and time ranges but it requires a lot of background and experience. Before radiocarbon methods were available a primary system of dating was by stratigraphy. In excavating a mound (*Tell* in Arabic, *Tepe* and *Hüyük* in Turkish), a cave, a rock shelter or other occupation site, it is assumed that the oldest deposits are at the bottom and the youngest at the top. It is an obvious logical assumption and generally is true, but intrusions and inversions do occur and are not always detectable, no matter how much care is taken in the excavation. We are finding more and more cases of intrusive materials in strata where they do not really belong.

The best defense against errors for organic materials is the use of accelerator mass spectrography (AMS). The accelerator separates ^{12}C from ^{14}C by mass and radioactivity is irrelevant. This instrument can give a ^{14}C reading on very small samples such as a single grain of wheat, rice or other crop plant. Some examples are instructive. In the cave of Nahal Oren, Israel, two grains of emmer with domesticated morphology were found sealed in Kebaran context beneath a rock fall. Because of the rock fall, the time range was thought to be secure and Kebaran. This culture dates to the fourteenth–fifteenth millennia BC (Noy, Legge and Higgs, 1973). The earliness of that date was rather sensational and out of context with other finds. A testing with AMS, however, showed the seeds to be much more recent. Wendorf (Wendorf *et al.*, 1979) reported barley, wheat and some other seeds found at Wadi Kubbanya near Aswan, Egypt, dating to the sixteenth–seventeenth millennia BC. The dates were determined on charcoal associated with the seeds. Agriculture at such an early time seemed out of place. When AMS became available, the seeds themselves were dated and turned out to be about Roman age (Gowlett and Hedges, 1987). The charcoal, however, was old and Wendorf *et al.* had no way of knowing the seeds were intrusive. Phillipson excavated the Gobedra rock shelter near Lalibella, Ethiopia, and sent some material to me for identification. I identified some finger millet seeds and one of my students, Khidir Hilu, who was studying finger millet at the time, confirmed positively that they were of cultivated form. The dating was largely stratographic but Phillipson thought the seeds could have been from the third millenium BC. At the time this would have been the earliest trace of indigenous cultivated plants of sub-Sahara Africa. Later AMS tests indicated they were intrusive and only a few hundred years old (Gowlett *et al.*, 1987). The much discussed maize cobs of Tehuacan valley of Mexico turn out to be no older than 3600 BC under AMS analysis.

There are other cases, but it should be emphasized that these were honest errors. The excavators had every reason to believe their seeds belonged to the context in which they were found. There is something Oedipean about the situation. When the gods on Mount Olympus are at play, there is nothing a mere mortal can do. AMS shows promise of helping archaeologists out of victimization by fate. Other instruments are coming into play and the science is progressing.

Wendorf and his colleagues have recently found what appear to be sorghum seeds in the western desert of Egypt. They have already been dated by AMS and are, indeed, ancient and not intrusive. His archaeobotanist is Krystina Wasylikova of the Polish Academy of Sciences, Krakow. At Wendorf's request I met her at the Royal Botanical Gardens at Kew, where there is an extensive collection of African sorghum made many years ago when materials were more authentic than now. We matched the archaeological material with herbarium specimens. John Evans of the Polytechnic of East London used infrared spectroscopy to make scans of both the archaeological material and herbarium specimens. The scans are on the lipid fraction, which is extremely durable and can even survive charring. Lipids were extracted by both hexane and chloroform; the extraction does no damage to seed morphology so they can still be used as herbarium specimens. The infrared signals confirmed the morphological identification as sorghum.

The 'skull house' at Çayönü, Tepesi, near Diyarbakir, Turkey.
Courtesy of R. J. Braidwood.

Braidwood and Cambel, excavating Çayönü Tepesi near Diyarbakir,
Turkey, from 1964 to the present found a house with some 90 human
skulls, a large stone slab with stains on it and a large flint knife, also
stained suspiciously. The stains were field tested for human blood
(positive) by Loy and Wood (1989), and then identified by crystalliz-
ation and immunological techniques in the laboratory. The residues
were around 9000 years old, but the technique was so sensitive that
blood of humans, sheep, goats and the now extinct *Bos primigenius*
could be positively identified. Techniques are improving year by year
and more and more sensitive ones are being brought to bear on
archaeological problems. Our digging into the past also changes
through time and we retrieve more and more information each passing year.

Seeds and plants

Changes in vegetation and climate are best monitored by palynological (pollen) studies. Pollen can sometimes be recovered in excavation sites, but the yield is usually sparse and scrappy as pollen does not preserve well in aerated conditions. The ideal source of datable pollen is in lake sediments. The lake should be old enough to cover the time range of interest, neither too shallow nor too deep, and large enough to provide a body of still water. Pollen is produced in enormous quantities by wind pollinated species; some of it blows over the lake and drops into the water where it sinks to the bottom. Silts and other sediments are washed into the lake from above. Over time, layers of sediments are built up laced with pollen that is often well preserved under anaerobic conditions of the lake bottom. Pollen can often be identified to species, or at least to genus, although grass pollen is always difficult and may not be very diagnostic.

Special tools have been devised to extract cores from lake sediments. Under most conditions, it is not possible to extract a single intact core and repeated borings are required to piece together the total sequence. Careful attention to depths of each boring and all precautions possible against contamination are needed for a reliable sample. The cores tend to be stratified, reflecting the history of the lake, and some strata may contain enough organic material for radiocarbon dating, so that the rate of deposition can be monitored as well as relative ages of pollen recovered. Such lake sediments are invaluable in recording changes of vegetation and possible changes of climate over time. The pollen samples are heavily biased toward wind pollinated plants and favor certain species of this class that produce enormous amounts of pollen. Some pollen of insect pollinated plants may also appear in the samples and could be very diagnostic. In studying a region, it is desirable to obtain samples of the current pollen rain for comparison. This can be done easily by exposing microscope slides coated with Vaseline or some similar sticky substance.

Unfortunately for the Near East and North Africa, there are not many suitable lakes and sediment cores form a very coarse grid. Swamps and marshy wetlands can yield useful information, although usually for shorter time periods. Pollen sequences in desert to subhumid climatic zones are sparse and scrappy, but much better in areas of higher rainfall where soil cores and peat may yield information as well as lakes.

Most plant materials that survive over archaeological time are charred. Carbon is extremely durable as any camper, who has tried to take the black off a pot or frying pan after a camping trip, knows. A seed or plant part need not be charred completely through; a coating of carbon may suffice to preserve it for thousands of years. Charring can radically distort the shape of seeds depending in part on the moisture content of the seed at the time of charring. Many years ago we did some artificial charring in our laboratory to monitor distortion of common cereal and pulse seeds likely to be recovered in archaeological sites. Under some conditions, we found the thin, laterally compressed seed of einkorn wheat could swell up to look like bread wheat. In general, for cereals at least, charring shortens the grains and increases width and depth; they become rounder. Most modern archaeobotanical laboratories today do artificial charring to provide reference material for identification. Seed identification has been largely based on morphology, although infrared spectroscopy of lipid fractions may become an important source of verification. Criteria for separating domestic races from spontaneous races (wild and weed) are described in Chapter 2 as well as problems associated with the identification of wild and domesticated animals.

For most of the history of archaeology bones have come out of excavations much more abundantly than plant remains. Superb plant materials were found in Egyptian tombs, in coastal Peru and in Swiss lake dwellings, but most sites yielded little until flotation and wet screening techniques came into use in the last two or three decades. The method is still not being used as much as it should be, especially in the Far East and Africa. Flotation simply depends on the fact that most organic materials have lower specific gravity than minerals and float in water. The water can be varied by adding salt or frothing with detergent, but the most common flotation procedure is to use whatever local source of water is available. It is possible to pass an entire mound through flotation procedures but usually only promising samples are submitted for extraction. Plant remains are now much more abundant than formerly and are providing critical information on origins of agriculture and crop evolution.

The science of archaeology has changed enormously in the thirty odd years I have been associated with it. I remember a botanical colleague remarking nearly 30 years ago, 'Have archaeologists ever heard of statistics?' At the time, it was a valid question but they certainly have used the tool since. The sophistication of modern archaeological techniques has added a great deal of information about people of the past, their life styles, what they ate, what they wore, their health status, demography, even something of rites and ceremonies. The picture of agricultural origins is being filled out and times and places are becoming more secure. This is not to say that new findings will not change our current perceptions. The great fun of science is that ideas long held can be overturned by the turn of a spade or signals from outer space.

Some generalities from archaeology

Traces of the hominid family now go back a few million years but the early prehistory of the human race is very sketchy. The crudest and oldest tools are simply pebbles, apparently broken artificially to produce a sharp cutting edge. Some are so crude it is arguable whether they are artifacts or not. Very slowly, over millennia of time, tools improved and became more recognizable. Eventually a rather standardized tool developed, usually called a hand axe and thought to be some kind of chopper or cleaver. The first versions are rather crude and called Abbevillian after a Palaeolithic site in France. This evolved into a similar, more refined tool, Acheulean, after another site in France. Acheulean hand axes have been found in considerable numbers over vast reaches of Africa, Europe and Asia. They are all very similar and often found in little groups. The site of Olorgosaille in Kenya has an extensive area almost paved with them. Whenever we find human bones associated with this artifact, they appear to be of the *Homo erectus* type.

The tool is always pear-shaped in outline and rather heavy and solid; the range in size is not great. Its actual function is not known. The consensus of anthropologists seems to be that it was a cleaver to dismember the large game animals that *Homo erectus* hunted. But it is not a very efficient tool, and why is it always pear-shaped, fat and rounded at one end and rather pointed at the other? Experiments have been performed with Acheulean hand axes and animals can, indeed, be dismembered with them, but other tools would be much more efficient.

Not being an archaeologist or anthropologist I can let my imagination run free, unrestrained by traditional thinking. I believe the teardrop shape of Acheulean hand axes had an aerodynamic function. If they just wanted a cleaver, why make it pear-shaped? I suggest it was a projectile. It is much too heavy for any kind of spear or arrow, but all one need do is weave a small pouch of fiber, put in the 'hand axe' and attach a cord, swing it around one's body like a hammer throw and let fly. Imagine the impact of a stone of this weight. It could stun a mammoth or crush skulls of animals of lesser size. We know that slings in the hands of an expert can be very accurate. I do not imagine a hammer thrower could be as accurate as a sling, but who knows what might be achieved with practice? Even modern Olympic contestants must direct their hammer fairly well to get the distance required to win. Why does this sport persist in Olympic games? It now seems a skill without purpose, but there was a function at one time. I have suggested this use for the 'hand axe' to several anthropologists and received extremely negative responses.

In Europe and western Asia, at least, the *Homo erectus* was followed by the Neanderthals, named for the Neander Valley in Germany where the first remains were found. The Neanderthals were a *Homo sapiens* recognizably different from modern *H. sapiens sapiens*. Their tool kit was called Mousterian, and was much more varied than that of *Homo erectus* and included an array of fine tools. Hand axes are classed as core tools made by removing flakes and the tool is what is left after the flakes are knapped off. Flake tools are made by preparing a core and striking off flakes, which are used as tools and the remaining core is discarded. A nodule of flint or piece of obsidian will yield a great deal more cutting edge when used as flakes than when used as a core; the flake technique was a considerable advance in tool making.

The extreme Neanderthal morphology that developed in Europe differed most noticeably from modern humans in having prominent brow ridges, a low forehead and a larger back of the head; brain size was about the same or a little larger but the conformation was different; and there were some differences in long bones as well as in skulls. In southwestern Asia differences were less than in Europe, and at Mount Carmel in Israel there is some evidence of introgression among forms of *Homo sapiens*. The Neanderthals disappeared some 40 000 to 50 000 years ago and *H. sapiens sapiens* appeared as early as 100 000 years ago in some places and as late as 35 000 years ago in others.

The Neanderthals were evidently skillful big-game hunters and the tradition was carried on with improvements by anatomically modern man, *H. sapiens sapiens*. They began to specialize in killing mammoths, mastodons, wooly rhinoceroses, giant bison and other huge animals of the Pleistocene fauna, and many of these animals are portrayed with great artistic skill on the walls and vaulted roofs of limestone caves in southwestern France and northern Spain (see p. 19).

Toward the end of the Pleistocene, the whole earth moved into a very dynamic time. The enormous continental ice sheets began to melt; so much water had accumulated in them that sea levels were some 90 to 100 m lower than they are today. The ice melted rapidly in geological terms of time, sea levels rose dramatically, drowning coasts and coastal valleys. The Sunda shelf off Southeast Asia was drowned leaving the islands of the Philippines, Borneo and part of Indonesia. The land mass of Sahul was divided as Tasmania and New Guinea were cut off from Australia (Allen, Golson and Jones, 1977.) The English Channel, North Sea and Baltic were formed, as well as Chesapeake Bay and the mouth of the Amazon. In North America, 35 genera or some 70% of the mammalian fauna became extinct; horses and camels that evolved in North America succumbed but survived in Asia. Everywhere mammoths and mastodon, giant bison, giant ground sloths and others died out. Elephants and rhinoceroses survived in the Old World but not in the New. Large mammals were not the only species to die out. There were losses of small animals and even birds. Why should animals die out when the climate became warmer and conditions presumably improved? The question is easy to ask but not so easy to answer. Some theories, of course, have been proposed; some seem to provide plausible explanations for some species but not for others. We shall not go into them here, but the fact that mass extinctions occurred surely caused radical changes in human adaptation, but biotic migrations were, perhaps, even more dramatic (Ruddiman and Wright, 1987).

At the end of the Pleistocene, the rain forests of Amazonia, of so much concern today, were confined to a few refugia spotted around the periphery of its present or recent distribution. Desiccation during the last Ice Age had caused it to retreat (Meggers, Ayensu and Duck-worth, 1973; Vanzolini, 1973; Fig. 3.1).

The situation in Africa was very much the same (Fig. 3.2). These tropical rain forests migrated thousands of kilometers in the first few thousand years of the Holocene. What we are doing to them today is

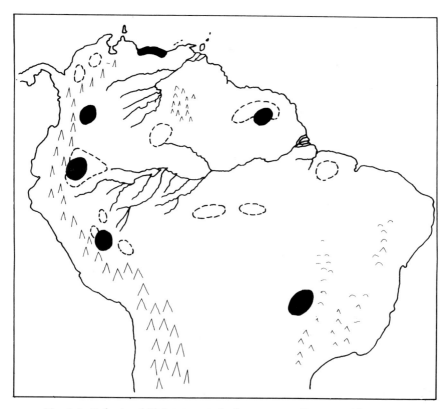

Fig. 3.1. Refugia of Pleistocene rain forests according to evidence from birds, dashed lines (Haffer, 1969), and reptiles and amphibans, black (Vanzolini, 1973).

not (yet) as devastating as what an ice age can do, and the processes seem reversible. In fact, one of the current theories to explain the enormous diversity of species in tropical forests involves the concept of pulsating floras. With each ice age the forest contracts to refugia, bringing about isolation of species for long periods of time. Then, with the return of an interglacial the forest expands rapidly, bringing isolation to an end and permitting introgression among related races and species. This is in fact a mechanism for rapid evolution that will be discussed later. The rain forest, despite its diversity, is a difficult environment for hunter–gatherers and again adjustments in human life were required for survival.

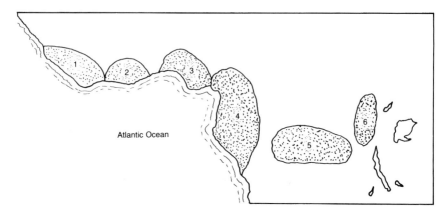

Fig. 3.2. Refugia of African rain forests in the Pleistocene based
on reptiles and amphibians (Vanzolini, 1973). 1, Guinea block; 2,
Ghanaean block; 3, Nigerian block; 4, Cameroon block;
5, northern and eastern Congo block; 6, southwestern Congo block.

Home sapiens was forced to make adjustments to these dramatic
changes. First of all humans adjusted to a watery habitat. They learnt
to build rafts, canoes, hide boats and other means of water transportation; they invented harpoons, fish hooks, weirs and fish traps; they
shifted their attention to a wider range of small animals as the
megafauna became extinct. Plants became more important in the diet.
People began to craft still smaller, more refined and efficient tools. In
most areas they lost stature and sexual dimorphism was reduced as
men lost relatively more in height than women. In some areas, for
example, eastern Mediterranean, skeletons suggest infection by *Plas-
modium falciparum*, the organism causing malaria (Angel, 1984).

It has been suggested that the loss in height and sexual dimorphism
was due to a change in the food procurement system. As the
megafauna became extinct, attention shifted to smaller animals and
plant gathering and women shared more equally in harvesting food.
Palaeopathology has indicated, however, that the diet remained good.
Preagricultural hunter—gatherers had excellent teeth, and there is
little or no evidence of starvation or chronic disease. The suggestion
of malaria in the eastern Mediterranean may have been an omen of
things to come.

The melting of continental glaciers must have been dramatic at times. Mountain glaciers flow down-slope carving out U-shaped valleys. They remove material and deposit it down-slope in lateral or terminal moraines when they retreat. Continental glaciers also flow from some focus where ice is building towards the face of the glacier. The flowing action continues even when the glacier is retreating. The retreat is due to ice melting faster than the forward thrust of the glacier. Retreats are not smooth and even; the glacial front may remain stationary for some time, the melting and thrust in balance. Then, it may pull back or even advance again temporarily. The result is deposits of material in moraines where the front has been stalled and the meltwater then forms lakes behind the barriers. Some of the best farmland in temperate regions of the world are derived from lake bottoms of temporary glacial meltlakes. Continental glaciers smooth and build the landscape in contrast to mountain glaciers that carve and cut. Sometimes the meltwater backs up to the point that it overtops its moraine dam and cuts through, dumping the whole lake on the terrain below. The sudden draining of a glacial lake will have dramatic results, flushing over thousands of square kilometers and perhaps creating new lakes in a matter of days.

The rapid rise of sea levels must have been traumatic for coastal dwelling people. This would be especially true where continental shelves were drowned by shallow incursions as in Southeast Asia and the South Pacific. The transgression extended over vast areas, sharply reducing land area and flooding out foraging ranges. Where continental shelves were deeper and/or steeper, the changes would have been less dramatic. Nevertheless, the rapid rise in sea levels everywhere must have forced many people to adapt to radically new situations.

Is it possible that the worldwide experience with flooding is the basis of so many flood stories in the creation legends of the world? Floods are a part of creation myths in North and South America, Africa, Europe and Asia including, of course, the Biblical and related accounts of the Near East. Even desert dwellers have stories of cosmic floods. Could this be traced to a universal early Holocene experience? I suppose there is no way to find out, but it seems a reasonable possibility.

CHAPTER FOUR

The Near East

The archaeological record

The archaeological record of humans in the Near East is respectably long, although not as long as that in Africa. Acheulean Man (*Homo erectus*) wandered over the whole region and left a scatter of character-istic 'hand axes.' Later, the Neanderthals occupied many of the caves in the hilly or mountainous areas and left tools and artifacts of the Mousterian tradition. In the Near East, the Neanderthals 'bowed out' about 35 000 years ago and there was a break in the evidence of human activity until the caves were reoccupied by anatomically modern humans (*Homo sapiens sapiens*) over 20 000 years ago. The artifacts left evolved into epipalaeolithic traditions with striking regional differentiation. The tools and weapons became smaller, more efficient and there was a trend toward compound pieces; that is more than one blade mounted on a haft to form a sickle or several very small razor-sharp bladelets on a shaft to make a spear. Local differentiation increased with time.

The time of interest for the evolution of agriculture begins at the suture between the Pleistocene and Holocene. For the Near East this may be taken as about 12 000 to 11 000 years ago, somewhat earlier than that for North America. The palynological information at that time range lacks data from most of Syria, all of Iraq, Saudi Arabia and Jordan, but what we do have shows a floral distribution strikingly different from the recent past. Figure 4.1 shows, in a somewhat crude way, the present distribution of the major plant formations of the region. Of particular interest is the oak woodland, which is found today along the Levant, the Taurus and the Zagros mountain ranges at median elevations. This formation is of particular interest because the earliest domesticates we have found so far are of emmer, einkorn and barley, and all three are found in the oak woodland. Einkorn may range well above the oak in the mountains and barley may range far below it into the deserts. But emmer is rather strictly confined to the oak woodland formation. All of the earliest sites containing plant domesticates have emmer remains. The oak woodland, therefore, is critical to the story.

It should be stressed that both forest and woodland have been seriously degraded in recent centuries and what we find today are relicts of former distributions. Quite often, one can see a whole mountainside bare of trees except for a patch or grove of relict woodland. One familiar with the region knows, without going to investigate, that there is a cemetery in the grove; the people do not cut trees in a cemetery. The spacing gives us some idea of what the ancient woodlands looked like. One may also find well developed mature trees standing alone where some saint or holy man was buried. Such trees are often decorated with colorful yarn or strings of blue beads. In a grove where there is a choice of trees, the ones decorated are usually the hawthorne (*Crataegus*). If there is no crataegus available, an oak will serve.

At the end of the Pleistocene and start of the Holocene, the oak woodland belt was not where it is now. It was confined to a few refuges in a narrow strip along the Mediterranean coasts of the Levant, and where the oak woodland belt is now was, at that time, an *Artemisia* steppe. The movement of the oak belt into the hill country of the Zagros and the Taurus was critical in setting the scene for the first plant domestications of the region. At least some of the oaks were in place by 10 000 years ago and this marks the approximate beginning of prepottery Neolithic A (PPNA) and the first evidence of domesticated plants in the region (Bar–Yosef and Kislev, 1989).

There is no hope that we will ever uncover the real beginnings, and they surely did not evolve in any one place. As of now, the first traces of cereal cultivation are found in prepottery Neolithic A and date to just a little before 8000 BC. Barley and emmer appear to be the first crops. PPNA is not abundant and as of this writing is known only from the sites of Gesher, Netiv–Hagdud, Gilgal and Jericho, all of them within a radius of 15 km in the Jordan rift valley, and from Tell Aswad in the Damascus basin.

The sites in and around Jericho are not in the oak woodland; they are too far down the valley and occur in a desert climate. They are, however, located at the apex or flanks of alluvial fans with copious springs for irrigation. The site in the Damascus basin was wetted by a high water table. Farther up the valley, but still well below sea level,

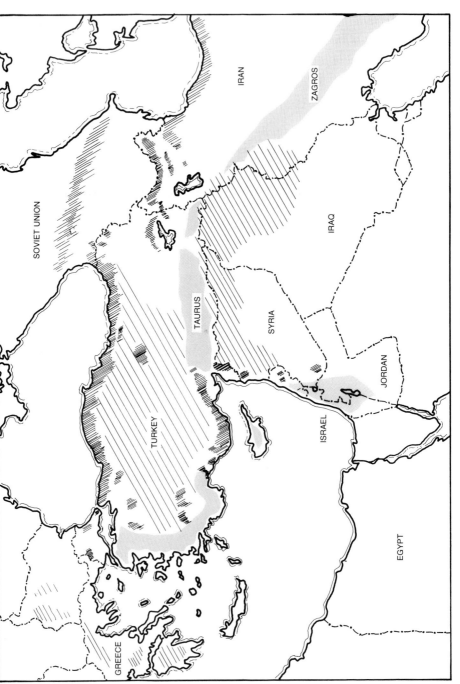

Fig. 4.1. Vegetation of the Near East. Dark shading, forests; light shading, oak woodlands; light hatching, steppe.

an oak woodland does appear and wild emmer is extremely abundant there today.

There are sites that span the time range between the epipaleolithic and the Neolithic. Two important ones are located near the Euphrates in Syria: Tell Abu Hureyra and Tell Mureybit. The earlier levels show considerable evidence of wild cereal harvests – wild einkorn, wild emmer, barley and rye are all found. Accelerator dates range from 9100 to 8250 BC. The epipalaeolithic culture however terminated about 8500 BC and there was a hiatus. The sites were reoccupied about 7500 BC by fully agricultural prepottery Neolithic B (PPNB). There was no transition (Hillman, Colledge and Harris, 1989). Both sites are now under an artificial lake behind a dam on the Euphrates.

The Natufian culture should also be mentioned. The lithic industry was first discovered in 1928 by Dorothy A. E. Garrod in Shouqbah cave and is now known from a good many sites, from Beidha in the southern Jordan highlands near Petra to basal Jericho, to Mallaaha near Lake Houleh and westward to the coast. Of particular interest is the presence of sickle blades, sickle handles and even some intact sickles. The blades often have a sheen or gloss, which is taken to indicate that they had been used to harvest cereals, either wild or tame. Grinding and pounding equipment, both stationary and moveable, was also abundant. At Mount Carmel, mortars were found ground into solid rock; at Mallaaha, well made decorated boulder mortars were found together with plastered storage pits. Unfortunately, we have yet to find actual grains of the harvests.

All the equipment for cultivating cereal grains is present in the Natufian industries, but there is no indication that either plants or animals were domesticated. The Natufian people lived in an area in which wild wheat and barley are abundant today and presumably were abundant at that time. It may be that natural stands were adequate to supply their needs and cultivation was unnecessary. Harlan and Zohary (1966) raised the question:

> Why should anyone cultivate a cereal where natural stands are as dense as a cultivated field? If wild cereal grasses can be harvested in unlimited quantities, why should anyone bother to till the soil and plant the seed? We suspect that we shall find when the full story is unfolded, that here and there harvesting of wild cereals lingered on long after some people had learned to farm and that farming itself may

have originated in areas adjacent to rather than in the regions of greatest abundance of wild cereals.

Figure 4.2 together with Table 4.1 document the spread of this early Neolithic agriculture. Many of the sites covered a considerable range of time and the evidences of domesticated plants were not always found in the lower or earliest layers. However, the general picture that is developing indicates that by 7000 BC a fully effective agricultural system had evolved.

In the Near East, animal domestication was closely coordinated with plant domestication. Archaeological sites yield bones in much greater abundance than plant remains, but they also pose problems of interpretation. The earliest domesticates must have been morphologically identical to wild types but differences did appear in due time. Goat horns became twisted and this can be detected in horn cores often found in sites. Cattle, pigs and sheep became smaller than wild types. Often there is a shift in the kill to a higher percentage of juveniles and toward more males than females. At Mehrgarh in Baluchistan, two graves were found that included an adult human and five kids in each grave. The goats were less than three months old. In several sites a striking shift from gazelle and deer to sheep and goats has been detected. At Mehrgarh, goats were domesticated when the village was founded but sheep and cattle may have been domesticated on the spot, independent of activities farther west (Meadow, 1984). The spread of animal husbandry generally coincided with the spread of Neolithic farming, but there are some intriguing features. Sheep appear suddenly in southern and southeastern France in late Mesolithic, in this case sixth millennium BC, well before the arrival of other domesticated animals, cultivated plants or pottery (Davis, 1987).

The incorporation of animals into agricultural rituals and sacrifice is more than hinted at in some of the sites excavated. Çayönü, excavated for almost three decades by the Turkish–American team of Braidwood and Cambel has revealed some strange and mysterious features. For one thing, the people had been working to some extent with native copper before making pottery. For an early site (*c.* 7200 BC) it has remarkably advanced architecture. One building contained a large polished stone slab, about two meters by two meters, surrounded by plastered floor and about 90 human skulls together with some complete and partial human skeletons (see p. 77). Blood

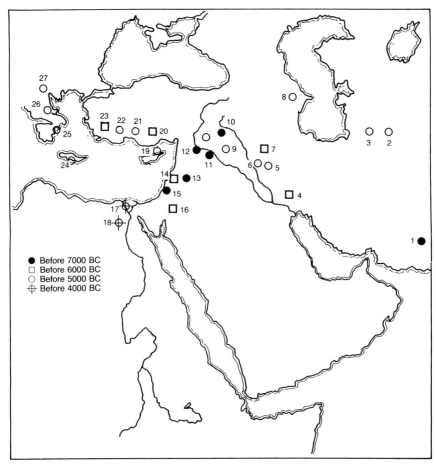

Fig. 4.2. Early Neolithic sites. 1, Mehrgarh; 2, Altyn Tepe; 3, Djeitun;
4, Ali Kosh; 5, Choga Mami; 6, Tell es-Sawwan; 7, Jarmo; 8, Chokh;
9, Yarym Tepe; 10, Çayönü; 11, Tell Abu Hureyra; 12, Mureybit;
13, Ramad; 14, Tell Aswad; 15, Jericho; 16, Beidha; 17, Merimde;
18, Fayum; 19, Andreas Kastros; 20, Can Hasan; 21, Çatal Hüyük;
22, Erbaba; 23, Hacilar; 24, Knossos; 25, Franchthi Cave; 26, Sesklo/
Agrissa; 27, Nea Nikomedia.

residues from the slab were analyzed by Loy and Wood (1989). The
traces proved to be blood of humans, sheep and wild cattle. Traces of
both wild cattle and human blood were also found on a large black
flint knife. Skulls of the wild cattle with horns were also found in the

Table 4.1 *Plant remains from selected early villages*

Sites	Approximate dates (bc)	Plants
Tell Abu Hureyra	9200–8500	ek, b, wild rye, l
PPNA (see text)	8000	EM, B2
PPNB sites	7600–6500	ek, EK, em, EM*, b, BN, o, L
Jericho PPNA	8000–7300	EM, B2*
PPNB	7300–6500	EK, EM*, B2, P, L, F
Tell Aswad	7800–7600	EM*, b, P, L
" "	7600–6600	EK, EM*, W, b, B2, BN, P, L
Çayönü	7200–6500	ek, EK, em, EM*, b, P, L, V*, F
Ali Kosh	7500?–6750	ek, EK, EM*, b, BN
" "	6750–6000	ek, EK, EM*, B2, BN, B6, o, L
Beidha	7000	EM*, b, o
Hacilar	6750	ek, EM*, BN, L
Jarmo	6750	em, EM, B2, P, L
Can Hasan	6500	ek, EK, EM, W*, B2, L, V
Tell Ramad	6250–5950	EK, EM*, W, B2, L, F
Tepe Sabz	6000–5000	ek, EK, EM, W, B2*, BN, B6, F
Tell es-Sawwan	6000–5000	EK, EM, W, B2*, BN, B6, F
Choga Mami	6000–5000	ek, EK, EM, W, b, B2, BN, B6, P, L, F
Yarym Tepe	6000–5000	EM, W, B2, BN, B6*, P
Çatal Hüyük	6000–5000	EK, EM*, W, BN, P, V
Erbaba	6000–5000	EK, EM*, W*, B2, BN, P*, L, V
Andreas Kastros	6000–5000	EK, EM*, B6, L, F
Chokh	6000–5000	EK, EM, W, B2, BN
Mehrgarh	6000–5000	EK, EM, W, B2, BN, B6
Franchthi Cave	6000–5000	EM, B2
Sesklo	6000–5000	EK, EM*, B6, L, V
Nea Nikomedia	6000–5000	EK, EM*, BN, P, L, V
Agrissa	6000–5000	EK, EM, B2, B6, L, millet
Knossos	6000–5000	EM, W*, B2

Notes: PPNA and PPNB, prepottery Neolithic A and B

Lower case bc are uncorrected ^{14}C date estimates.

Lower case, wild; upercase, domesticated; ek, EK, einkorn; em, EM, emmer; b, B, barley; B2, two-rowed barley; BN naked barley; B6, six-rowed barley; o, oats; W, naked (free threshing) wheat; P, pea; L, lentil; V, vetch; F, flax; *, most abundant.

Sources: Zohary and Hopf (1988) and from site reports; see also Fig. 4.2.

buildings. Çayönü appears to be a remarkably early ceremonial center and suggests that agricultural sacrificial rites were established very early in the history of farming.

The site of Çatal Hüyük has already been mentioned with its racks of bull horns and other evidences of cattle worship. But Near Eastern agriculture was founded upon four species: sheep, goats, wheat and barley. In many ways these are still the basic commodities of the system. Cattle were domesticated later.

The crops

Wheat

The wheats: einkorn and emmer were the first wheats domesticated. Einkorn is a diploid adapted to cool uplands. Figure 4.3 shows the known present distribution of wild races; each dot on the map can be documented by a herbarium specimen, recent collection or citing by a reputable botanist. There are weedy races that infest fields of modern wheat and races that thrive in fairly primary habitats. These are indicated on the map. Because of its weedy potential, the distribution of wild einkorn may have spread with agriculture. There are two major races, one with one grain per spikelet, as the name 'einkorn' implies, and one with two grains per spikelet. The two-seeded race is found in southeastern Turkey, Iraq and Iran. In central Anatolia it gives way to the one-seeded race found in western Anatolia and the Balkans. In the two-seeded race, the upper grain is about twice the size of the lower and lacks dormancy. The smaller, lower grain may be dormant for several years. This is an adaptation to the difficult environment of the region. If the fall rains come and cause the grains to sprout, then fail and the seedlings die from drought, there will still be seed in the soil to sprout another year (Harlan and Zohary, 1966).

Wild einkorn is abundant in Tell Abu Hureyra and turns up in Çayönü, Ali Kosh, Hacilar, Can Hasan, Tepe Sabz and Choga Mami. Thus, it seems to have been an important wild grain resource. As a crop, however, it has always been minor compared to emmer. Einkorn spread with Neolithic agriculture across the Balkans and into western and northern Europe. It apparently did not reach Egypt or Ethiopia but is reported from Mehrgarh in Baluchistan, perhaps its most easterly

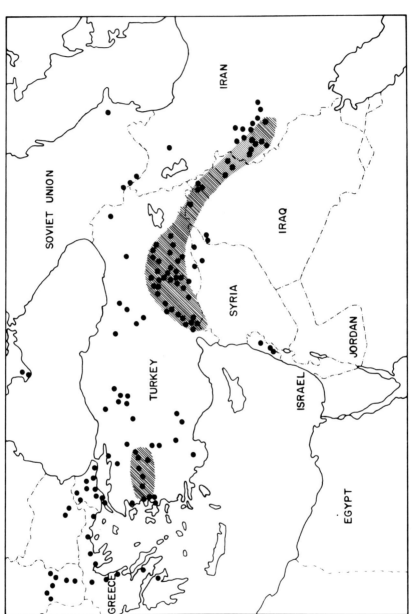

Fig. 4.3. Known sites of wild einkorn: fairly primary habitats in shaded areas.

penetration. The crop is still grown on a small scale in parts of Europe and North Africa and has staged a modest comeback in France because of health food enthusiasts who feel that a wheat so primitive must be good for you. The crop was never much of a rival for emmer.

Emmer is a tetraploid. The known present distribution of wild emmer is shown in Fig. 4.4. It is not weedy and its range could have decreased with the disturbances of agriculture. There is an obvious congruence with the oak woodland belt and presumably it migrated with the oaks in early Holocene from Mediterranean refugia into the Taurus and Zagros mountains. The wild forms of emmer bear the epithet *Triticum turgidum* subsp. *dicoccoides* and the cultivated races that of *T. turgidum* subsp. *dicoccum*. The genomic constitution is AABB and cytologically identical with all the major forms of tetraploid wheat including the derived durum or macaroni (pasta) wheat. There is another sibling tetraploid species with the genomic constitution AAGG; the wild forms are essentially indistinguishable from wild emmer but hybrids between the two are sterile. A race of this species was taken into the *domus* in Soviet Georgia and called *Triticum timopheevii*. The wild race is *T. timopheevii* subsp. *araraticum*. The Georgian domesticate remains strictly endemic, grown on a small scale and has little to do with the wheat crop elsewhere. It has been exploited to some extent in wheat breeding programs because of the resistance to several diseases. The distribution of the subspecies *araraticum* is shown in Fig. 4.5 (Zohary, 1989).

Both wild tetraploids have two grains per spikelet and as in two-grained einkorn, one is dormant while the other germinates readily. This is again an adaptation to erratic rainfall. The race found in the Palestine area (Israel, Lebanon, southwest Syria and Jordan) has very large seeds, often larger than those of cultivated wheat. This feature probably evolved from intense seedling competition. When the rains do come in the fall, the first seeds to germinate and the most vigorous seedlings have an advantage over later and slower growing seedlings and will contribute more to the next generation. All of the wild cereals of the area, wheat, barley and oats have very large seeds.

Emmer and barley were the two major cereals of the Near Eastern Neolithic from the very start in prepottery Neolithic A and spread together across Europe and to India and Ethiopia. Emmer persists today, generally as a relic crop but still locally important. I have seen it grown on a substantial scale in Ethiopia, Turkey, Yugoslavia and

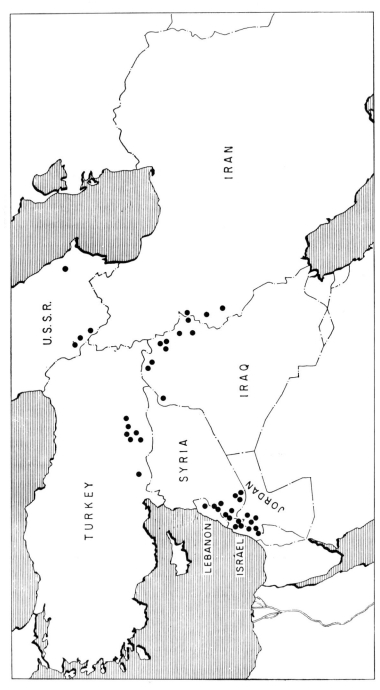

Fig. 4.4. Known locations of wild emmer. This species is not very weedy and the range has probably been reduced by agriculture and overgrazing.

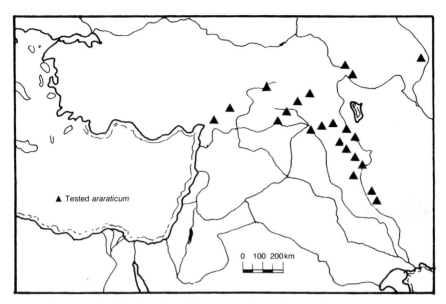

Fig. 4.5. Distribution of *Triticum araraticum*. After Zohary (1989).

the hill country of south India. It is reported from mountainous parts of Germany, Switzerland, France and elsewhere in Europe, but it is usually a minor crop in these areas. One reason for its persistence in south India is a higher level of disease resistance than more modern wheats. The Ethiopian, Yemeni and Indian emmers are closely related and differ from European emmers in having more vascular bundles in the coleoptile. A scattering of emmer collections from remote regions of Turkey, Iran and Transcaucasia belong to the Afro–Indian group and probably represent relics of the initial Neolithic expansion. In about 1910 the average yearly production in Russia was some ten million bushels, mostly from the mid- and lower Volga regions.

It is easy to understand the preference for emmer over einkorn, but it is not easy to understand the preference for a glume wheat like emmer over a free threshing naked wheat. Archaeology tells us that naked wheats were available from the early Neolithic onwards. A few grains were found in Ramad, Syria, at *c.* 7000 BC and a large sample, nearly 3000 grains from Knossos, was found by Dr Helbaek to consist almost entirely of naked grains. The uncorrected date is *c.* 6000 BC and the corrected one would be at least 7000 BC. Naked grain has also been reported from prepottery Neolithic B in Baluchistan at over 6000 BC, yet emmer remained king of the wheats for several thousand years. Naked wheats have turned up in small quantities in many sites of the European Neolithic and Bronze ages but did not dominate wheat growing until later (Harlan, 1981*b*).

The world of emmer and barley

The wheat of ancient Egypt was emmer but this may have been due to prejudice. Herodotus in the fifth century BC wrote: 'While other nations live on naked wheat and barley, it is considered in Egypt the greatest shame to live on them. They prepare their bread from Ολυρα which some call *Zeia*.' (Herodotus, II, 36).

Wooden tomb models give us an insight into the processing of grain in ancient Egypt. The brewery and the bakery always occupied the same building. Figures (usually male) are shown using mortar and pestle to hull the emmer. Adjacent groups (usually female) are shown grinding hulled grain into flour. This is then mixed with water and baked. Some of the bread is put into water in jars, innoculated and allowed to ferment in the brewer's section of the building. Presumably sources of sugar were added or some of the grain was malted. Additives mentioned in Egyptian texts include figs, dates and grapes, and various kinds of yeast cultures were given separate names. In Cairo today, a wheat beer called *bouza* is still made the same way, but in the modern recipe a part of the wheat is malted, crushed and added to the bread in the jars. The loaves are baked only lightly so as not to kill the yeast mixed with the dough. According to Lucas (1962), the alcohol content is rather higher than that in traditional barley beers.

Emmer wheat and barley were the predominant cereals of Hittite cuneiform literature and are the only cereals listed in Hittite laws (Chadwick, 1973.) According to Hrozny (1913), the ancient Babylonian word for emmer was *ziz*, but various modifiers such as *ziz-gar*, emmer for bread and *ziz-kas*, emmer for beer turn up. It is written $\nabla\nabla$.

There were other words for cereals but we do not know if the ancients of Mesopotamia distinguished between durum and bread wheats. Kislev (1973) has suggested that the ancient Hebrew word *kassemet* meant emmer. The word *ḥiṭṭa* meant naked wheat, probably durum in Palestine and bread wheat in Mesopotamia, and the word *šifon* referred to einkorn.

Emmer was traditionally deglumed in a mortar throughout the Mediterranean and Near East. The Mycenaean glyph for flour was a figure holding a pestle ⚲ or ⚲ (Chadwick, 1973).

Roman bakers were called *pistores*, from the verb *pinsere*, 'to pound'. The emmer heritage was strong in Rome even after it was little used. It was a sacred grain and called *semen adoreum* or simply *ador* for short and this in turn became the word 'glory' (Pliny, XVIII, 3). Pliny (XVIII, 11) cites Verrius as stating: 'Emmer was the only cereal used by the Roman nation for 300 years.' A yearly celebration called The Feast of the Ovens was established by Numa, in which emmer was roasted for a sacrificial meal (Pliny, XVIII, 2). Protocols for sacrificing to the gods using emmer are given by Cato and Pliny. Roman recipes even in imperial times often called for emmer groats.

Another Latin word for emmer was *far*, from which the words farina and farinaceous were derived. The harvest ceremonies of ancient Rome were called *farnacalia* and traditional marriage vows were *confarati* in which *far* was ritually consumed by the partners. North of the Alps, the same root word was pronounced *bar* and attached to a different cereal. It meant originally a bearded grain from which such words as barb, barbe, beard, barber, beer, brew, brewing and brewery were derived. For grain, it was first used as an adjective as in barlic korn or barlie korn. It was finally reduced to barley. A 'barn' is a place to store barley and 'Barton' a village where barley grew well (Andrews, 1964).

Despite the availability of naked wheat, whether it was durum or bread wheat, the picture given us in early historic times is one dominated by emmer and barley. The Romans rejected barley for human food at an early date, but the Greeks clung tenaciously to their *maza* porridge. Greek tradition asserted it was the strongest and healthiest of cereals. Athletes and soldiers were trained on barley and gladiators were called *hordearii* or barley men (Pliny, XVIII, 14).

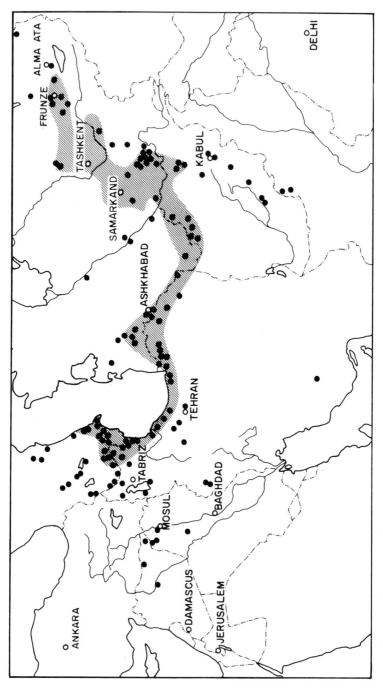

Fig. 4.6. Known locations of *Triticum tauschii* populations. This is the only species of the wheat group with a continental distribution. Its contribution of the D genome is probably responsible for the adaptation of bread wheat to the semiarid steppes of the world.

Bread wheat

The major wheat of the world today is a hexaploid (*Triticum aestivum*) with the genomic constitution AABBDD. The D genome was added to a cultivated tetraploid, probably emmer, at some date unknown. It came from a wild diploid goat grass, *Triticum tauschii*. The location of this hydridization event is also unknown, but it seems likely that it occurred within the present range of distribution of *T. tauschii*. Of all the wheat group, this species ranges the farthest into central Asia and occurs on semiarid steppes of the region. This adaptation is probably responsible for permitting modern wheat to be grown on the semiarid and subhumid wheat belts of Asia, North America, Argentina and Australia. Bread wheat is the most drought resistant and cold tolerant of wheats. The known distribution of *T. tauschii* is shown in Fig. 4.6.

The initial hexaploid hybrid was a glume wheat called spelt (*T. aestivum* subsp. *spelta*.) Many artificial hybrids have been made between various tetraploid wheats and an assortment of collections of *T. tauschii*, and all are nonfree threshing glume wheats. Several lines of evidence suggest the original hybrid occurred near the southern end of the Caspian Sea. Spelt has not turned up archaeologically in the Near East or the Mediterranean regions. It made its way to central and northern Europe by a different route and at a later time from the migration of barley and emmer. Soviet archaeologists have reported remains in the Caucasus dating to the fifth millennium or possibly the sixth millennium BC. Spelt turned up in Moldavia between 4000 and 3000 BC and more has been found in Bulgaria and the Black Sea littoral. Janushevich (1978) suggested two routes of dispersal from the traditional nuclear area: across Anatolia to Greece, then to the Danube and central Europe; the second from Transcaucasia northward across the Caucasus, the lower Don and Dnepr valleys and then to central Europe.

Spelt became closely associated with some of the Germanic tribes and although it is a glume wheat and considered primitive, it lingered on in some abundance in central Europe, competing well with naked bread wheat. As late as the first decade of this century, the area sown to spelt exceeded that of bread wheat in Württenberg, Swabia, Baden and in a number of other districts in southern Germany and German-speaking Switzerland (Gradmann, 1909.)

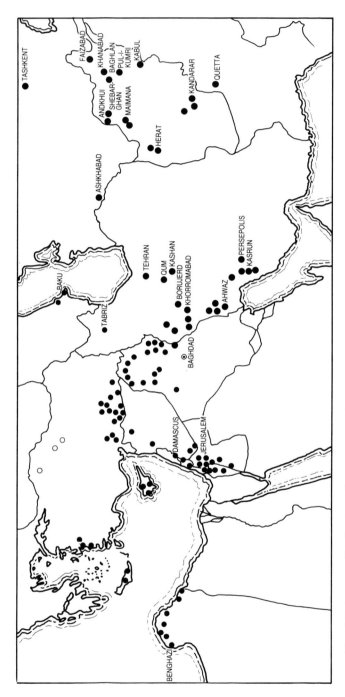

Fig. 4.7. Known distribution of spontaneous barley: in addition outlier weedy populations have been found in Morocco and Tibet.

Barley

Barley was the other primary cereal of the Neolithic expansion. Wild barley, *Hordeum vulgare* subsp. *spontaneum*, has a wide distribution although the outlying colonies are of weedy types and may be due to relatively recent expansion. Known sites are shown in Fig. 4.7. In addition there are outliers as far away as Morocco and Tibet. Races found in reasonably primary sites are in the shaded area. Barley may have been the most important cereal in the world at one time. In Mesopotamia, where writing originated, barley was the chief crop. In the south especially, barley almost completely displaced wheat as a cereal crop by 2300 BC. This is taken to be not so much from preference as from necessity, since there is independent evidence that the irrigated lands were salting up. Barley is much more salt tolerant than wheat. However, even before this shift to a near monoculture, barley was apparently the more important of the two (Adams, 1965).

Barley also held a dominant position even into classical Greek times. It was the food of the poor and the ration of the soldier. It is not an attractive cereal from a dietary and culinary point of view; the covered sorts especially are very high in fiber and difficult to digest. The culture of naked varieties improved the diet considerably, but even naked barley is less desirable than wheat. From Table 4.1 we can see that naked barley appeared rather early and spread quickly. Today it is found only where barley is a significant part of the human diet.

In the cuneiform literature of Mesopotamia, barley is mentioned much more often than wheat. There is a myth concerning the divine origin of barley but not one for wheat. The relative value as indicated by price, taxes or rations shows barley and emmer, probably in the glume, about equal and about half the value of naked wheat. Yields at about 2400 BC were calculated by Adams (1965) from a number of records and show: barley – 2537 liters per hectare; emmer – 3672 liters per hectare; and wheat – 1900 liters per hectare. The emmer was presumably in the glume and therefore about 75% as heavy as wheat. The yields are quite respectable but similar computations only a few centuries later indicate a sharp decline that again may be attributed to salinization. In 2100 BC the yield of barley was only 1460 liters per hectare and wheat had virtually disappeared as a crop in the southern region (Jacobsen and Adams, 1958).

All of the earliest remains are of two-rowed barley but the six-rowed morphology appears at Alikosh at the 6750 to 6000 BC time range and in a number of sites dated from 6000 to 5000 BC. As a general rule the two-rowed kinds are best suited for dryland farming and the six-rowed ones are grown under irrigation; but there are exceptions. Barley spread with emmer and beyond, eventually becoming an important crop from China to western Europe and the most productive crop of the Ethiopian plateau.

Because of its short life cycle, maturing earlier than wheat, barley can be grown at the fringes of agriculture, higher up in the mountains, further into the Arctic and at the edges of deserts. Because of its salt tolerance it can be grown in desert oases and as pointed out above, in lands salted up by inadequately drained irrigation systems. There are even strains that can tolerate irrigation by sea water where adequate drainage is provided. It is today one of the world's greatest cereals, ranking in production only behind wheat, rice and maize. Some of the production is used in the brewing industry; more is fed to livestock, but barley continues to contribute significantly to the human diet especially in Asia, Ethiopia and parts of Europe.

Pulses

In addition to the cereals, pulses were an integral part of the Near Eastern crop complex. Lentil may have been the first of the legumes domesticated. Remains of wild lentil turn up in the earliest levels of Tell Abu Hureyra, 9200 to 8500 BC and domesticated races in the 7500 to 6500 BC time range. Domesticated lentil remains are found in most of the later sites of the region. The natural distribution of wild lentils includes the oak woodland of the Levantine–Taurus–Zagros arc, but spreads out from there across southwest Anatolia and along the Elbrus mountain chain in northern Iran into central Asia. There are several chromosome races differing by one or more interchanges, but the domesticated lentils are all of one kind indicating a single domestication. The wild races occur as scattered bushy plants and were probably harvested by uprooting, which is still the customary mode of harvesting to this day. The plants may be allowed to dry briefly in the field and are then brought to the threshing floor for further treatment.

Pea was another early domesticate, showing up before 7000 BC at

Jericho, Tell Aswad and Çayönü and was widespread in somewhat later sites. Wild peas are widespread from the Levantine–Taurus woodlands across much of Anatolia and the Mediterranean maqui. There are two cytotypes differing by a single reciprocal translocation. The race identical to the domesticated pea is confined to the Levantine–Taurus zone and is most likely to be the immediate progenitor. Once again, the open park forest or woodland zone is the genetic source of an early Near Eastern crop (Zohary and Hopf, 1988).

There are several species of vetch (*Vicia*) in the region. They are important soil builders and many are weedy, growing in and around cultivated fields, along roadsides, etc. The one most commonly found in early sites and the one most used for food in early times is bitter vetch (*Vicia ervilia*). Vetch seeds have a rather characteristic angular shape and are easily identified. The progenitor race is found in the Taurus arc and adjacent parts of southeast Turkey. It is still grown on some scale in the Near East but is seldom used for human food.

The chickpea is the major edible legume from Iberia, where it is called garbanzo, across the Near Eastern mountains to India and southward to Ethiopia. *Hummis*, a ground chickpea paste, is very important in Arabic cuisine and chickpea plays a large role in Indian cooking. Archaeologically it does not appear as early as the pulses just mentioned. Wild chickpea is confined to a relatively small area in the Taurus in southeastern Turkey.

The broad bean, field bean or faba bean (*Vicia faba*) was also brought into the *domus* at a later date than lentil, pea and vetch. The wild form has not yet been identified and we are not sure of its origin. The earliest archaeological finds are of a small seeded race; the large seeded form, more familiar to us, came later. It has been an important crop over much of Europe, the Near East, Ethiopia and India. It is a cool season plant that has filled important niches in the Andes, highland Mesoamerica and even the mountains of Indonesia. It does produce alkaloids that can lead to favism in those who eat a lot of them.

Flax

Flax is a common component of archaeological remains from pre-pottery Neolithic B onward. The wild races are found in wet places near springs, marshes, river banks and coastal areas from the Near

East across both sides of the Mediterranean and on to western Europe, even to the coasts of England. Such a distribution does not help to establish the area of origin, but since the seeds turn up in the same archaeological sites as other Near Eastern crops it is presumably another component of the complex. Wild flax was available from the Levantine–Taurus oak woodland arc. After domestication, two general types evolved: a taller one generally for fiber and a shorter one, primarily for the grain. The fiber is long and extremely strong, producing thread of high tensile strength and linen cloth of fine quality. As the primary fiber of ancient Egypt, it was also used for cordage, ships' rigging, ropes for hauling stones to build pyramids and so on. Today the grain is used for the production of linseed oil, used in paints and other protective finishes. In Ethiopia it is still used as a cereal grain but in small doses.

The animals

Sheep and goats appear to be the first animal domesticates. The most common bones recovered in archaeological sites are not very diagnostic and it is difficult to tell *Capra* (goat) from *Ovis* (sheep). Consequently, many site reports simply indicate sheep/goat or caprid. If the right bones are found, or skulls with horns, diagnosis is unequivocal. The two animals occupy rather different habitats and very likely were initially brought into the *domes* separately. Wild sheep were once common from the mountains of central Asia to western Europe and North Africa. There were several races or species, and they have been hunted to near extinction over much of the range. The race available for domestication by people of the Levantine–Taurus–Zagros arc is now reduced to very small populations. These animals prefer open rolling country and range to high elevations in summer and lower elevations in winter.

Wild sheep have no wool. The hair is rather like that of a deer and, at first glance, they do not look much like our sheep. They are large, rangy and stand taller. Hair sheep are still found in parts of Africa; however the conformation of these breeds is similar to the domestic sheep. The appearance of wool is a sure sign of domestication and so is the loss of horns in the females. Other criteria that have been used are reduction in size and the kill rates. Harvest of domestic sheep is likely to include more immature animals and more males than the harvest of wild flocks. Trends in this direction, however, occur in wild populations without domestication so that caution in interpretation is warranted. The fat tailed mutation appeared about 2000 BC in both the Near East and northern Africa (Muzzolini, 1988).

Reduction in body size could be a natural adaptation to desiccation and less forage available, and the appearance of female sheep with small horns, or no horns, might have been due to natural variation and/or inbreeding of isolated populations. Long tails in sheep, whether thin or fat, are more secure criteria as are corkscrew horns developed in some breeds. But these came after 4000 BC.

The wild goat (*Capra*) had originally a wide distribution. It prefers crags, cliffs and rough precipitous slopes, and is a hardier and more independent animal. In mixed flocks goats take the lead and sheep follow. It too became reduced in stature with domestication, and in due time evolved twisted horns quite different from the arching sickles of the wild *Capra ibex*. The long-haired Angora type came later.

Swine (*Sus scrofa*) were widely adapted and abundant in marshy lands right across Eurasia. Despite heavy hunting pressure, they still thrive in some places. Travelers in the last century frequently commented on their abundance in the canebreaks near the Dead Sea, marshy areas in the Jordan Valley and the lower Tigris–Euphrates valleys. The Dead Sea population supported a few leopards that preyed on wild boar. According to murals at Taqui Bustan, Iran, shooting wild boar with arrows was a popular diversion for Assyrian royalty. Pigs also became smaller with domestication, but as they became feral so easily there was often much introgression and crossbreeding among wild and tame races.

Swine were domesticated somewhat later than caprids; the earliest remains, as of this writing, were found at Çayönü about 7000 BC. Pig bones have been found in many sites in the Near East and Egypt. Around 2400 BC, the taboo against pork and pigs set in, or at least pig bones became scarce and caprid bones more abundant over a large area. This could have been due to other causes, however, such as destruction of oak woodlands for agriculture. Swine herds are mentioned in the Bible as being in the midst of Old Israel, and bones and teeth of pigs have been found in ancient Jewish settlements. The Egyptians herded swine to trample in seeds as Nile flood waters receded. Herding swine in the oak forests of Europe was a regular practice in the fall to exploit the acorn mast.

Wild cattle had an enormous range across Eurasia and North Africa. They were widely hunted, some tribes specializing in them as a food source. They were worshipped, revered and sacrificed. Domestication came rather later than for sheep and goats, but with the same usual reduction in stature and change in conformation (Isaac, 1970.)

The time and manner of domestication are both obscure. According to Muzzolini (1989*a*), a fully established animal industry had been established and widely distributed over North Africa and the Near East by 4000 BC. Before that time the evidence tends to be more suggestive than proof and often subject to various interpretations. The fact that the system was so widespread by 4000 BC surely indicates there were many earlier tentatives, but evidence is often tenuous. Eric Higgs and his school at Cambridge have suggested that at least for early time ranges, the term 'domestication' be dropped and the term 'husbandry' be used. One can manage wild herds and flocks; one can kill selectively. The trend toward more young animals and more males can be detected in bones of deer and gazelle that were not domesticated, as well as in sheep and goats that were.

One can be a herd follower rather than a herder or perhaps one can be both. One can attract grazing animals by skillful use of fire; people can cooperate in herding wild animals into kill sites. The term 'husbandry' covers the management of both wild and tame animals without the need of distinguishing between them.

Domestication of mammals in the Near East led to an impressive dairy industry. This was done with no refrigeration whatever. Animals milked include cows, water buffalo, nanny goats, ewes, mares, donkeys and camels. The milk is preserved by fermentation, producing mostly cheese and yogurt. These products are extremely durable and will keep well for a matter of years without refrigeration. The keeping quality of cheese may be enhanced with salt. Two general types of nomads evolved: short term and long term. The short-term nomads live in villages, farm, and take their flocks after the harvest to nearby mountain pasture and return to their villages in the fall. Long-term nomads range widely, from the mountain pasture in summer to winter foraging in desert lowlands, and live yearlong in black tents woven of mohair. Some live in poverty and some are affluent. Meat, wool, cheese, yogurt and hides are sold to villagers or to urban dwellers. A number of tribes produce the characteristic knotted oriental rugs as an important source of supplemental income. Tribes on the move, to the mountain pasture in spring and on their return in the fall, hack and mangle the woodlands for firewood on their way; and tribes on the mountain pastures lower the timberline by cutting the trees for fuel, to process the milk into cheese and yogurt. Woodlands are also exploited for charcoal; and there is also a small class of snow dealers who bring the snow from the mountains by donkey or horseback and sell it in lowland city markets. As road building has made mountains more accessible, a new class of nomads has arisen. They are bee keepers who take their hives to mountain pasture in summer and to desert pasture in winter.

A number of cattle-keeping tribes evolved in Africa. Systems vary considerably. In some, women and children stay in a village and raise sorghum, 'the cattle of women,' while the men and young boys take the cattle to a succession of camps for forage. In camp the basic diet is blood and milk with sometimes a little urine to coagulate the milk. The women may bring sorghum meal to the camps from time to time and receive milk and fresh blood in return. Other tribes take their herds into the desert in the rainy season and retreat as forage dries up. They often plant a small patch of millet in the Sahel or savanna en route to desert pasture. The patches are fenced with branches from thorny acacias but not otherwise tended. On their return from the desert range, they harvest what remains after pillage by birds, rodents, baboons or thieves. Apparently the reward is worth the effort for the custom continues.

Among cattle tribes, I was particularly taken by the Massai. They are tall, handsome, athletic people who seem to sparkle with amused tolerance as they look down on you. They are not of Watusi height but can look down on most of us. Their diet of blood and milk is high in cholesterol and one does not see many old people in the population. Several of the cattle tribes do not customarily wear clothes. It is not uncommon to see naked men walking across the open savanna with a small wooden stool-headrest in one hand and a spear in the other. The lack of pockets results in some interesting adaptations long forgotten by people who wear clothes. The Turkanas make circular knives that slip over the wrist like a sharp-bladed bracelet. There are small fighting knives worn on the thumbs; horns containing snuff or tobacco are hung about the neck. The inventory of personal possessions is small but must be suspended from the human frame in some fashion. The artifacts are interesting for collectors of folk art.

Some noteworthy adaptations evolved in African cattle. In and near the central delta of the Niger, the Ankole breed became adapted to the watery landscape. Many individuals have huge, inflated, spongy horns that serve as floats, keeping the head, or at least the nostrils, above water while swimming. The breed also has very large feet, adapted both for swimming and walking on mud. The Ndama breed of Sierra Leone and adjacent parts of West Africa is small but highly resistant to tsetse fly-borne sleeping sickness. In general because of diseases, neither horses nor cattle have been able to penetrate beyond the savanna into the forest zone but the Ndama breed has done fairly well.

Goats and sheep have had problems in the high rainfall belts. Both have responded by evolving dwarf or pigmy breeds. They are very small indeed and probably not very productive, but the small body size has some advantage in surface to mass ratio and the dwarf breeds tolerate the heat and humidity better than normal sized breeds. Hair sheep are also found in the region and may have some advantage over wooled sheep.

Of the equids the wild ass has a wide distribution in Africa and Asia. The donkey is thought to have been brought into the *domus* first in Egypt and adjacent Nubia. There is a small figurine from Mesopotamia showing what appeared to be onagers hitched to a cart (*c.* 2500 BC).

The true horse is a relatively late domesticate; the earliest remains, so far, were found in the Ukraine about 3500 BC. It had become important in warfare by Hyksos times in Egypt when war and hunting chariots were introduced.

The camel was also a rather late domesticate but had a profound effect in opening up long distance caravan routes across the deserts of both Africa and the Near East. Archaeologically the domesticated camel shows up in Saudi Arabia about 3000 BC and the Bactrian at about the same time in south Russia. There could well have been earlier and more widespread domestications in central Asia or western China.

From Egypt to Mesopotamia and southern Anatolia, pigeon raising is an important part of the agricultural system. Dove cotes, at the edge of towns or villages or sometimes interspersed among the dwellings, may be very large. Built from the same materials as the houses, at a distance the only way to tell human dwellings from dove dwellings is by the size and number of windows. Pigeon manure is considered the very best for raising melons. A common practice for melon growing along the Tigris and Euphrates rivers is as follows: after the main threat of flood is over and temperatures are high, holes are dug in the exposed sand and gravel bars down to ground water, usually no more than a meter in the river bed; melon seeds are planted and as the vines grow up out of the hole, it is filled in with a mixture of soil and pigeon dung. With an assured moisture supply, high nutrition and hot weather, the melons are highly productive and have a reputation for fine flavor and sweetness. The doves that produce the manure forage at will over the grain fields and must consume large quantities of wheat and barley and do considerable preharvest damage. After harvest, of course, the gleaning by birds does little or no damage to the farmer. Both squabs and adult birds are eaten.

The very beginnings of animal domestication will probably never be revealed to us, but animal domestication, or at least manipulation, has been an important element in human development and civilizations of the Old World. Over millennia people have tried to domesticate a wide range of animals; some successful, some failures. In Europe people tried to domesticate deer, elk and the local mouflon; the Lapps, of course, did domesticate reindeer. In Egypt, tomb murals show the keeping of several kinds of antelope, hyenas and cheetahs, as well as the force feeding of cranes and other animals.

Neolithic expansion

Once the various elements of the Near Eastern agriculture became integrated, the system became expansive. It spread along the shores of the Mediterranean on both the African and the European sides. It spread to Greece, the Balkans, up the Danube and down the Rhine, eventually reaching England and Scandinavia. It spread southward to Egypt and the Ethiopian plateau and eastward to the Indus to form the base of Harappan and Mohendjodaro civilizations.

The temporal sequence is now rather well documented archaeologically, but there is a lively debate as to the nature of the spread.

Ammerman and Cavalli-Sforza (1984) argue for a wave front of farmers advancing across Europe at approximately 1 km per year. Dennell (1983), Barker (1985), Gregg (1988) and others disagree, insisting that the temporal sequence was due to the propagation of a mosaic or patchwork of interactions between Neolithic and Mesolithic cultures.

The wave of migration theory gets support from plotting dated sites of both Neolithic farming settlements and terminal Mesolithic occupations. The distribution of human gene alleles is also suggestive (Ammerman and Cavalli-Sforza, 1984). The opposing views point to the fact that the early Neolithic settlers in each region occupied small scattered sites on loess soils, avoiding the clayey soils. Mixed assemblages indicate a considerable period of trade and interaction between the two cultures. Diffusion was also erratic and jumpy, and the jumps seem to correlate with changes in climate. The pattern does not fit that of a tidal wave of farmers. In the mosaic view, Mesolithic people took up farming slowly from their neighbors and the result was the temporal progression observed in archaeological research. Both sides of the debate concede that the diffusion across Europe could have been due to a mixture of developments; some farmers probably did migrate and many Mesolithic cultures probably did opt for agriculture. Farmers no doubt increased their own hunting–gathering activities when the crops were bad, and poor yields were probably common. None of the suite of crops from the winter rainfall–summer drought zone could have been initially well-adapted to central and northern Europe. The different food procurement systems are not mutually exclusive nor does the development of European agriculture depend on one or the other mode of diffusion.

Agricultural vulnerability

After a fully functional agriculture became established, populations increased in relation to the increased food supply. However, the threat of famine was ever at hand and starvation became an integral part of agricultural history. It still is. Recent headlines have pointed to Africa, but famines are well-known in the recent past in India, China, Europe and elsewhere.

As we come into the historical time range, Egypt emerged as the nation with the most stable and reliable agricultural system. Egypt had the Nile with its annual flood of life-giving and life-maintaining silt laden waters. Mesopotamian agriculture was also based on irrigation and large public works, but the Tigris and Euphrates were much less dependable and more erratic. The irrigation system was based on long canals that were constantly silting up and required a stable political system to function and, as we have seen, they also had inadequate drainage provision so that the land salted up. Egypt, protected by seas and deserts, was less susceptible to raids from neighboring people. The Israelites and other tribes might be burned out by drought when the rains failed, but Egypt flourished with or without rain. Egypt had the Nile.

The rise of the Old Kingdom can be briefly sketched. By 3100 BC King Menes had unified the kingdoms of the north and south and had pushed Nubian peoples back beyond the first cataract. Mines were in operation in Sinai and vessels of copper and gold were being produced for the royal household. By the second half of the second dynasty, reliefs and statues adorned stone temples. The building of royal estates, strongholds and public works, such as irrigation canals and dykes to produce basins, indicates a great national prosperity during the first two dynasties.

The pyramids were built during the third and fourth dynasties, a striking testimony to the prosperity and power of the nation. The fifth dynasty kings were high priests of Re, so naturally they channeled national resources into the building of vast temples. It was during this period that hereditary succession in the offices of local government became the rule. Throughout the fifth dynasty, the power of the temple priests and local governors increased as that of the Pharaoh waned. In the sixth dynasty, weak Pharaohs presided over very powerful governors. The collapse of the Old Kingdom followed the death of Pepi II about 2160 BC. For approximately 171 years we have almost no major monuments and do not even have a reliable record of all the kings' names.

What happens if the Nile fails? What if the floods are too low to cover the land and fill the basins? There is evidence to show that the First Intermediate Period was brought on by such a catastrophe. The Old Kingdom collapsed and Egypt went into eclipse.

Egyptian records, which are very few in number during the 'dark' period, give us only a limited idea of the problems of the times. But

one piece of evidence to which we may turn is the inscription on the
tomb of Ankhtifi, a monarch of Hierakonopolis and Edfu:

> I kept alive Hefat and Hormer . . . at a time when . . . everyone was
> dying of hunger on this sandbank of Hell . . . all of upper Egypt was
> dying of hunger to such a degree that everyone had come to eating
> his children. But I managed that no one died of hunger in this nome.
>
> *Bell, 1971*

From the lament of Ipuwer, we read:

> Plague stalketh through the land and blood is everywhere. Many men
> are buried in the river . . . the towns are destroyed and upper Egypt is
> become an empty waste . . . the crocodiles are gluted with what they
> have carried off. Men go to them of their own accord . . . Men are few.
> He that layeth his brother in the ground is everywhere; . . . Mistresses
> of the houses say . . . 'Would that we had something to eat' . . . Grain
> hath perished everywhere . . . The storehouse is bare and he that hath
> kept it lieth stretched out on the ground . . .
>
> *Erman 1927*

Toward the end of the Intermediate Period, Neferty states: 'The whole
land has perished . . . the river of Egypt is empty . . . Men cross over
the water on foot . . . the south wind drives away the north wind . . .'
(Erman, 1927).

Egypt was not alone with its problems. The First Intermediate Period
of Egypt had its counterpart in Palestine at the end of Early Bronze
and beginning of Middle Bronze. Towns, cities and even villages were
abandoned and nomads took over the land. There was a convulsion
that shook the whole eastern Mediterranean from Greece to Mesopotamia. The Akkadian Empire of Mesopotamia collapsed about 2130 BC,
and the wealthy city of Troy II was destroyed about 2149 BC. Masson
(1968) has detected a marked deterioration in the agricultural communities in southern Turkemania during the middle of the second
millennium BC, culminating about 2100 BC, which interrupted urban
development until early in the 1st millennium BC. There appears to
have been a general exodus from the Libyan desert in sixth dynasty
times as evidenced by cessation of rock paintings and the abandon-
ment of Neolithic sites.

In due time Egypt and the rest of the Near East recovered. The
Middle Kingdom arose and flourished for about one thousand years.
Then a Second Intermediate Period occurred and a dark age descended

upon Egypt once more. The Middle Kingdom went into eclipse. This may have been aggravated by the arrival of the Sea People and Rameses III took credit for defeating them in a battle. However, murals depict them not as an army, but as a people coming in wagons with women, children and household goods. They were people fleeing drought in their homeland and probably came from Anatolia. Again there are records of low floods on the Nile. It has happened before; it can happen again.

What then did it profit the human race to domesticate barley, wheat, sheep and goats? What was gained by the development of effective food producing systems? Obviously it was not an assured or stable food supply. But when the system works well, large numbers of people can be supported and civilizations can emerge from an agricultural base. We must realize, however, that famine and starvation are an integral part of agricultural systems and agricultural systems are fundamentally unstable.

CHAPTER FIVE

Africa

The African pattern

The picture for Africa is of a different order from that of the Near East. As pointed out in Chapter 2, the pattern in Africa has a noncentric character. As of now, at least, we cannot detect a temporal sequence of events. There is no 'center' where crops originated and out of which they were dispersed. Activities of plant domestication were diffused all across sub-Saharan Africa from the Atlantic to the Indian Ocean (see Fig. 2.2, p. 55). More than that, activities were diffuse in both time and space. There seems to be neither a geographic center nor a temporal one, whereas, as far as the evidence now goes, the Near East shows both rather clearly. Future research may change the picture.

To be sure, there are many endemic crops in Africa. Some are clearly Ethiopian in origin and some are clearly West African, and others originated between the two, but there seems to be no detectable place (or time) where agriculture itself began, except that it is basically a savanna phenomenon and this was mostly north of the equator and south of the Sahara.

Another feature of the African scene is that this vast noncenter is a model crop evolution laboratory. The wild races are easily identified; the origins of the weed races are clear; steps in the evolution of cultivated races from the most primitive to the most advanced and specialized are easy to follow. Could this mean that indigenous African agriculture evolved later than on other continents? We do not know, but so far archaeology has not come up with very early dates for known domesticated races.

Another difference is that proto- or para-agricultural activities persist in Africa more than in the Near East. The Africans left a conspicuous stamp on the native vegetation as did the Australian Aborigines. For one thing, they encouraged certain species by discouraging others. The white barked acacia (*Acacia albida*) is adapted to the wadis that fan out into the desert from local highlands or massifs. These are dry washes on the surface for most of the year, or sometimes all year, but there is moisture below infiltrating from the highlands. The cultivators of the Sahel believe that crops grow better under an open park-like stand of white acacia than without the trees. They have managed to spread the acacia out of its wadi habitat and across their farm lands without deliberately planting a tree. The species has the peculiar habit of shedding its leaves at the beginnings of the rains and going through the rainy season in a more or less dormant condition. It then leafs out at the start of the dry season. This reverse habit reduces competition with interplanted crops.

Some research (Dancette and Poulain, 1968) indicated the local beliefs have merit. As a legume, the tree may contribute some fixed nitrogen by nodulation, but possibly more important are the shed leaves and pods that are consumed by village flocks of sheep and goats. These in turn spread the seeds and manure the crop. The farmers protect the acacia trees, or at least do not cut them down unless they become too thick. The white acacia, then, has spread over large areas from its natural habitat.

Another savanna tree is the *karité* (*Butyrospermum*), but it is better suited to the broad leaf savanna than the Sahel proper. It is encouraged because an edible oil can be extracted from the fruit. Among some tribes it has the status of a sacred tree and is never cut down, while other species are used for construction or hacked for firewood or charcoal production. In this manner extensive areas of the broad leaf savanna become covered with a nearly pure stand of widely spaced karité trees. A land owner can sell the land and keep title to the trees, and individual trees may be inherited from father to son. Nearly pure stands of the African oil palm (*Elaeis*) evolve in the same way, but assisted by a more elaborate set of beliefs to be described later.

The harvesting of wild grass seeds may also be classed as a proto-agricultural practice and has persisted in Africa more than elsewhere. Wild grass seeds are still harvested in Africa, but not on the scale of 100 years ago when it was a large commercial industry. The first European travelers to reach central sub-Sahara Africa all describe the wild harvests, and remark on the warehouses full of the grains and on the export from areas of surplus to deficit regions (Harlan, 1989*a,b*). There were no figures on production at that time, but they described warehousing by the ton and export by camel load or even whole caravans. The wild grains were staples of a number of tribes and export reached to central Sahara.

The primary grasses harvested in the Sahara were, and are, *Aristida pungens* and *Panicum turgidum*, the former in the northern part of the desert and the latter more in the central part, although it is harvested wherever it occurs as far as Afghanistan and Pakistan. As late as 1963 Nicolaisen pointed out that a single household might gather 1000 kg of wild grain in a year. In the southern Sahara, a sandbur, *Cenchrus biflorus*, was harvested on a huge scale and is still important to some tribes. Barth (1857), after reaching the Niger from Tripoli, provisioned himself and his horses with the grain of this grass because he could find no other. It is called *kram-kram* over a large area. The sandbur is a pest, because of its thorny fascicles that cling to fur and clothing and penetrate flesh with ease, but it is good grazing before maturity and yields a relatively large seed in abundance. I have seen nearly pure stands, many square kilometers in size, on sandy land. After shattering the spiny fascicles may adhere to each other in masses and roll in the wind. Harvesters sweep them up with a broom or a wooden rake, throw them into a mortar and pound them to release the naked grain. The caryopses are nutritious and rather high in fat.

In the broad leaf savanna, the primary harvests are wild rice (*Oryza barthii*) and a complex of a dozen or so species called *krebs* or *kasha*. The wild rice is sometimes tied in bunches before harvest so that seed can be more easily gathered. Both kinds are often harvested by a swinging basket technique.

Wild grass seed harvesting has persisted elsewhere as well, including Europe and North America. Until recently, crabgrass, *Digitaria sanguinalis*, and a wetland grass, *Glyceria fluitans*, was harvested in commercial quantities in central and eastern Europe and exported around the Baltic and to western Europe. Wild harvests of the American wild-rice, *Zizania aquatica*, persist in USA and Canada because it is a delicacy and commands gourmet prices.

The patterns with respect to domesticated animals also differ from those of the Near East. Animals are much less integrated with cropping. A Mediterranean–Near Eastern integrated system, with village flocks, draft power for working the soil, planting and threshing the produce, etc., is found along the Mediterranean coasts, up the Nile Valley to about mid-Sudan and on the high plateau of Ethiopia, but

Harvesting wild grass seeds by the swinging basket technique, near Lake Chad, Africa. Courtesy of Jean Pernès.

in these regions the animals, the crops and the agricultural systems are all of Near Eastern origin. Indigenous African agriculture is based on the hoe, not the plow. There may be small village flocks, but most of the livestock are reared by specialists and involve at least some migration. The evolution of cattle rearing has followed a different path in Africa as we shall see.

Archaeological background

The prehistoric history of human beings in Africa stretches farther back in time than anywhere else in the world. The genus *Homo* seems to have evolved some two to three million years ago, perhaps even earlier. *Homo erectus* is well represented in Africa, not so much through skeletal remains as from the typical Acheulean hand axes. These are found in some abundance scattered widely over the continent, and at sites like Olorgesailie in Kenya the ground is literally strewn with these artifacts. *Homo sapiens sapiens*, anatomically modern humans, appeared some 100 000 years ago and spread out over the entire world reaching all but the most uninhabitable places late in historic times. However, our interest begins with the end of Pleistocene and start of Holocene.

At that time, some 10 000 to 12 000 years ago, the African vegetation map was very different from what it is today. It was in a hyperarid mode; the forests had retreated to small refuges near the Atlantic coasts and in the high mountains of East Africa; the Sahara was essentially uninhabited (see Fig. 3.2, p. 84). Pathways from that condition to the present are complex and difficult to interpret. The Sahara expanded and contracted, forests advanced and retreated. At one time Lake Chad was 10 times its present size; Lake Rudolf was so deep that it overflowed into the Nile watershed. Terraces along the Nile indicate rises and falls in river levels of considerable extent. Periods of desiccation were interrupted by pluvials of various intensities. Changes in climate were not synchronous over the whole continent and events north of the equator were not necessarily reflected by events south of the equator. The whole pattern is too complex to describe in detail here.

In the Sahara, a pluvial set in *c.* 10 000 BC that peaked at *c.* 6 to 7000 BC. This wet phase was abruptly terminated by a short arid phase peaking at *c.* 5000 BC, which in turn was relieved by a 'Neolithic pluvial,' *c.* 4500 to 3000 BC, when there was more rainfall than now. Desiccation set in again reaching more or less the present rainfall levels by *c.* 2500 BC (Muzzolini, 1989*a*).

In the early Holocene, a culture developed along the Nile called 'Nilotic adaptation.' These people were big-game hunters and wild cattle were one of their favorite foods. They also exploited aquatic resources, such as hippopotamus and fish. Fishing was probably assisted by 'wild' flooding of the Nile during an episode 11 000 to 10 000 BC. At that time, flood waters spilled out over the alluvial plain leaving fish stranded in shallow pools when the waters receded. The resources were sufficiently abundant that people were more or less sedentary and occupied the same sites for long periods of time. The stone tool kit was epipaleolithic, featuring microliths and small blades, but at several sites grinding stones, including heavy mortars and blades with sickle sheen, were found. The equipment suggests heavy reliance on wild grass seed harvests.

The Nilotic adaptation rather suggests the sedentary fisherfolk that Sauer (1952) thought would be the most likely people to start plant domestication (see p. 22). But these cultures along the Nile began to fade as increasing rainfall brought improved conditions in the Sahara. There is no evidence that either the Nilotics or the people of the Sahara at that time cultivated plants or raised domesticated animals.

Farther west in North Africa, we find traces of hunter–gatherers who, although not fully sedentary, hunted large animals and sometimes occupied sites off and on for millennia. Different groups specialized in hunting particular species: wild sheep, in this case *Ammotragus* rather than *Ovis*; aurochs (*Bos primigenius*); and various antelopes and so on. These people had a few grinding stones. The best known and most widespread of the North African cultures was the Capsian. It developed in early Holocene and lingered on to about 4000 BC. The stone tool assemblage was epipalaeolithic throughout but demonstrated an evolution toward smaller and more finely made microliths and blades. There is no convincing evidence of either plant or animal domestication. The Capsians were noted for their fondness for snails and large middens of shells are found. This was probably not a major part of the diet, however, because they are highly seasonal in availability.

Nomadic pastoral economies became established across the Sahara during the Neolithic pluvial of 4500 to 3000 BC. Livestock tending and ceramic production were developed in the Sahara by people with an epipalaeolithic tool inventory well before ceramics and domestic animals were known in the Nile valley. These people often camped on the shores of playa lakes that expanded in the rainy seasons and contracted in the dry seasons. They exploited aquatic resources, hunted upland game and probably harvested wild grass seeds. Grinding equipment was abundant and blades with gloss were part of the inventory. Pottery was fragile and rather poorly made but much earlier than any in the Nile valley or Mediterranean North Africa (Clark and Brandt, 1984).

About 4000 BC, fully developed farming systems began to appear in the Nile valley. The earliest so far excavated are Merimde, on a branch of the Nile in the delta, and Fayum, on the shores of a lake fed by the river some distance upstream from the delta. Merimde covered some 18 ha, and had houses arranged by streets. Plastered pits and large ceramic jars for grain storage, as well as bones of domestic cattle, pigs, dogs, sheep, goats and donkeys were found. The sheep were larger than those of the later Old Kingdom. Fully domesticated crops included emmer, covered six-rowed barley, lentil, peas and flax, but the cereals were by far the most abundant. At Fayum, granaries were found containing emmer, two- and six-rowed barley and some flax. Within a few centuries, many sites of a fully Neolithic economy had spread up and down the valley, and Egypt was prepared to move into the Old Kingdom and historical times (Muzzolini, 1989*b*).

Clearly Egyptian agriculture was not truly African. The crops came from the Near East and the Mediterranean, but the stone tools used by the people were African in character. Native African crops evolved south of the Sahara and were tropical in adaptation. They did not fit the flooding regimes of the Nile. The Nile floods in late summer, and planting begins as the waters recede in the fall. Therefore the crops that are grown must be adapted to the cool season of the year. All the early Egyptian annual crops were of that nature; emmer wheat, barley, peas, lentils, chickpeas, lettuce and so on. They did have perennial crops, such as figs, olives, pomegranate, palm trees and the like, but the tropical annuals were not suited to the system.

The evolution of tropical African crops has not been well-documented archaeologically. Linguistic studies suggest indigenous agriculture may have been in place by 6000 BC in West Africa and by 4000 BC in the central Sudanic zone. Yet archaeologists have failed to turn up any evidence whatsoever for agriculture at such early dates. We must therefore depend, more than is desirable, on evidence from the plants themselves (Clark and Brandt, 1984).

Figure 5.1 shows a climate-vegetation distribution for Africa. On a coarse scale climate and vegetation coincide. It will be noted, as with other continental land masses, that there is a certain rough correspondence of zones north and south of the equator. For Africa, there is a zone of Mediterranean vegetation along the northern coasts and in South Africa. These are flanked by deserts, the Sahara in the north, the Kalahari in the south. There is a forest zone close to the equator and this is flanked by broad savanna zones. In addition, there are highlands in eastern Africa. In describing African crops we shall follow roughly an ecological order.

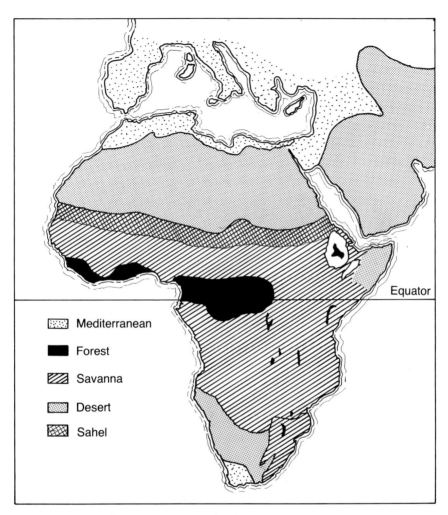

Fig. 5.1. A climate–vegetation distribution map for Africa.

The crops

Cereals

The Mediterranean formation contributed virtually nothing to indigenous tropical African agriculture, and the desert zone, understandably, contributed few crops – the date (*Phoenix dactylifera*) probably being the most important. Whether the date was derived from the African oases or from the Near Eastern deserts we do not know, but it is an important desert crop. The other possible contribution is pearl millet; it is the most drought resistant of all the millets and its wild races are still found in the Sahara (Fig. 5.2). The supposition is that it was domesticated at a time when people were living in the Sahara and camping along the margins of playa lakes. This is yet to be substantiated by archaeological results. Whatever the origin, pearl millet is a major crop of the Sahel and the dry savanna. Our analysis showed four major races, each with its own geographic, ecological adaptation. There is a northern pearl millet belt stretching from Mauritania and Senegal to the Ethiopian border. There is a second, but less well defined southern belt around the fringes of the Kalahari desert. The crop was taken to India at, we think, a rather early date where it is vital to the food supply of people living around the Indian desert (Brunken, de Wet and Harlan, 1977).

The interaction among wild, weed and cultivated pearl millet is conspicuous. Massive swarms of hybrid derivatives are built up in West Africa and again in the Jebel Murra part of Sudan. The weeds can be quite aggressive and do considerable damage to production in cultivated fields. They are not easily controlled because they are mimetic, that is they mimic the variety of crop with which they are growing. It is very difficult for the farmer to weed out these mimetic races until maturity when the seeds begin to fall and infest the soil. This kind of mimicry is found in many crops and will be mentioned from time to time throughout the book. In West Africa, the weed races are called *shibra* and are considered a serious pest.

Pearl millet provides the staff of life for some millions of people in the dry savanna and Sahel zone of Africa and dry zones of India. It may be treated as most other cereals, grinding it into flour, making flat breads or dumplings; it may be pounded and cracked in a mortar to make a gruel, a sort of breakfast cereal. It is one of the more nutritious of cereal grains and has one of the best amino acid profiles. Most Africans prefer pearl millet to sorghum for culinary purposes and therefore the crop is grown farther into the wet zones than its adaptation would warrant. As a desert grass, it is generally susceptible to many diseases of the wetter tropics. However, this cultural practice has led to some highly resistant land races of pearl millet from the wetter zones.

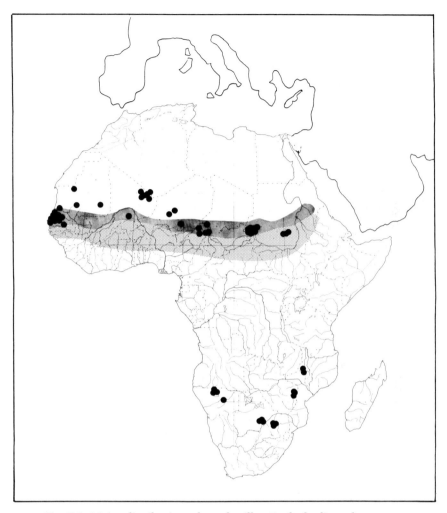

Fig. 5.2. Major distribution of pearl millet. Dark shading: the
northern pearl millet belt where it is the staff of life. Light shading:
adjacent belt where it is grown but less important than sorghum.
Dark circles: known sites of spontaneous races.

Moving into the tall grass savanna, sorghum becomes the most
important food crop. It has wild races that occur in enormous abundance in the African savannas. There are parts of Sudan where one
can drive for 100 km or more and as far as the eye can see there is a
tall grass savanna sprinkled with occasional thorny acacia trees. This

Pearl millet mimics. (a) Stand of wild pearl millet on wadi bank, Sudan. (b) Weed race of pearl millet, called shibra, Burkina Faso. (c) Cultivated pearl millet with long false spike, Burkina Faso. (d) Mimic weed race of pearl millet imitating the 'mil des Peuls,' Niger. It has a very long florescence, but shatters.

is a climax formation; there is no farming, not much grazing and these areas are subject to the usual fires associated with grasslands. The primary dominant of this formation is wild sorghum; in fact it is abundant through the savannas all the way to southern Africa. But in West Africa, the pattern is different. Here there is a race of wild sorghum adapted to the forest zone and rather closely associated with it; its natural habitat is along river banks or openings where sunlight can reach. It is not suited to a closed canopy situation, but when logging trails are opened up and a little light penetrates, the wild sorghum follows the trails. In city lots in the forest zone, for example in Lagos, Freetown, Abidjan or other cities, it is a very common weedy plant. This race, however, probably had little to do with cultivated sorghum because it grows in a region too wet for the range of adaptation of cultivated sorghum. The progenitor of cultivated sorghum would appear to be the race of the savannas. This race is hardly found at all in West Africa. It would seem, then, that the most logical part of Africa for domestication would be in the northeast quadrant, probably in the area from Lake Chad to the Ethiopian border. The evolution of weed sorghums by different routes are described in Chapter 2 (see Fig. 5.3).

The Crop Evolution Laboratory of the University of Illinois devoted a good deal of time to a study of sorghum. We read what literature we could find on the genus, especially *Sorghum bicolor* and its near relatives, and herbarium specimens at Kew, Paris, Brussels, Florence, Berlin, Lisbon, Nairobi, Pretoria and many smaller herbaria in Africa were examined. Wild, weedy and domesticated races from most of the countries of Africa were collected, and the accessions introduced into the USA where we made hybrids, studied fertility and chromosome pairing in the hybrids, conducted studies in numerical taxonomy, isozyme analyses, chromatography of the tannins and so on. A rational classification of the diversity was developed, based primarily on the work of John Snowden and his classification of some 60 years ago. We believe our system to be simpler and more practical, but it is grounded on Snowden's pioneering work (Snowden, 1936.)

In the classification system that we worked out (Harlan and deWet, 1972) there were five basic races of cultivated sorghum and four of wild sorghum. The five basic races are easily identified from spikelets and even seeds or caryopses, but there are intermediates among them all. We called the basic races bicolor, guinea, kafir, caudatum and

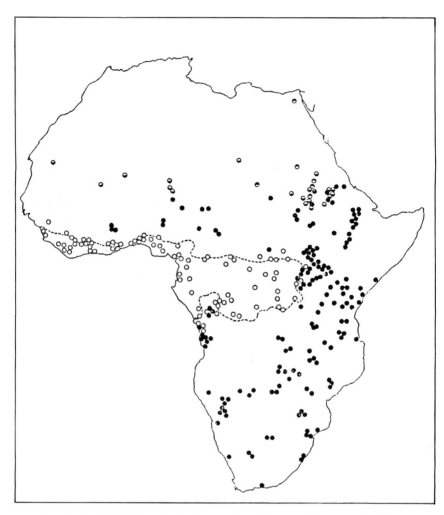

Fig. 5.3. Distribution of wild races of sorghum in Africa. Dotted lines indicate approximate limits of the tropical forest.

durra, and the intermediates guinea–bicolor, guinea–caudatum, kafir–bicolor, kafir–durra and so on. The total then came to 15 races. When these were plotted on the map, the resemblance to a language map of Africa was striking. There were guineas of West Africa that fitted quite well the distribution of the Congo–Niger language group; there were caudatums that fitted very well the

Chari–Nile language group; the kafirs fitted very well the distribution of Bantu tribes in southern Africa. The durras we found were most abundant in India, Pakistan and parts of the Near East, and in Africa were grown almost exclusively by Islamicized tribes. It was our feeling that perhaps the durra had evolved in India and had been returned to Africa during early Islamic times. There are other reasons to support this idea. The bicolor race is found everywhere sorghum is produced and therefore is not very helpful in establishing its origin. It is the most primitive of the five races and probably the progenitor of the other four. The general history, then, based on distribution of variation follows the sketch shown in Fig. 5.4.

In addition to the African sorghums, there is a group of Asian sorghums found primarily in China, but also in Southeast Asia and Indonesia. These probably have a different history and may, in fact, be derived from a local wild diploid *Sorghum* with which they are also compatible. The Chinese galiangs, as they are called, are very fibrous and have been selected, in part, for vanery and house construction, and include the broom corns whose panicle branches are used in the manufacture of brooms. The Chinese use this kind of sorghum a great deal in the manufacture of an alcoholic beverage called *mai-tai*. In Southeast Asia and Indonesia, the sorghums are also quite different from the African ones, often with very large, loose, open panicles – very handsome plants. It is not a major crop in that part of the world.

Another important cereal of the savanna zone is African rice, *Oryza glaberrima*. The progenitor is an annual wild rice adapted to water holes that are filled with water during the rainy season and dry up in the dry season. The annual adaptation fits this hydraulic regime. It is found abundantly in sub-Saharan Africa from Senegal to the Ethiopian border and sparingly and spottedly southward through the savannas surrounding the forest zone (Fig. 5.5). The wild form was harvested in enormous quantities a century ago and is still being harvested to some extent today. It is collected in sufficient quantities to appear for sale in the markets (Harlan, 1989*a,b*).

Oryza glaberrima, too, has its weed races, and although *Oryza* is mostly self-pollinating hybrids do occur between the wild forms and the cultivated forms; weed races are produced and these in turn hybridize with both cultivated and wild races. The results can be extremely complex hybrid swarms that often infest rice fields today. African rice was basically a West African crop and has been

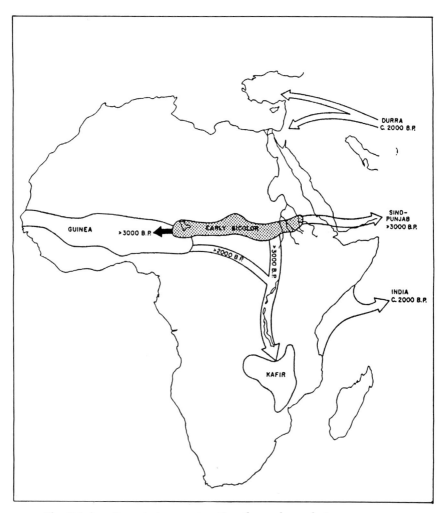

Fig. 5.4 An attempt at reconstructing the early evolutionary
history of sorghum. The earliest race to be domesticated is thought
to be 'early bicolor' that later gave rise to the guinea race in
western Africa, the kafir race in southern Africa and the durra
race, perhaps in India. After Harlan and Stemler (1976).

disappearing for some decades, being replaced by rice from the Orient.
The weed races and even the cultivated African rice are serious pests
as weeds in fields of Oriental rice now being grown in West Africa.

African rice is quite different in appearance from Asian rice; it is a

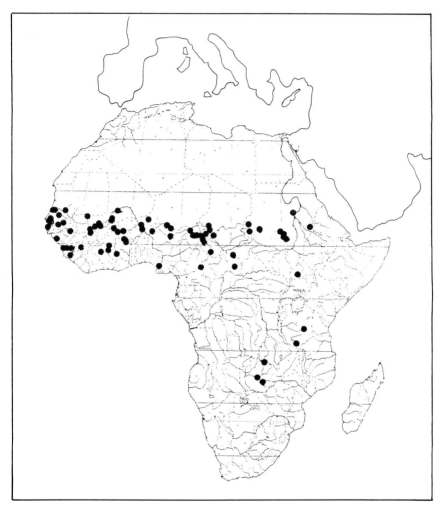

Fig. 5.5. Distribution of *Oryza barthii*, the progenitor of African cultivated rice.

separate species. Hybrids can be made between the two, but the hybrids tend to be highly sterile. Yet some offspring can be obtained, and rice breeders are trying to use African rices to introduce certain characteristics into Asian rice. Drought resistance would be one of the features and resistance to certain diseases. African rice, however, is very susceptible to the diseases of Asian rice and very difficult to grow outside of its native region of adaptation.

Other crops

The most important of the African edible legumes is cowpea, *Vigna unguiculata*. The wild forms of cowpea are plants of the forest. They are small viney plants that climb on understory trees of the forest zone. This probably was not the direct ancestor of cultivated cowpea, however, because a weedy form adapted to the savanna evolved from this forest race and is more likely to be the progenitor of the cultivated races. The savanna form is rather aggressive, a viney plant and moderately productive, and it was from this source that the cultivated forms, with their higher yields, were selected. But the same pattern prevails: there are weed cowpeas that may grow in the fields of cultivated cowpeas; they shatter, infest the soil with their seeds, and cause considerable damage to subsequent crops.

The yams are important crops in Africa and especially basic to some West African tribes. Different species of the true yam, *Dioscorea*, have been domesticated in Africa, Asia and tropical America. The yam-eating tribes of West Africa are today largely found in the forest zone; the yams can tolerate high amounts of rainfall. Their progenitors, however, were savanna plants. The underground tuber is an adaptation to a long, dry season; the vines can dry up and survive drought and fires because of the underground tuber.

The genus *Dioscorea* is very large with probably more than 600 species, which are found mostly in the tropics around the world. Those adapted to the forest tend to be more perennial in nature, usually very woody and not suitable for food. It is the yams of the savanna, adapted to the long dry season, that are most useful. The African yams of most importance are *Dioscorea rotundata* and *Dioscorea cayenensis*. These were taken into the forest zone at some unknown time where some tribes became almost completely dependent on them for food. The rice-eating tribes and the yam-eating tribes have very different cultures, but live side by side in the forest zone. If one goes down the Bandama River, Ivory Coast, people on the right bank are rice-eaters, people on the left bank are yam-eaters (Fig. 5.6). Both rice and yams are enormously important to their respective tribes who have developed elaborate rituals and ceremonies around their particular crops. The yam festivals are the major events of the year to yam-eating tribes; the rice festivals are the major events for the rice-eating tribes.

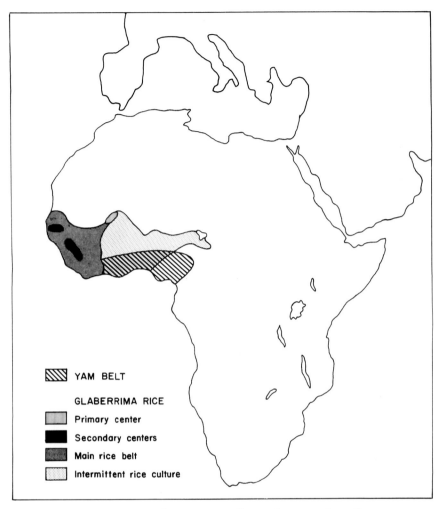

Fig. 5.6. Distribution of rice-eating tribes and yam-eating tribes,
Ivory Coast area, West Africa.

The close association of yam-eaters and rice-eaters probably has
historic origins. From the distribution of wild rice, it is apparent that
African rice culture must have originated in the savanna. This produced an expansive agriculture that moved in to the forest zone,
since rice is adapted to wet areas. But there, the rice-eating tribes
encountered yam-eaters who were already well entrenched and well
established. Both crops, however, are of savanna origin.

In fact, indigenous African agriculture is basically a savanna agriculture. The crops originated there and were dispersed into the forest zone or out toward the deserts as far as ecological limits would permit.

Décrue agriculture

In French *crue* means flood and *décrue* refers to the recession of the waters after the flood. Since there is no convenient English term, we borrow the French word. The hydrology of the central delta of the Niger River is extremely complex but the local cultivators have developed a remarkably sophisticated agriculture in order to deal with it. Crops, varieties and cultural practices are sensitively adjusted to variations in the height of the flood, soil texture, storage hazards, bird damage, nutritional needs and food preferences.

The headwaters of the Niger River lie in southern Guinea near the borders of Sierra Leone and Liberia where the rainfall usually exceeds 1.5 m per year. Several branches are gathered together and the water flows past Bamako and Ségou through relatively confining banks. Below Sansanding the slope becomes very slight with a fall of 15 m in some 250 km. At Diafarabé the main river takes on all the characteristics of a delta (Fig. 5.7). The Bani River follows a somewhat parallel course and discharges a considerable volume into the Niger at Mopti. The result is a flood that spreads water over vast areas at rather shallow depths. The hydrology is remarkably complex. While the slope in the present delta is very slight, the topography itself is undulating, so that during the annual flood the spreading waters follow an intricate lacework of channels, flats, ponds, marshes and lakes with a pattern that varies from year to year according to the height of the flood. The area covered is so vast and the slope away from the main channels so slight that the waters rise and fall very slowly. The main region of décrue agriculture is in the Diré-Goundam, Lake Faguibine area. Here the waters start rising in September but do not reach maximum until December or January, and it is not until March that the waters have receded enough for an appreciable amount of planting. Even within a single lake system with direct connections to the river, the flood may cover fields near the main stream a full month before it covers fields at the far end of the lake system.

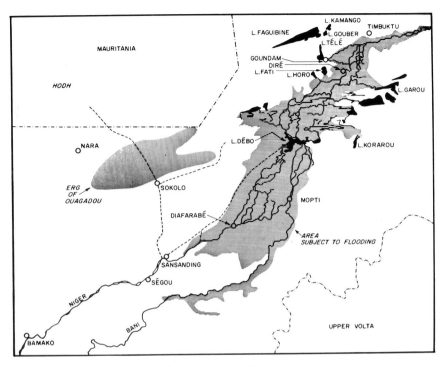

Fig. 5.7. The central delta of the Niger River.

On flat lands with direct connections to the river, the amount of land that is available for décrue culture depends almost directly on the height of the flood. During years of maximum flood, two to three times as much area is available for planting as in years of minimum flood. In some areas, flood waters enter the lake and marsh system over sills of such an elevation that some water is trapped and does not drain out with the décrue. The height of the waters in these lakes varies on a long-term cyclic basis of some fifteen to twenty years. A series of years with high floods will fill up the lakes leaving but scant acreage for planting; a series of years with low floods will expose considerably more land.

Cultivators have responded to this remarkably complex system by developing a very sophisticated sort of agriculture. Crops and even varieties are selected very carefully in order to fit the patterns of each flood separately. The main crops of décrue agriculture in the region are pearl millet and sorghum. Pearl millet is preferred from a culinary point of view and is better suited to sandy soils and sorghum is better suited to soils with high clay content. There are early and late land-races of each of the crops and these are selected according to the height of the flood. Understandably, lands farthest from the main channel receive water last and the water drains off first. It is necessary to use short season landraces in order to mature seed before the moisture supply is exhausted. As one approaches the main river channel, water during the flood is much deeper, goes off later in the season, and again short season types may be required so that grain is matured before waters rise again in the next season. In between there may be areas where long season varieties have an advantage. Close to the main channel rice is sown; in those fields nearest to the river, floating types are used. These may be seeded in dry soil in anticipation of the flood, or there may be sufficient summer rains to plant in moist soil before the flood comes. Farther from the river, ordinary kinds of rice of the nonfloating kind may be used.

The general sequence from the upper fields to the lower is as follows: pearl millet, long season durras, midseason durras, guinea corn and rice. The rice is harvested as the waters go down, but in the deepest areas this harvest must be done from a canoe. The guinea corn is harvested as the waters rise and a canoe is frequently used for it as well. The other varieties are not so tolerant to flooding before maturity but hold their seed well, and in the years when the floods are early even some pearl millet may be harvested from a canoe.

In areas where the waters recede very slowly, planting may go on for a period of three months or more, starting with the millets in the upper fields and proceeding through the durras to the guinea corn. The very lowest fields present the problem of getting the plants sufficiently mature before the floods rise again. A great deal of transplanting is done in these lower sites. The guinea corn is sprouted in seedling beds like rice and transplanted to the field in order to get the plants off to a faster start. Transplanting is done primarily where the threat of early flooding could be damaging, but the cultivators feel that there are other advantages to the practice including some control of shootfly and fungal diseases.

Landraces are also selected by maturity cycles in order to avoid the major depredations of the 'mange-mil' (*Quelea*), a small passerine bird that migrates through the region in vast cloud-like flocks in August and early September. The time of planting a given field is more or less fixed by the décrue, but the variety selected depends to a considerable degree on the number of days to the end of September when most of the mange-mils have passed through. The choice of variety for a given field will, therefore, vary according to the height of flood and time of décrue. When the crop matures too early, it may be a total loss due to the birds; when it matures too late, the flood may cause extensive damage (Harlan and Pasquéreau, 1969).

Cowpeas are sometimes grown as a décrue crop between the hills of millet and durra. They must be harvested before the rise of water in the fall. Some form of décrue agriculture is usually practiced along the banks of most rivers throughout the world, but the décrue of the inner delta of the Niger in Mali is probably the most sophisticated of all.

There is a modification of décrue practiced widely throughout the savanna of Africa, where land that stands under water during the rainy season is exploited after it begins to dry out. Often the land is covered with native grasses; the grasses are burned and sorghum or pearl millet is transplanted into the moist area and must mature a crop on residual moisture. Seedlings are started in sand beds and transplanted by use of a large dibble, perhaps 1.5 m in length, rammed into the moist soil; the seedling is put into the hole; a little moisture is added from a gourd and the plant is on its own from then on. Yields are not likely to be large but it is a method of using land that cannot be exploited otherwise. In some cases transplanting is not necessary. One practice observed in Chad is to broadcast the seed in standing vegetation and then hoe it in, planting the seed and destroying the weedy vegetation in one operation. This does not yield very well but it is a reasonably efficient method for using wetlands.

Ancient Egyptian agriculture was, of course, a décrue agriculture. However, the time of the flood (late summer) made it impossible to grow native tropical crops. As I have pointed out, seeding had to be done in the fall and therefore cool season crops such as barley, emmer, flax, chickpea, lentils, etc. were imported from the Near East. It was not until the arrival of the shaduf, the water wheel and other water lifting devices, that it was possible to grow summer crops along the banks of the Nile.

The forest zone

As we move into the forest zone with its higher rainfall, pearl millet and sorghum are left behind as they are not suited to such a high rainfall. Yams and rice, however, penetrate to the coast and can be found throughout the forest. An important crop is added in this region; the native African oil palm is well suited to a high rainfall, although its native habitat is at forest margins or along river banks where it can receive more light than in a closed canopy forest. In traditional African agriculture, the oil palm was not planted in plantations but dense stands were developed by the simple practice of cutting down other trees and protecting the oil palm. The management was very much like that practiced for the white barked acacias and the karité of the savanna. Distribution was also assisted by some religious beliefs. It was thought, for example, that if the fruits of the palm were beaten off in the village, the flying fruits signified people leaving the village. Therefore, the bunches of fruits were taken into the forest and beaten off there or beaten where they were harvested.

Traditional management of the oil palm has resulted in some genetic selection. There is a gene in the crop that governs the production of the kernel inside the fruit. One allele in homozygous condition essentially suppresses kernel formation. Consequently, most of the fruit is pulp, it is sterile and cannot reproduce itself. The other allele in homozygous condition produces a thick-shelled grain, while the heterozygous condition produces an intermediate form with a thin-shelled grain. The thick-shelled kind is called durra, the thin-shelled kind, tenera and the kind with no kernel, pissifera. Natural selection would tend to favor the durra allele because pissifera kinds are sterile. But the cultivators prefer pissifera and are more apt to tap the durra trees for a toddy that is palm wine. Repeated tappings will kill the tree. The result is a selection pressure favoring the heterozygous condition, which is the one preferred by the cultivators. The African oil palm has become a major supplier of edible oil for the world in this century. Most of the production, however, is in Malaysia and adjacent parts of Southeast Asia, and African production is relatively small.

A major contribution to world agriculture from the forest zone is coffee. *Coffea arabica* is the coffee of quality, the most desired in the coffee trade, and its wild forms are found as understory trees in the forests of Ethiopia. We do not know when Ethiopians first began to use coffee, but apparently it was taken to the Yemen at least by the fourteenth century and coffee drinking became popular in Arabic culture. It was from there that Europeans first learned of it. Coffee was taken from the Yemen to India, Ceylon, Java, New Guinea and the Philippines around 1700. Later it was introduced into the Dutch colonies in South America by way of Amsterdam, and by 1725 it had been introduced into French Guiana via Paris. Most of the coffee in South America is derived from these limited introductions. The other coffee of commerce is *Coffea canephora*, which is native to the forests of the Congo and adjacent areas. It is used primarily in the production of instant coffee and has become important in world trade.

Cola nuts are important to many peoples, particularly in West Africa. There are several species but *Cola nitida* is the most common, Cola is important in social affairs: there are welcoming ceremonies; people of note are presented with cola nuts upon arrival; guests are served cola nuts, often in beautifully carved wooden bowls designed especially for the purpose and the best bowls are much appreciated by collectors of African art. Cola is high in caffeine and is used extensively as a fatigue plant. One can buy three or four nuts for a penny and after chewing one or two, one is no longer hungry and fatigue is reduced.

East African highlands

In the uplands of Ethiopia, Uganda and Kenya, a small suite of crops evolved adapted to the cool to mild climates of the region. Except for coffee, none has become important on the world scene. The one with the greatest distribution is finger millet, *Eleusine coracana*. It is a small-seeded millet, formerly used for food in the region but now used mostly for beer. Finger millet made its way to India at an early date and became an important crop for the people of the hills, both in the south and in the north of India. There it evolved races that are peculiarly Indian in character. The Indians use it more for food than the Africans.

In Ethiopia a more important millet is tef, *Eragrostis tef*. It is perhaps the smallest seeded of all the millets and is grown on a larger hectarage than any other cereal in Ethiopia. It has a large ecological amplitude being grown from the lowest parts of the country to the highest parts of the plateau. Yields are rather good for a small-seeded millet, and as a whole grain food it has an excellent nutritional profile.

The grain is prepared by grinding into flour, adding water, allowing the dough to ferment for some hours or even a day or two. Then the dough is thinned, poured on a large clay skillet, baked, and it is then ready to eat. It has a spongy texture, a rather sour taste from the fermentation and is an excellent bread to go with the hot, peppery stews of Ethiopian cuisine. This is a cereal that could be much more widely used.

Musa ensete is a crop of great importance to some of the tribes of central and southern Ethiopia. It is not much used elsewhere. The plant is a relative of the banana but the fruit is not the edible portion. The base of the pseudostem is harvested, sacrificing the whole plant, and is wrapped in leaves of the enset and buried for a matter of some days to ferment and render the flour more easily extracted. It is then dried and pounded, and the flour used in cooking.

Noog, *Guizotia abyssinica,* is an oil crop commonly used in Ethiopia. It is a composite, a relative of sunflower and safflower, and produces a highly edible cooking oil. The crop is grown on a small scale in India and elsewhere but its primary area of use is Ethiopia. It follows the same path of evolution as most other crops in that there are wild and weedy races that interbreed, producing hybrid swarms that are quite conspicuous. The flowers are yellow and fields of *Noog* are very attractive in the landscape.

A crop of commercial importance for Ethiopia is chat, *Catha edulis.* It is a mild narcotic, and produces a sort of euphoria and is very popular around the Red Sea. The upper leaves and twigs are chewed, sometimes with lime added to the quid. However, it must be chewed fresh, so chat is exported from Ethiopia by airplane and distributed to Arabia and adjacent countries.

The animals

The documentation of animals in Africa has been a matter of controversy for some time. This revolves primarily around the status of sheep and goats, but cattle and swine are also in question. There are some who maintain that wild sheep and goats were not in Africa in early Holocene and were not available for domestication. Therefore, the appearance of ovi–caprid bones at sites in North Africa must signal the arrival of domesticates from the Near East where they had been domesticated earlier. As Muzzolini has pointed out, we are not so sure of the distributions of wild forms at that time range: distributions do change over time. There were times in Holocene when rhinoceros, elephant, Cape buffalo and lion ranged up from the savannas of sub-Sahara almost to the Mediterranean, but no one claims that the rhinoceros was domesticated and introduced by humans (Muzzolini, 1987).

There was, in fact, a wild sheep in North Africa assigned to *Ammotragus* rather than *Ovis*, but the bones found in archaeological sites cannot easily be distinguished between the two or even separated from *Capra* (Higgs, 1967). There is no question that wild cattle (aurochs) ranged widely over northern Africa and were targeted by a number of hunting people. Wild boar also occurred at the appropriate time range in northwest Africa. Domestication of all of these animals, independent of the Near East, is certainly possible but no real proof is as yet available. The evidence before *c.* 4000 BC is all tenuous and/or ambiguous (Muzzolini, 1987).

By about 4000 BC there is evidence that animal husbandry was entrenched and widely practiced from the Maghreb to the Nile Valley. This could not have happened without antecedents but the antecedents, as of now, are hazy and uncertain. The early sheep of Egypt were hair sheep, with corkscrew horns sticking out horizontally from the head. In the second millennium BC, they were largely replaced both in Egypt and Mesopotamia by fat-tailed sheep. Wild sheep have short tails; some breeds of domesticated sheep have long thin tails, while the fat-tailed sheep has an enormously enlarged tail of fat, often dragging on the ground. It seems to be well-adapted to the hot dry zones of the Near East and Africa, but has not successfully penetrated Europe or other temperate mesic zones.

The ancient Egyptians experimented with domestication or at least rearing of a number of African animals, apparently with little lasting effect. The Egyptian goose may have been reared for a short period and the hunting cheetah was used for the sport of the rich. It is still used for this purpose. One indigenous domesticate of sub-Sahara is the guinea fowl. This noisy bird is reared in Europe and North America for the gourmet market, but is less popular in Africa than the imported chicken.

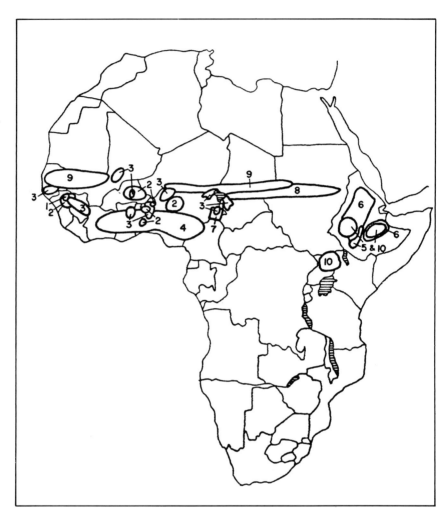

Fig. 5.8. Probable areas of domestication of selected African crops.
1, *Brachiaria deflexa*; 2, *Digitaria exilis* and *D. iburua*; 3, *Oryza
glaberrima*; 4, *Dioscorea rotundata*; 5, *Musa ensete* and *Guizotia
abyssinica*; 6, *Eragrostis tef*; 7, *Voandzeia* and *Kerstingiella*; 8, *Sorghum
bicolor*; 9, *Pennisetum glaucum*; 10, *Eleusine coracana*. From Harlan
(1971): copyright by the American Association for the
Advancement of Science.

Our common house cat, the beloved pet of so many people, was first brought into the *domus* in Egypt. The wild form is very similar to our present day tabby cat. Cats had a special place in Egyptian culture and were revered, sometimes mummified and buried with ceremony. Many cultures perceived the cat to have mystic and magical powers, often of a malevolent nature.

Conclusions

Indigenous agriculture in Africa has its own special characteristics. The cattle-keeping tribes living primarily on milk and blood are endemic to Africa (see also p. 109). Nomads in Eurasia may be heavily dependent on their flocks, but not in the African fashion. The list of plants domesticated from the African flora is impressive and includes cereals, pulses, oil-seed crops, fruits, spices, vegetables, medicinal, magic and ritual plants. The list is short on fruits, nuts and vegetables compared to Asia and the Americas, but the African supplements the diet freely with harvests of wild plants.

The geographic pattern is noncentric in that no one region stands out in either time or space as an overall center of origin. The pattern is rather a mosaic of cultures, crops and farming practices. These features seem to be characteristic of noncenters. The activities of domestication of indigenous African plants seems confined to the sub-Saharan belt from the Atlantic to the Indian Ocean with few, if any, contributions from south of the equator. Nearly all of the domesticates are native to the savannas of that region (Fig. 5.8).

CHAPTER SIX

The Far East

Prehistoric record

While the prehistoric record of *Homo* in China is not as long as that for Africa, it does go back to *Homo erectus* some 1.5 to 1.7 million years ago. The Chinese race of that species (Peking Man) differed in his tool preparation traditions from the *H. erectus* races who ranged over Europe, Africa and central Asia. Peking Man did not make the classic pear-shaped Achulean 'hand-axe' but invented a characteristic 'chopper' of his own. It looks cruder and less refined, and for a long time the Chinese *H. erectus* was thought to have been backward. But Pope (1989) noted a close correspondence between the geographical distribution of 'choppers' and the large bamboos of East Asia, and suggested that the choppers might have been designed to cut and process bamboo from which much more refined and elegant tools could be made. True or not, the inhabitants of China seem to be developing a unique endemic tradition at a very early time.

Geological evidence indicates that from mid-Pleistocene and perhaps earlier, western China and central Asia had a semiarid steppe environment and occasionally may have been desiccated even further to form an arid region over vast reaches of the interior. One result has been an extraordinary accumulation of loess, some alluvial but most of it windblown. Deposits over 250 meters thick are found over large sections of Shaanxi and Gansu, and still larger areas with 150 meters or more down slope. Huge tracts of Hebei, Henan, Shandong and Anhui are covered with redeposited loess (Fig. 6.1).

The end of Pleistocene and start of Holocene in China was, as elsewhere, a dynamic time. The Tali glacier was melting, the Pleistocene fauna was being reduced by extinctions, sea levels rose rapidly, etc. A climate similar to the present emerged from 10 000 to 12 000 years ago, although sea levels continued to fluctuate by a few meters in elevation throughout most of the Holocene (Chang, 1986). At the end of the Pleistocene, much of China was inhabited by a variety of

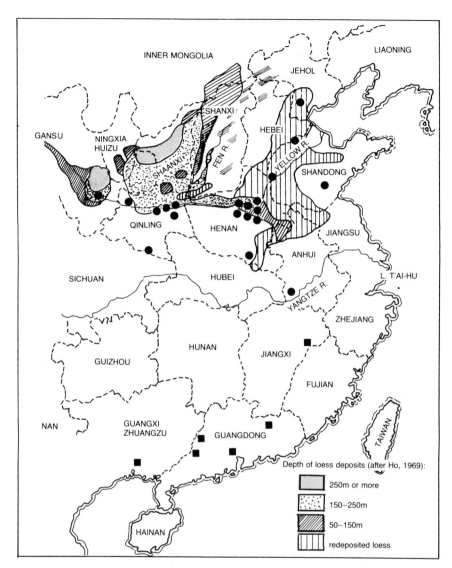

Fig. 6.1 Early Neolithic sites in China. (●) P'ei-li-kang and related cultures; (■) south Chinese Neolithic sites.

populations living by sophisticated hunting–gathering–fishing techniques. The several populations had different and specialized tool assemblages. The pattern was similar to that of the Near East and Africa, in that it consisted of a mosaic of Mesolithic cultures showing considerable local and regional diversity, and the same trends toward smaller and more finely made tools.

On the loess terraces of north China, the Mesolithic/Neolithic threshold was crossed around the middle of the seventh millennium BC. The earliest Neolithic culture of the region we now know is P'ei-li-kang. It is now well known from some forty sites in Henan and other provinces (Fig. 6.1). The dates cluster between 6500 and 5000 BC. There was little change in the stone tool assemblage and the people continued to hunt deer and other game. In addition, they had domesticated pig, dog and chicken. Crops included proso and foxtail millets and a *Brassica* of some sort. Hazelnut, hackberry, acorns, walnut and jujube were gathered and some might even have been grown. They had pottery, elaborately made grind stones and buried the dead in special cemeteries. P'ei-li-kang culture gave rise to the well-known Yang–shao with its handsome pottery and well-developed village layouts. This culture spanned the period 5000 to 3000 BC, and flourished on the loess soils of northern China (see Fig. 6.1).

In south China other Neolithic cultures were evolving independently. Some caves have yielded cord impressed pottery that may have some connection with impressed wares of Thailand and Indochina, further south. Early pottery in south China and Southeast Asia is usually cord impressed. The technique seems to consist of wrapping a paddle with cord and beating the wet clay of a freshly shaped pot or bowl with it before firing. The patterns that result are often attractive and the rough surface may be useful in the firing process. The earliest pottery so far found in China may come from Tsing-'i-Yen. The site has been dated at about 6400 BC by radiocarbon and between 5160 and 8370 bc by thermoluminescence. Another cave, P'ao-tzu-t'ou, in South China has yielded pottery dated at about 7350 bc by radiocarbon. No plant remains have been recovered as yet and there is no real evidence for farming.

In the Yangzte delta around Lake T'ai-hu, yet another Neolithic culture evolved in a watery landscape. Plants grown or gathered include lotus (*Nelumbo*), arrowroot (*Sagittaria*), water 'chestnut' (*Eleocharis*), water caltrop (*Trapa* spp.), wild rice (*Zizania*), reed (*Phragmites*) and rice (*Oryza sativa*). There are over 50 known sites of this culture in the area and the dates range from 5000 to 3000 bc.

Much more detail is given by Chang (1986), but the general picture is that a mosaic of Neolithic cultures had evolved over most of China

Clones of *Zizania* infected with smut produce swollen stems used as a vegetable.

by 5000 BC and evident linkages began to appear by about 4000 BC. The Mesolithic/Neolithic threshold was crossed at least twice, once in the north and once in the south. Or it could well have been crossed several times independently. The northern Neolithic was founded on the millets and the southern Neolithic was based on rice. The wet lowland roots and vegetables are still basic to much of Chinese cuisine. Chinese Neolithic sites appear on Taiwan dating to about 4400 BC.

The early Neolithic that developed on the loess terraces of north China gives the appearance of a center of origin, but it is not earlier than sites in south China, which suggest some relationship to developments in Southeast Asia and may be outposts of that noncenter.

Recorded history

Chinese civilization emerged from previous Neolithic cultures and is said to have begun with the founding of the Shang dynasty sometime before 1500 BC. At about 1300 BC the Shang capital was established at An-Yang, and this city was captured by the Chou tribe in 1027 BC. The legendary ancestor of the Chou tribe was Hou Chi, the god of millets. The dates for An-Yang became important in Chinese history for several reasons. Essentially all the Shang literature falls between 1300 and 1027 BC and consists of oracle bone inscriptions and writing on cast bronze objects. Art had reached a high state of development and Shang bronzes are world famous for their style and technique of casting.

It is from An-Yang that we detect the first real evidence of contact with the West. Foreign importations of the time included wheat and barley, probably the domesticated goat, the horse chariot and some art motifs borrowed from the Seima cultures on the Volga. There is external evidence that the nomads of the Eurasian steppe were particularly active during the thirteenth century BC, with much warfare, raids, and the sacking of towns and cities. It will be noted that this time range roughly corresponds to the Egyptian Second Intermediate Period, the migration of the Sea Peoples and other cataclysmic events. Could it have been the workings of a drought of continental magnitude?

Among the earliest compilations of Chinese literature is the *Book of Odes* (*Shih-Ching*), an assemblage of fragments from the eleventh century to the middle of the sixth century BC. Botanically, it is the most informative of the early literatures and mentions about 150 plants, as compared to 55 in Egyptian literature, 83 in the Bible and 63 in Homer (Ho, 1969). In the Odes, panicum millet is mentioned 27 times, the mulberry 20 times, and *Artemisia* is mentioned 19 times with 10 varieties.

The soybean was first mentioned in 664 BC in connection with a tribute paid to the Chou by the Shan-Jung, the mountain Jung tribe. Hemp (*Cannabis*) was not mentioned in the Shang oracle literature but occurs seven times in the Odes. Iron implements for agriculture became significant about 400 BC. Manuring, crop rotation, double cropping and intensive agriculture, as well as the first large scale irrigation projects all date to the third century BC (Ho, 1974).

After Alexander the Great (d. 323 BC) and the establishment of Greek states from Afghanistan to the Mediterranean, regular contact was maintained between China and Persia by way of the silk routes. Laufer in his scholarly study, *Sino–Iranica* (1919), traces the arrival in China of a number of Near Eastern cultigens. Grape and alfalfa were introduced in 126 BC, cucumber, pea, spinach, broad bean, chive, coriander, fig, safflower, sesame and pomegranate arrived from Iran at various times from the second to the seventh centuries AD.

The Chinese crops were very slow to spread out from their homeland. The millets constitute a special case that will be discussed later. But cultigens of certain Chinese origin were unknown to the West until very late. The peach is said to have reached India by about the second century AD. Many authors credit the Chinese with domestication of the apricot but, since the wild races range from Turkey to China, it seems likely that other peoples were also involved.

The West did not know rice until after the time of Alexander the Great. Theophrastus gave a good description of it and called it 'the emmer of the Indians.' On the whole, Far Eastern agriculture may be characterized as introverted, with very little dispersal until well into modern historical times. And many crops did not move out until the arrival of European shipping in the late fifteenth and early sixteenth centuries. There is, in fact, a notable lack of long range diffusion, as illustrated by the fact that the Chinese were casting iron for two thousand years and using the cross bow for a thousand years before the Europeans began to do the same.

As we move into the tropics south of China, we find contributions coming from different ecological zones as expected. The savannas with their long dry seasons present us with annual cereals like rice and coix, and with yams that behave like annuals. Wetlands yield aroids like *Colocasia* and *Allocasia*. The forest margins provide such cucurbits as *Mamordica*, *Benincasa*, *Trichosanthes*, *Luffa* and the ubiquitous bottle gourd. More species of citrus, cinnamon, ginger, turmeric, black pepper and others add spice to food, and the betel nut–betel leaf combination becomes a popular masticatory.

The Malay Pennisula and South Pacific islands have provided a bewildering array of fruits, roots and spices. Some of the best known and most popular include mango, durian, rambutan, jambos, mangosteen, nutmeg, clove, sugar cane and coconut. The coconut is primarily a coastal plant and probably of island origin. The rest tend to be forest margin plants adapted to more light and less shading than is found in the rainforest climax.

Many of these crops are not familiar to people who have not been in the region. I will therefore give a few brief notes. *Coix* is a small genus with several species mostly native to southeast Asia. The one of interest here is Job's-tears or 'hippie beads', *Coix lachryma-jobi*. The widespread weedy form is now found adventive or naturalized around the world in warm humid climates. The cultivated races are quite different in appearance. They are tall with few or even no tillers and the 'beads' are large with thin shells. It is now mostly a relic crop but is still grown in south China, the Philippines, New Guinea and elsewhere in the region. The large grains are extracted from the shells in a mortar and used as other cereals.

The crops

If we look at the crops individually and in some detail, they present a pattern in general conformity to the center and noncenter concept proposed for the region. Crops of the north Chinese center form a cohesive unit or complex; those of the noncenter form a mosaic related to cultures and agricultural practices over a wide area. Plants were domesticated out of the native flora wherever the people found them. For that reason they may be grouped according to ecological adaptation which surely reflects something about their origins.

The agriculture that evolved in the north China uplands was based on the millets, soybean and a suite of fruits and vegetables. Li (1970) had pointed out that several of the ancient vegetables are no longer grown but linger on as weeds of waste places or in fields of modern crops. The most important to the ancient Chinese was a mallow (*Malva verticilata*). Others that were once cultivated, then abandoned, include *Lactuca denticulata*, *Viola verucunda*, *Angelica kiusiana*, *Polygonum hydropiper*, *Nasturtium indicum* and *Xanthium strumarium* (Li, 1970). We have no familiar English names for these. They are mostly pot herbs and presumably would have been lightly boiled for consumption as in typical Oriental cuisine. Modern vegetables are strong in Cruciferae, *Brassica*, radish, onions, leek, chives, shallot, garlic, etc. They also include a number imported from abroad: pea, cowpea, lettuce, etc. But the imports have been modified in typical Chinese fashion. Peas are used in the green pod form and the famous Chinese snow pea is the result. Cowpeas are used as green pods also and are typically of the 'yard long' kinds. Lettuce was selected for succulent non-bitter stem and reduced leaves and is very different in appearance from Western lettuce.

The fruits of north China were selected from the temperate forest flora and are strong in Rosaceae. Pears, apples, cherries, plums, peach, apricot and hawthorn, all in great diversity, make up most of the inventory to which can be added the persimmon (*Diospyros kaki*) and the jujube (*Zizyphus jujuba*). Mulberries were and are grown more for silkworm fodder than for their fruits. The Oriental persimmon is the large soft and delicious one, sometimes found in the West in specialist markets. The jujube looks something like a date but has little flavor. It is an extremely hardy tree, however, and can be grown on dryland in semiarid zones where other fruits fail.

Soybean. The wild soybean is a small, slender, creeping vine bearing a few small pods with small, black seeds. The plant is widely distributed from southern Siberia through Manchuria, along the eastern coastal plain of China and westward to Sichuan. It is rather weedy and is often found in city parks under shade trees. Presumably it was once a woodland or temperate forest plant before the natural vegetation was destroyed for agriculture. The changes under domestication have been enormous.

Evolution of bush types from vines is common under domestication. It has occurred in American beans in both common and lima types, African cowpeas, lablab beans, pigeon pea, oriental soybeans and other legumes. The viney ancestral types are usually retained as well and trailing forms of soybeans and cowpea are still grown for fodder. Soybeans are prepared for food in many ways, often including fermentation with special strains of yeast and fungi cultured for the purpose. Tofu and soy sauce are the products best known outside the Orient. While soybean is a major Chinese contribution to agriculture, it has a relatively low status in China. On the world scene, soybean ranks fifth in production of edible dry matter, but is behind the major cereals; wheat, rice, maize, barley. The world's major producers of

Stem lettuce (center), vegetable market, Beijing.

soybeans are the USA and Brazil, most of which is fed to animals.

Cannabis was a north China domesticate, but could well have been taken into the *domus* elsewhere. It was the principal coarse fiber; the grains could be eaten and oil can be expressed from the seeds as well. Its narcotic properties were well known, Another technical plant was *Rhus verniciflua*, the lac plant. Silk production and weaving and lacquer ware are two Chinese artistic crafts that have contributed much to the elegance of the high civilization that emerged in north China.

In the watery lowlands of the east China coastal plain, another group of plants was selected from the native flora for domestication. From the Nymphaceae came at least three: the Oriental lotus (*Nelumbo nucifera*), the prickly water lily (*Euryale ferox*) and the water shield (*Brassenia shreberi*). Others include the popular water 'chestnut' (*Eleocharis tuberosa*) and the water caltrop (*Trapa natans*), the water mustard (*Brassica japonica*), oriental 'celery' (*Oenanthe stolonifera*), arrowroot (*Sagittaria sinensis*), *Ipomea aquatica*, a sort of morning glory with edible leaves, wild rice (*Zizania latifolia*) and common rice. The rhizomes of reed and cattail were, and are, gathered as well.

The wild rice belongs to the same genus as the American wild rice, and it is said that it was once grown as a cereal in north China. It became infected with a smut (*Ustilago*) that caused the stems to swell and resulted in sterility. The plant is now grown as a vegetable and is propagated vegetatively. As we have seen, the wetlands suite of plants was domesticated early in the Neolithic and after some thousands of years is still a major part of Chinese cuisine.

In the south of China still more plants were domesticated. These include several species of *Brassica*, the red bean (*Vigna angularis*), velvet bean (*Stizolobium hassjoo*), the Chinese yam (*Dioscorea esculenta*), the day lily, etc. But the major contributions from the south came from the subtropical forest and woodlands. Sour orange, sweet orange, mandarin orange, kumkwat, loquat, wampi, litchi, *Canarium*, and other fruits were brought into the fold. Fiber plants included *Boehmeria niveae*, *Abutilon avicennae* and *Prueria lobata*. The tung trees, *Aleurites* spp., produce commercial oil and tea is a major crop on the world market.

The millets

Setaria italica and *Panicum miliaceum* were basic to the north Chinese Neolithic and were presumably domesticated in the region. Yet both are found in a sprinkling of Neolithic village sites over Europe throughout the fourth millennium BC. They were seldom important components of plant remains. For example, they were reported only from Niederwil among the Swiss lake dwellers; but they occurred in sufficient sites that there can be little doubt of the presence of both millets in fourth millennium BC Europe. *Panicum* has also been reported from Jemdet Naser, Mesopotamia, about 3000 BC and possibly Argissa–Maghula, Greece, about 5500 BC (Renfrew, 1969).

The Tripolye of the Ukraine was the only European culture that grew *Panicum miliaceum* on a large scale. That culture flourished from 3800 to 2900 BC and panic was one of the major crops. Neither millet has been studied intensively, and archaeological investigations on the vast Eurasian steppe between China and the Ukraine are not yet sufficiently advanced for us to choose between possible alternatives. The possibilities are:

1. the millets were domesticated in China and dispersed to Europe before 4000 BC in Neolithic times;
2. they were domesticated in the West and were dispersed to China; or
3. there was more than one domestication.

The presumptive progenitor of *Setaria italica* is *Setaria viridis*, a ubiquitous weed originally found from Japan to England and now widespread in North America and elsewhere. *Panicum miliaceum* is a weedy plant; the shattering allele is easily recovered and it is now a serious weed in the upper Mississippi valley of North America. It is reported as weedy, naturalized or escaped and common from European Russia to eastern Siberia. It is difficult, if not impossible, to separate wild from weedy races without very careful analyses.

Both millets are adapted to the summer rainfall belt of temperate Eurasia. They were well known to the Greeks and Romans and to Indians of ancient times. It is significant, however, that a number of Indian names for panic suggest that it came to India from China. In Sanskrit, the name is *chinaka*, meaning Chinese; in Hindi, *chena, cheen*; Bengali, *cheena*; and Gujarati, *chino*. The Persian word is essentially the same as the Chinese, *shu-shu* (Laufer, 1919).

No other known crops had such a distribution in that time range. Wide dispersals in the fifth millennium BC are certainly possible, but one might have expected more than the two millets if this was the explanation. The Chinese crops did not disperse until very late. In our present state of ignorance, independent domestications appear to be the most likely answer, but new information could easily lead to other conclusions.

There were two cereals in the ancient agricultural systems of Southeast Asia: rice and coix. There is some evidence that coix was the older of the two, at least in the rainforest zones. It spread into regions of the Philippines, Borneo and New Guinea where rice did not penetrate. At one time, the great swampy deltas of Southeast Asia probably supported vast stands of wild rice, but the rice in such environments was mostly, if not entirely, of the perennial floating kinds. Seed was, no doubt, harvested by gatherers in canoes or from the tangled mass after flood waters receded at the end of the rains. However, the perennial races are shy seeders compared to the annuals, and the environment is extremely difficult to exploit for agriculture. It is most unlikely that rice was domesticated in the delta zones, which must have been sparsely settled until social and political systems evolved permitting the construction of dikes, canals and other water control measures. Rice in Africa was domesticated in the savanna. The situation in Asia must have been the same.

The domestication and diffusion of Asian rice has been reviewed several times by T. T. Chang, who has studied this subject more than anyone else. Figure 6.2 is adapted from a recent paper and graphically shows the most likely region of origin and subsequent dispersal (Chang, 1989). H. I. Oka has studied the genetics of rice domestication for many years and anyone interested should consult Oka (1988).

Within modern historical times, the traditional digging stick and hoe-shifting cultivation has been replaced in many places by wet rice cultivation. The lower swamp areas in particular were intensively cultivated only in the last century or two, and much of the settlement was so late that some census figures are available. In the 1850s, Burma planted about 600 000–800 000 ha to rice; the current figure is about 5 000 000 ha, 80% of it in the lower Burma Irrawadi swampland delta area. Thailand in the 1880s reported just over 1 000 000 ha of rice and today about 10 000 000 ha are being planted. Much of the increase has been in the lower Chao Phraya valley (the Bangkok plain). In Vietnam, diking and draining of the Mekong delta began in the nineteenth century. The delta as a whole is still not fully occupied but the increase in rice acreage has been phenomenal. In modern Vietnam about 6 000 000 ha of 6 500 000 ha in cultivation are planted to rice. The rice area of Indonesia is about 10 000 000 ha, much of it in Java and in the mangrove swampland of northeastern Sumatra. In the Philippines, there are about 1 000 000 ha in shifting cultivation but some 3 500 000 ha of wet rice land. In Laos, much of the agriculture is still of the original indigenous kind. Most of the country is mountainous upland and the human population is sparse. Malaysia is also

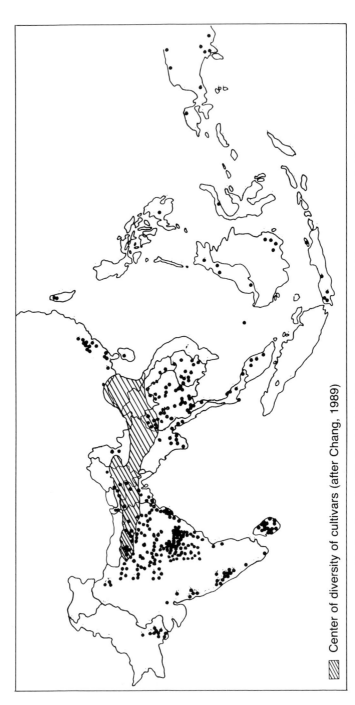

Fig. 6.2. Known distribution of wild rice in Asia. The gaps in Burma and Vietnam are probably due to inadequate collections.

sparsely populated especially in Borneo. This permits the development of plantation crops on a large scale. On the whole, wet rice dominant landscapes are new in Southeast Asia and have replaced shifting cultivation of root and tree crops only in recent centuries.

Although the origin and antiquity of wet rice cultural techniques are uncertain, there seems to be little question that wet field taro production had been developed earlier. Well engineered but small-scale terraces were constructed and water was led by canals to flood them. Such practices persist among tribes in New Guinea who have not yet taken up rice growing. The suggestion has been made that rice was domesticated from wild or weed races that infested the flooded taro fields. This idea has merit for limited regions of the southeast Asian mainland and the larger islands but, if this sequence took place, it was probably in addition to rice domestication in the savanna zones with their prolonged dry seasons, as in India, southeastern China, Burma and Thailand.

The evidence for early rice cultivation in Thailand suggests that the cleavage between cereal agriculture and vegeculture is exaggerated and may never have been real. As a matter of fact, there are more tropical cereals than temperate ones and cereals play at least some role in all tropical agricultural systems. Wild rice is a food resource that could not be overlooked by gathering people and, as we have seen, is still harvested. The archaeological evidence suggests that domesticated rice was grown in China, India and Southeast Asia by 5000 BC. Rice has been available for a long time, but a rice-based agriculture did not really become expansive until population densities and social and political structures were such that intensive agriculture was not only demanded but could be practiced. The historical evidence of Ho (1974) indicates intensive agriculture got under way in China in the third century BC. We do not know when it developed in Southeast Asia.

Sugarcane

The basis of modern sugarcane production probably started in New Guinea as a mutation in *Saccharum robustum*. This species is an octoploid with 80 chromosomes and has large, stout, hard canes. It is often used to build fences in New Guinea, to keep pigs out of the garden or to keep them in the pen. At some unknown time, mutations occurred that blocked the pathway from sugar to starch, and sweet canes resulted. These were the 'noble' canes that were taken across the Pacific by the Polynesians and that diffused westward to Southeast Asia. In southern China and perhaps Assam, the cultivated canes came into contact with wild *Saccharum spontaneum*, a widespread weedy plant of Asia and Africa. As a result of introgression, the thin caned types evolved. These have been grouped under the epithet, *Saccharum sinense*, and have variable chromosome numbers from $2n = 82-124$ or thereabouts (Simmonds, 1976*b*) The noble canes are traditionally exploited by chewing, and syrup was extracted from the thin canes. The syrup could also be boiled down to make a dark brown sugar.

The Arab invasion of Europe brought sugarcane into southern Spain, and the Spaniards introduced it to the New World where sugar production became intimately associated with slavery. The abundant cheap white, refined sugar is a recent development on the world scene.

Bananas and plantains

The wild diploid bananas are native to the Malay Peninsula and major Pacific Islands, especially Borneo. They reproduce by seeds that are numerous and extremely hard, rendering the fruit unattractive as food. Some genotypes, however, appeared that are parthenocarpic, that is they produce fruits without seeds. They were, of course, sterile and had to be vegetatively propagated and would have died out without human assistance. There are two species involved in the evolution of commercial bananas: *Musa acuminata* (A) and *Musa balbisiana* (B). The A genome tends to produce sweet dessert bananas, and the B genome tends to produce the dry cooking banana or plantain. Natural hybridization and polyploidy have produced nearly all the combinations of the two genomes. The most common are AA, AAA, AAB and ABB, the others being relatively rare. Quadruple A (AAAA) is not known to have arisen naturally, although it is frequently produced in breeding programs (Simmonds, 1976*c*.)

We do not know when bananas were first cultivated. They spread from their homeland to India and southern China, probably rather early. The Polynesians took them to Madagascar when they colonized the island at the beginning of the Christian era. From there they made their way to Uganda where an important banana-based culture evolved, and bananas were found on the west coast of Africa when the Portuguese began to explore it in the fifteenth century. The Arabs knew of the banana and called it muza, hence *Musa* and Musaceae. In their travels, the Polynesians took it to the remote islands of the Pacific.

Bananas of the Australomusa group are native to New Guinea and adjacent islands, and these were taken by the Polynesians to some of the islands they colonised. In this group, the fruit bunch remains erect rather than drooping as in the familiar Eumusas or true bananas. They are seedy and some have escaped and become naturalized in Tahiti and other islands. Another species of the Australomusa group is *Musa textalis* or Manila hemp. This was once a major source of marine cordage. The long strong fibers are resistant to sea water and are extracted from the leaf sheaths. Another member of the family important in Ethiopia is *Ensete ventricosa*, which was domesticated and became a staple of some Ethiopian tribes. The seedy fruits of *Ensete* are not eaten, but the starchy stem base can be processed into flour.

The coconut

There has been some dispute and controversy over the origin of the coconut, some of it due to poor taxonomy and much due to lack of information. The nearest to a consensus we now have is that the coconut was originally a native of the South Pacific islands from New Guinea westward through Sulawesi, Borneo and northward to the Philippines. The large fruits with their thick fibrous husks and hard shells are adapted to dispersal by sea. Violent storms have probably played a role in casting the nuts far beyond normal high tide where they may sprout away from sea water. Humans have also played a major role in both dispersal and in the selection of special types. The exploitation of the coconut as a plantation crop is a recent industrial age phenomenon. In traditional agriculture, it was fundamental for the settling of smaller Pacific islands and atolls. The low coral islands had few natural resources and Polynesian colonizers had to establish their cultigens before many of them could be inhabited. Coconuts, pandanus, *Cyrtosperma* and taro were among the most important on low, relatively dry islands where bananas, breadfruit and sugarcane did not do well. Excavations to reach fresh water lenses was often required for cultivation of the tubers.

The coconut was reported on Cocos Island and west coast of Panama by the Spanish natural historian, Gonzalo Fernandes de Oviedo y Valdes II (1944). His first description was written in 1519, giving almost no time for European introduction of the plant. The possibilities are:

1. Oviedo's account was garbled and the coconut was not there;
2. the coconut reached the west coast of Central America through natural means of dispersal not very long before Columbus; or
3. the plant was brought to the area by human agency not very long before Columbus.

Oviedo's account was indeed garbled and early European observers gave contradictory accounts. Oviedo's description of the coconut is accurate, detailed and unmistakable, but he then supplies us with a line drawing of a palm which is *not* a coconut. He said it was particularly abundant in Cacique Chiman (Panama) yet Wafer (1903), a very good and reliable observer, passed through Cacique Chiman in the 1680s and could not remember seeing a coconut on the mainland. Wafer did, however, report a very strange account of a 'frolik' on Cocos Island by several of the ship's company in which they cut down a number of 'coconut' trees, harvested some 80 liters of milk, toasted the Queen until they were benumbed. Cook (1939) found a palm on Cocos Island that is 'remarkably similar in size and appearance' to the coconut but is entirely unrelated. Despite the garbled reports, it seems most likely that the coconut had, in fact, established a foothold on American shores before the arrival of Europeans. Jonathan Sauer has studied the populations in Panama and considers them to be naturally introduced (personal communication.)

The orange

Little is known of the early history of the orange. It is thought to have originated in northeastern India and western Burma. Its adaptation to the subtropics with some frost resistance suggests that it came from the hill country, and perhaps its range extended into southern China.

The sweet orange probably arose as a mutant of the sour orange. The latter is rather weedy and readily distributed by parrots in both the Old and New Worlds. It was introduced to southern Europe in late historical times and to the New World by 1493. The seeds of most oranges are produced asexually, but there is sufficient sexuality in the species for breeding programs. As a fruit of commerce, it is a recent development but we know little of its antiquity.

The original name began with an n: in late Sanskrit, *naranga*; in Hindi, *narangi*; in Persian, *narang*; and in Arabic, *naranj*. The original n is preserved in the Spanish, *naranja*, but lost in the French, *orange*, the Italian, *arancia* and in English, due to the absorption of the n of indefinite articles – an-norange, une-orange and so on. The House of Orange, the royal line of Holland, derived its name from a town on the Rhone in France. In some regions, regardless of the local language spoken, the orange is called *portugal* because it is perceived as being introduced by the Portuguese.

The mango

The genus *Mangifera* is a native of the Far East and the wild forms confined to it. The largest number of species is found on the Malay Peninsula, Borneo and Sumatra. *Mangifera indica*, however, is found wild primarily in northeastern India and into western Burma. Domestication seems to have been straightforward without contributions from other species. The wild forms are highly fibrous and have a strong taste of resin or 'turpentine.' Selection has been toward less fiber, more juiciness and less resin. Some cultivars are exceptionally fine and their fruit enjoys great popularity throughout the tropics. Distribution out of India into Southeast Asia and offshore islands may have been in the first millennium BC, but dispersal to the rest of the world has been only in recent centuries.

Yams

Several species of yams, *Dioscorea*, are cultivated in the region, but by far the most important are *Dioscorea esculenta* and *Dioscorea alata*. They have 'annual' type tubers and are derived from savanna environments with long dry seasons. Both species have complex polyploid series with a base of $x = 10$, while the African domesticates have a base of $x = 9$. The principal Asian yams probably originated in the north-central part of the Malay Peninsula. Papua New Guinea is probably the center of diversity today, but that is, in part, due to a decline in importance of yams on the mainland.

In the Pacific Island area, the yam is considered a dry crop and taro a wet crop. Soil is mounded or ridged up for yams; ditches are dug to keep taro wet. Yams are tended by males, and females are excluded from yam gardens. Taro is cultivated by females, and males, even babes in arms, are excluded from taro gardens. There are sexual implications in the phallic shape of the yam tubers and the vaginal shape of the taro leaf. In New Guinea, ceremonial yams are grown each year with great care and ceremony. Contests are held among villages to see who can grow the longest and heaviest tuber, and records are kept from year to year. The male gardeners who tend the ceremonial yams must refrain from sexual intercourse while yams are growing and other rites are practiced. These and other details are discussed in a charming essay by Barrau (1965); also see Coursey (1976).

Aroids

Colocasia is the familiar taro that produces *poi* in Hawaii and elsewhere in Polynesia. There are other ways to prepare it including boiling and roasting. The Polynesians developed special *poi* pounders, often elegantly made of stone, and these are archaeological artifacts that help document the spread of taro over time.

Allocasia is also an aroid but much larger than the taro. It has huge elephant ear leaves, often taller than a man. The tuber is coarser and less palatable than taro but the yield can be impressive.

Fruits

Jambos are highly variable fruits of *Syzygium*. In general, they are sweet and pleasant to the palate, red or white in color and range in size from a cherry tomato to a plum tomato.

Mamordica is a cucurbit, sometimes called 'bitter gourd.' The fruits

Allocasia, Philippines.

are borne on a vine, have a warty surface and the flesh is red and seedy. They are cooked like a squash.

Benincasa, a cucurbit, is sometimes called a winter melon, because it can be harvested in the fall, stacked with straw insulation, and kept all winter. The fruits are the size of a medium watermelon, which they resemble; the flesh is relatively tasteless but used for soups. It is not uncommon to cook the soup inside the melon shell.

Trichosanthes (cucurbit) or snake gourd, has rather large undulating twisting cucumber-like fruits. It is an attractive vegetable, usually blended with others in oriental dishes.

Luffa (cucurbit) is the sponge gourd. The elongate fruit contains a network of fibrous bundles that remain after the flesh is retted away.

They make good scouring pads and bathing sponges. However, the fruit can be eaten when young.

Mangosteen (*Garcinia mangostani*) has no relation to the mango. It has been called 'queen of tropical fruits' and I heartily agree. The purple fruits are only a little larger than a crabapple and have a thick rind, but inside are eight to twelve segments of pure white flesh that are a delight to the palate. A mangosteen is truly nectar for the gods.

Durian (*Durio zibethinus*) is of a different order. For the novice, this should be approached with caution. The odor can be overpowering but, once past the nose, the flavor can be delightful. It is all a matter of taste and some people are repulsed; others become addicted. It is hard to be neutral about a durian.

Rambutan (*Nephelium lappaceum*) is a fruit that has an exterior like a burr with many short spines. The interior is delightfully sweet with some mulled aromatic flavoring. There are other fine fruits in the same genus.

The betel nut

The betel (*Areca*) palm in mature plantations is a very tall and very slender palm. Harvesting by climbing tree after tree is very slow and tedious. In many plantations, if not most, the harvesters learn to set the tree to swaying to the point that they can reach the next tree without coming to the ground. The tall thin trunks are tough but supple and bend rather easily under the weight of a human being. The harvesters are always small, wiry and agile people but there is, of course, some danger of a bad fall. The nut meat is reddish and rather soft and used as a masticatory. It may be chewed in pure form but most commonly it is wrapped in betel leaf to form a quid. The betel leaf is not from the palm but from a vine of the same genus as black pepper (*Piper betle*). Throughout Southeast Asia, from India through to Indonesia, street vendors prepare quids for sale to passers by. The quid also has some social standing. A good host would provide quids for his guests as they depart. There is caffeine and some alkaloid-like compounds in the nut that can make chewing addictive. Chewers spit red spittle and it stains the teeth. I have tried it and found it refreshing but have no ambition to become addicted. Betel chewing

The betal nut palm, *Areca*.

is an entrenched cultural trait throughout the region, practiced by both men and women and starting at an early age.

The South Pacific

Human remains in southeast Asia and Indonesia are of respectable antiquity and include *Homo erectus* in Java (*Pithecanthropus* or Java apeman). Our interest in agricultural origins, however, focuses on the end of Pleistocene/start of Holocene suture. At that time, the land configuration of Southeast Asia and adjacent islands was very different from the present. Islands on the Sunda shelf west of the Wallace line were joined to the mainland.

Sahul was an island continent, including New Guinea, Australia and Tasmania, forming a separate land mass. Sahul had been inhabited by anatomically modern humans from 40 000 years ago or possibly earlier. Even at glacial maximum, with sea levels about 90 m below present, there were water gaps between Sunda and Sahul of some 100 km or more. Somehow, Pleistocene man was able to cross the gaps and become a representative of a third order of placental mammals to inhabit Sahul – after bats and rats. This early colonization extended to New Ireland with a date of about 32 000 years ago and to the Solomon Islands by 29 000 years ago (Allen and White, 1989).

People were probably inhabiting margins of the ancient shorelines in early Holocene but nearly all traces have been drowned by rising seas. Here and there, coastal uplifting has exposed Pleistocene shorelines, but for the most part the archaeological record of early coastal settlement has been buried by sea water. Tasmania became separated from Australia about 12 000 years ago and New Guinea from Australia about 8000 years ago. More or less present sea levels were reached in the neighbourhood of 6000 years ago (White and Connell, 1982). The early Holocene evidence is, therefore, closed to us, although a fair number of later sites are known and have been studied (Higham and Maloney, 1989).

In the uplands on the Asian mainland, evidence of exploitation of local plant and animal resources has been uncovered. Of special interest is the Hoabinhian culture named by Madeleine Calami in 1927 after the province of Hoa-Binh in Old Tonkin. A number of sites have been located in Burma, Thailand and Vietnam among the earliest of which is Spirit Cave, dating to more than 9000 BC, and other sites like Banyan Valley Cave, lingering on as late as AD 900 (Higham, 1976; Hutterer, 1983). Among the plant remains found in Spirit Cave, 8000–7000 BC time range, were seeds or fruit fragments of *Aleurites, Canarium, Madhuca, Terminalia, Castanopsis, Cucumis, Lagenaria, Trapa, Ereca* and *Piper*. A few other plants were reported in the original report that seemed ecologically and geographically out of place and were challenged, but the list of tropical materials is impressive. A second excavation added *Celtis, Ricinus, Mamordica, Nelumbium, Trichosanthes* or *Luffa*. The Ban Kao Caves in Thailand yielded remains of an edible fruit, *Syzygium*, the bark of which has medicinal properties, and a palm, *Licuala* (Pyramarn, 1989). The Hoabinhians preferred karst typography, hunted a variety of animals and were noted for a pebble tool and large flake technology. They may also have been making sophisticated tools, traps, snares and nets of bamboo, woody vines and other perishable materials. The economy is described as broad spectrum hunting and gathering and their late persistence among farming people is of interest.

On Timor and Sulawesi, Glover (1986) reported that dry caves were occupied from 12 000 BC to about AD 0. Before 3000 BC, plant remains included *Aleurites, Celtis, Erica, Coix* and *Piper;* and after 3000 BC, no *Celtis* but *Inocarpus,* bamboo, *Lagenaria* and possibly *Setaria* have been recorded (Hutterer, 1983).

From these studies we are developing evidence for people in early to mid-Holocene living in caves, hunting and exploiting tropical forest products. None of the sites has yielded any real evidence of early agriculture. Sites that do reveal unequivocal evidence of farming are relatively late. At Ban Chiang and Non Nok Tha in Thailand, the people had domestic cattle, pig, dog, water buffalo, rice and cord impressed pottery. Dating has had some problems but the sites were probably of the fourth millennium BC. Xom Tria Cave in northwest Vietnam yielded domesticated rice about 3000 BC (Chang, 1989), and other agricultural sites are later.

Meanwhile, something was going on in New Guinea. There is some evidence for an early attack on the tropical forest; heavy ground axe heads make an appearance by 26 000 years ago, and pollen sequences show disturbance of the forest of some kind by 30 000 years ago (Groube, 1989). What this means in terms of forest exploitation we do not know, and the disturbance could be by natural causes. Other tropical rain forests were altered by the ice age changes in climate during the Pleistocene. At Kuk swamp in the highlands, clear evidence of land form modification turns up dating to about 7000 BC.

Buried under peat in a natural swamp (Kuk), Golson (1984) found an extensive drainage/irrigation canal system. One canal was some 10 km long, 1 m deep and 10 m wide. There were extensive fields with raised beds surrounded by ditches for water control, whether for drainage or irrigation we do not know. One immediately thinks of taro, *Colocasia,* or *Cyrtosperma* production, but no plant remains have yet been found. Ample evidence for the presence of the pig appeared about 4000 BC. The pig as a placental mammal was absent from New Guinea before 4000 BC and was almost certainly brought by man at least somewhat before that date. It was taken everywhere in the

Pacific colonized by farmers. The source is obscure, however, because the date seems to be earlier than farming is known in the Philippines or Borneo (Bellwood, 1985). At about this time, the rather Hoabinh-ian-like core and large flake industry of Australia was suddenly changed to a highly developed micro-lithic complex. But if this was introduced, the pig was left behind (Moore, 1976).

The implications of the irrigation/drainage systems are clearly in favor of some independent experimentation with horticulture. The effort required to put in the system with digging sticks was very con-siderable; there must have been some worthwhile reward. In New Guinea, colonies of spontaneous taro have long been considered to be recent escapes but they proved to be diploids, while the common cultigen of Southeast Asia and India is a triploid (Jones and Meehan, 1989). The case is not proven, of course, but it is a strong one for another independent origin of plant husbandry if not domestication.

Of course there were other environments in Southeast Asia. There were savannas and forest–savanna ecotones that offer far more food resources than the rainforest, and it is from such environments that most of the indigenous domesticates came.

The archaeological evidence, to date, does not document a transition from hunting–gathering to farming in Southeast Asia nor does it supply sure evidence of an indigenous development. This may be partly due to insufficient excavation, but could also be due to the manner in which the threshold into the Neolithic was passed. The Hoabinhian peoples kept their traditions long after their neighbors were farming and there was, no doubt, considerable interaction among the different cultures. This again shows that hunting–gathering is a viable alternative to farming and that agriculture is not always readily adopted. The lack of clear beginnings in either space or time may be characteristic of noncenters as in Africa and lowland South America.

The spread of farming systems across the Pacific islands has been reviewed several times. Among the most recent are Kirch (1982), Bellwood (1985) and Spriggs (1989). The picture may change in the future with more information. The oldest Neolithic on Taiwan is called Ta-p'en-k'eng and comes from southeast China. Cord marked pottery was present, which may have some relation to the cord impressed wares of Indochina. The tradition on the island began about 4400 BC and continued to about 2500 BC. Early Neolithic, as of current information, is no earlier than 3500 BC in the Philippines and probably later. It had definitely been established on Luzon by 3000 BC; on Mindanao, Borneo Sulawesi and Maluka by 2500 BC; and on Timor soon after (Bellwood, 1985; Spriggs, 1989). The agricultural complex at this time included pig, chicken, breadfruit, *Allocasia*, taro, yams, bananas, sago, betel nut. Cereal culture declined as farmers moved eastward. The millets dropped out one by one, coix alone reaching New Guinea, and rice stopped in the main Indonesian islands. New Guinea had its own Neolithic and was skirted by the Polynesians. By this time, sailing canoes were available and long distance travel was feasible.

The peopling of the islands beyond New Guinea and its immediate islands, that is New Ireland, New Britain, etc., by farmers began with the Lapita complex about 1600 to 500 BC. The Bismarck archipelago, Santa Cruz Islands, New Hebrides, New Caledonia, Fiji, Tonga, Samoa were settled by Lapita horticulturists. They had a distinctive pottery and used characteristic stone adzes for woodworking. Pig, dog and fowl were domesticated, and plants included taro, yams, breadfruit, bananas and plantains and a varying selection of other food crops.

The Marquesas may have been reached by 150 BC and eastern Polynesia no later than AD 300. The earliest ^{14}C dates run: Marquesas, about 100 BC; Society Islands, AD 890 and 900; Hawaii, AD 390, 610 and 795; New Zealand, AD 1050 and 1230; Cook Islands, AD 1020; Easter Island by AD 400.

India

In the plan of presentation in this book, India falls between the Near East and the Far East. It seems to have had that position in terms of the evolution of agriculture. A wheat, barley, lentil, chickpea, lathyrus, flax, etc. culture arrived from the west and a Harappan civilization arose. Rice, fruits and roots arrived from the east; and sorghum, pearl millet, finger millet and cowpeas came from Africa. India was receptive to all. The north Gangetic plain adopted the Near Eastern complex; peninsular India adopted the tropical complex of Southeast Asia and Africa. But the Indians also domesticated plants from the local flora. We have seen that northeast India reaches into the primary region of rice domestication and that the mandarin orange is likely to have been brought into the *domus* there. Sesame, pigeon pea, eggplant, guar, several minor millets, several pulses and some tubers were domesticated locally. The processes of domestication swept across Asia from the Levant and Anatolia to the Pacific Ocean. Except for North China, the concept of center of origin does not apply to the Far East any better than to Africa.

The animals

The several kinds of Bovidae, common cattle, humped backed cattle, water buffalo, yak and mithan have been mentioned. Wild cattle of various kinds ranged well into the south Pacific islands, west of the Wallace line, and local domestications took place from time to time. Throughout the Far East, bovines had been used as beasts of burden, pulling carts, wagons, ploughs and other agricultural implements. Their use for milking is more restricted. Simoons (1970) was able to draw a sinuos line through Southeast Asia indicating a dividing line between people who used milk to the south of the line and those who did not to the north. People who do not use milk are likely to lack the gene for the production of lactase but the correlation is far from perfect. Those who do not use milk often substitute soybean products like tofu and meiso. The two sources of protein are not mutually exclusive and some cultures use both.

For China and adjacent regions, pork is the primary source of animal protein. Pigs have been a basic feature of Oriental agriculture from early Neolithic on. Wild boar were available for domestication over most of China. Pigs are very efficient at converting waste materials into edible food. Meat is used sparingly in Oriental cuisine, more as a seasoning for vegetables than as a main dish. This makes sense for an area of high human population density. In the system that evolved, nothing is wasted and pig manure is used as a substrate for mushroom culture. Mushrooms are also an important feature of Oriental cuisine. Certain breeds of Chinese pigs produce very large litters, and germ-plasm has recently been imported into the USA in an attempt to increase the litter size of American breeds.

The domestic chicken is thought to be derived from the red jungle fowl native to Southeast Asia. It can interbreed with other pheasants, however, and more than one kind of wild fowl might be involved.

Certainly the diversity among breeds is enormous. The chicken is easy to rear and select, has a short generation turnover, reproduces at a high rate and is an ideal animal for proliferation of diversity under domestication. There are breeds selected for egg production, meat production, cock fighting, crowing, plumage, etc. Some of the more spectacular variants include indeterminate growth of tail feathers, feathered legs and even toes, frizzled feathers that have lost barbets, reduced or enlarged combs, etc. Archaeological evidence suggests the chicken moved northward from Vietnam to China where it is found at Peiligan and Cishan *c.* 6000 BC. It was well documented at Mohenjodaro in the Indus Valley *c.* 2000 BC, but there are some 16 sites in China and seven to eight in southeastern Europe earlier than that. The spread to western Europe may have been via Russia (West and Zhou, 1988.)

The Peking duck is world famous both as a breed and as a culinary delight. It is thought to be descended from the common mallard that has a circumboreal distribution, and was probably domesticated independently in Europe. The wild birds adapt easily to domestic life and it would be surprising if there were not several domestications across Eurasia. It shows up archaeologically in the Near East about 2500 BC. Diversity in domesticated duck is not so extensive as in chicken but a number of breeds have been selected. The common white Peking is by far the most popular. It plays an important role in Chinese agriculture where duck herding can be a profession. Ducks are herded through fields for insect control and for weeding grass out of some crops.

I was once shown the Peking way of preparing duck in a restaurant in Beijing that specializes in this delicacy. Ducks should be very fat; they are plucked, gutted and sewn up, so the body cavity can be filled with boiling water. Several are suspended on a metal hook that is turned slowly around a fire of jujube (*Zyzyphus*) wood. It is asserted that this was the only appropriate wood for a true Peking duck.

Cormorants are trained and exploited if not actually domesticated. Their use for fishing was once much more important than it is now. In Japan it is not much more than a tourist (mostly Japanese tourists) attraction. A string is carefully and skillfully tied around the neck of the bird so it can function but not swallow anything except a small fish. Fishing is done at night from small boats with a bonfire in a metal basket projecting from the bow. A fisherman has several or perhaps a dozen birds, each on its own leash. The birds catch fish and are periodically brought into the boat to disgorge them. They are very efficient fishers and a night's catch can be considerable.

My wife and I were treated to a delightful evening in Japan. Several pleasure boats were beached on a gravel bar at dusk; as we waited for dark of night, there were a few small fireworks, a delicious meal prepared by a local hotel, much saki (rice wine), a platform with dancing girls (well covered by kimonos) and in the boat next to ours, some young business men and two geisha girls who sang and played on stringed instruments. When it was dark enough, a line of cormorant fishing boats came past, floating downstream with their bonfires blazing and their birds working industriously. The whole affair was lovely, but I think in China cormorant fishing is more serious business.

The agriculture of the Far East is incredibly rich. A local market displays fruits and roots in bewildering array. In Southeast Asia and the island nations of the Philippines and Indonesia, mixed orchards are common. I once took an inventory of an orchard in Indonesia and counted over 40 species of fruits and nuts. There were only one to three specimens of each. The diversity mimics to a degree the complexity of a rainforest, and pollination did not seem to be a problem partly because the orchards are often grouped together. But then, forest trees are normally pollinated as widely dispersed individuals. Gathering from wild plants is also common. After being guided to some of Kyoto's finest temples by a Japanese professor, my wife and I invited him to lunch, he to choose the restaurant. He took us to a traditional vegetarian restaurant and, knowing my interest in food plants, identified the elements of our meal. There were 15 species treated in a total of 22 ways. Six of the 15 were gathered from the wild. This on one of the most densely populated islands in the world and in one of the most industrialized nations. Wild plants still have a place on the menu today.

CHAPTER SEVEN

The Americas

Archaeological background

The archaeological record of humans in the Americas is not nearly as long as that in the Old World. We have not found any *Homo erectus*, no Achulean hand axes or Chinese choppers; we have not found Neanderthalers or Mousterian stone tool traditions. The conventional wisdom has been that the Americas were peopled by big-game hunters who crossed the Bering land bridge in late Pleistocene when sea levels were low and one could walk from Siberia to Alaska on dry land. There was supposed to be an ice-free corridor between the eastern and western glaciers down through Canada to ice-free land to the south. This theory has had problems in the testing.

There were indeed big-game hunters to the south of the ice sheets. They manufactured a distinctive projectile point called 'clovis' after a site near Clovis, New Mexico, where a point was found embedded in the skeleton of a kind of bison now extinct. The date is about 12 000 years ago and clovis points have been recovered over an enormous range of both North and South America. The people were specialists in big game mammals – mammoth, mastodon, horse, camel, giant bison, ground sloth, etc., and the culture seems to have died out as these animals became extinct at the end of Pleistocene. But clovis points have not been found in Beringia or Siberia, and the evidence for pre-clovis people south of the ice is difficult to establish. Stanford (1983) reported a short list of possible sites, but there is some problem in dating or in stratigraphy with each of them. For instance, Meadowcroft is a cave on the border between Ohio and Pennsylvania and has several ^{14}C dates in agreement at 21 000 to 22 000 years ago, but the flora and fauna do not seem to fit the time range (Shutler, 1983). The Pleistocene animals that later became extinct and a boreal flora are missing.

As of now, the earliest reports of human activity come from South America, not North America, but these are few and have not been precisely dated. Pebble flake industries are reported from eastern Brazil dated to about 30 000 to 35 000 years ago (Bryan, 1983; Schmitz, 1987). Other dates of 20 000 years ago or earlier for humans in America have been reported and they could well have been there earlier (Bryan, 1983; MacNeish, 1983). The early human skulls in both North and South America were of long-headed people; the later ones were short-headed (Carter, 1980). Ancient Mongoloids were short-headed and modern ones have the highest known frequencies of B and Rh_2 genes, while both are low to nonexistent in Australians and North American Indians (Shutler, 1983, p. 45). Still, absolute proof of pre-clovis man in the Americas is elusive (Dincauze, 1984).

Basic to the Bering land bridge crossing theory is the perception that both the Pacific and Atlantic oceans were impassable to human traffic in Pleistocene times. This perception is not altogether secure. As we know, Thor Hyerdahl has shown that it would be possible for humans to cross both oceans by raft, either sailing or drifting on currents. The rafts could be made of rushes or of balsa wood logs. Bednarik (1989) has proposed a theory to account for both early Americans and the settlings of Australia at some 40 000 years ago or earlier. There could have been, he suggested, a Pleistocene coastal seafaring people who settled both Australia and South America, and rising sea levels have since covered the evidence. How they got to South America and from whence, remains to be worked out. Lathrap has suggested an early colonization from Africa (Lathrap, 1977).

The earliest evidence of human activity found so far in North America comes from the Old Crow and Bluefish basins in Yukon Territory, Canada. In Bluefish caves, remains of the late Pleistocene fauna are preserved in excellent condition and include horse, bison, mammoth, wapiti, sheep, caribou, together with human artifacts, especially worked horn, bone and ivory. The dates are about 25 000 to 29 000 years ago, but a mountain of ice separated them from the hunting grounds to the south. The upper layers of the caves had an impoverished Holocene fauna but no evidence of human beings. Archaeology has not supported the conventional wisdom very well, not that people did not cross the Bering land bridge but there are possible, or even likely, alternatives to the scenario. With the present soft evidence for early humans in the Americas, one is entitled to promote one's own theories and speculations. If one has faith in early cross-oceanic travel, one can make a good case for that. If one wishes to believe that *all* American Indians are descendants of hunters who crossed Beringea from Asia, I suppose one can make a case for it although there are problems with this scenario, as we have shown. In due time, evidence will probably become firmer and more detailed. In any case, people were in the Americas long before agricultural activities began. Our focus is, once again, at the end of Pleistocene and start of Holocene.

The punctuation period for North America is now well dated at 11 000 to 10 800 years ago. Large mammal extinction was more or less completed by 10 000 years ago with loss of some 33 genera or 70% of the large mammals including mastodon, mammoth, horse, camel, ground sloth, a large cat, etc. (Bonnichen, Stanford and Fastook, 1987). In South America, the Amazonian rain forest was not where it is now. It was restricted to several relatively small refuges around the perimeter of its present range (Haffer, 1969; Meggers, Ayensu and Duckworth, 1973; Vanzolini, 1973). Rapid changes in fauna and flora followed and the scene was set for plant domestication. A few of the more important sites will be mentioned.

Guitarrero Cave in Peru is located in an inter-montane valley on the west slope of the Andes at 2580 m elevation. It was excavated by Thomas Lynch (1980) and has a record over 12 000 years long. At the bottom, a bifacial 'knife' was found dated to about 12 500 years ago. Some projectile points were found above this and plant remains were found in complex II dating 8600 to 5600 BC. Plants included *Phaseolus vulgaris, Phaseolus lunatus, Oxalis, Capsicum, Solanum hispidum, Cucurbita* sp., *Igna* and some grasses, perhaps for bedding. The common bean and pepper were from IIA dated 8600 to 8000 BC and are of domesticated kinds. The upper levels of II, 6600 to 5500 BC, had both common and lima beans, lucuma, oxalis and solanum. Complex IIA also had textiles, the second oldest in the New World. The oldest found, so far, is from Danger Cave, Utah, radiodated at 9599 BC. It seems that beans were definitely domesticated before 8000 BC. Wild beans and wild peppers are found on the eastern slopes of the Andes, and were probably domesticated there and introduced to the west slope later. The evidence now indicates plant domestication in the Americas was as early, or perhaps earlier, than similar activities in the Old World.

Pachamachay Cave in the central Puna of Peru at about 4000 m elevation has a record from before 9000 BC. The earlier dates are rather hazy but from 9000 BC become much clearer. The site was excavated, 1974–5, by John Rick (1980) and the abundant plant materials studied by Deborah Pearsall. The people were heavy exploiters of vicuña.

Domesticated beans and peppers appeared by 8500 BC, confirming the finds of Guitarrero Cave. Sites on the coast yielded abundant plant remains in superb condition, desiccated, not carbonized, but dated in later time ranges. The coast of Peru is almost rainless and agriculture depends on irrigation with water coming from the highlands or by excavating to subsoil moisture, also of mountain origin. It is an unlikely environment for the beginnings of agriculture. Skeletons were also well preserved and show that the earlier people were of the long-headed type, but by ceramic times short-headed types had become dominant (Keatinge, 1988).

Guilá Naquitz Cave in Oaxaca, Mexico, was excavated by Kent Flannery and the site report published in 1986. The time range covers the transition from hunting–gathering to farming. The foragers ate cactus fruits, extracted syrup from mesquite pods, roasted maguey, leached acorns, used wild bean flowers and wild onions. They had the atlatl, coiled baskets, maguey fiber sandals, net bags, fire drills, snares, traps and grinding stones.

In the neighborhood of 8000 BC they, too, began to grow plants on a small scale, and again beans and cucurbits were among the earliest domesticates. Teosinte pollen shows up around 7000 BC but the record reveals very little about maize domestication. The whole process of agricultural development seemed to be very slow and deliberate, and the small scale efforts at gardening may not have been designed so much to increase the food supply as to make it more dependable or more convenient.

There are other sequences in the Americas which help to round out the picture (See Table 7.1). The full story of maize evolution is yet to be documented archaeologically, but maize farming is now well attested in Panama and Colombia by about 5000 BC (Piperno, 1989). The general picture that emerges is one of widespread and early plant manipulation. Beans, cucurbits and *Capsicum* peppers were generally among the first in each area regardless of the time range. These were grown on a small scale for a long time with additional crops being added from time to time, one by one, and with seeming reluctance. Eventually agricultural complexes evolved and fully agricultural

Table 7.1 *Some early American archaeological sites*

Date in millennia BC	Site	Plant remains
8.7–7.8	Guilá Naquitz, Oaxaca	*Cucurbita pepo* (seed fragment)
8.5–8.0	Guitarrero Cave, Peru	*Phaseolus, Capsicum*
8.5	Pachamachay Cave Peru	*Phaseolus, Capsicum*
8.2	Guitarrero Cave	*Phaseolus vulgaris, Oxalis Capsicum, Solanum*
7.4–7.2	Guilá Naquitz	*C. pepo* (seeds and peduncles) *Lagenaria*
7.0	Ocampo Caves, Mexico	*Lagenaria*
6.5–5.5	Tehuacán, Pueblo	*Capsicum*
6.0–4.0	Coastal Peru	*Lagenaria*
5.7	Guitarrero Cave	*P. vulgaris, Phaseolus lunatus*
5.5	Tehuacán	*Lagenaria, Zea mays*
5.5	Poro Ayacucho, Peru	*Lagenaria*
5.0	Koster, IL, USA	*C. pepo*
4.0	Ocampo Caves and Puebla	*P. vulgaris*
3.5	Tehuacán, Puebla	*Gossypium Amaranthus*
3.5–3.0	Eastern woodland complex, USA: MO, IL, IN, OH, MI, TN, KY, MS	*C. pepo, Lagenaria*
3.3	Real Alto (Valdivia)	*Canna, Canavalia Gossypium, Zea*
2.1	Eastern woodland, USA	*Iva, Chenopodium*

economies became established. The complexes range from the United States midwest to at least northern Argentina and evolved over several thousand years (Fig. 7.1).

The lowland infiltration into the rain forest was probably late and slow to develop because the undisturbed forest is an extremely difficult environment to exploit (Bailey *et al.*, 1989; Piperno, 1989). Man-modified rain forests are much richer in exploitable plants and the plants are much more concentrated than in climax situations. Piperno (1989) records evidence that in Panama the hunter–gatherers were very few and had little impact on the region until about 5000 BC when maize-based agriculture took over. Developments in Amazonia were later and probably slower because of the size of the area. There are a number of forest plants that provide significant amounts of food, brazil nut, cashew, peach palm, carrizo palm, etc., but the savanna plants

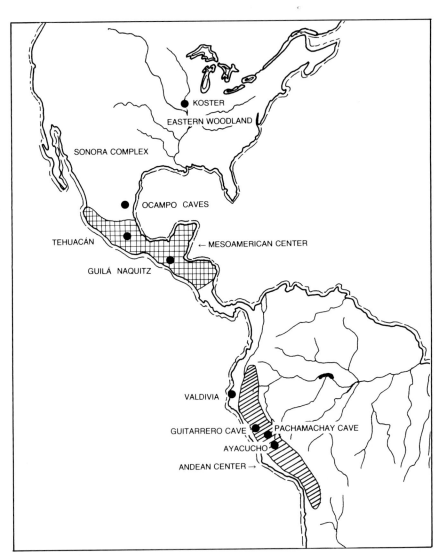

Fig. 7.1. Early sites with domesticated plants.

are generally more important and these must be adapted to forest conditions.

The vast area of the Amazon watershed is not totally covered by high forest; there are enclaves of savanna, often with gallery forests along the streams. Some of these were densely populated in prehistoric times. Civilizations did not develop comparable to those of the Olmec or Maya, but some degree of urbanization was achieved. Since the rain forest migrated into place in the early Holocene, the people were probably adapting continuously to changing conditions. Lévi-Strauss (1950) and Lathrap (1968), among others, have suggested that most, if not all, hunter–gatherers in South America are 'drop-outs' from farming. We have yet a great deal to learn about human occupation of Amazonia, but what developed seems to follow the pattern of other noncenters with the emergence of a mosaic of cultures, crops and farming practices with no evident center in time or space.

Cereals

Maize

The origin and evolution of maize has been a matter of contention and sometimes acrimonious debate for decades. For those not familiar with the materials, I shall try to explain the basis of the debate and present my own views, right or wrong. I did work with maize and related taxa for some twenty years and gained some experience in these matters.

Most people are familiar with the general morphology of maize or Indian corn with its tassel of male flowers at the top and one to several lateral compact ears of female flowers that develop into grain at maturity. At flowering time, each ovary bears a long stigma or 'silk' that protrudes through the tip of the covering husks. The tassels produce large amounts of pollen that is wind blown to the silks and pollination is effected. The pollen is large and sprouts quickly, pushing out a pollen tube through a pore provided, and within a few hours tubes from several to many pollen grains approach the embryo sac, penetrate and discharge their contents including two sperm nuclei. One fertilizes the egg cell to produce a zygote, the other fertilizes the polar nuclei to develop endosperm.

There is a plant native to Mexico, Guatemala and Honduras called teosinte with a similar morphology and appearance and life cycle. It is fully compatible genetically with maize and crosses readily with it in the field. It is now usually considered a subspecies of *Zea mays*. As with other cereal progenitors (see pp. 42–4; 124), it builds massive stands of weed races through repeated hybridization with maize and among the wild and weed populations. In fact, it behaves in the field exactly like wild wheat, wild barley, wild rice, wild sorghum, wild pearl millet, etc. The story is a familiar standard one, simple and straight forward, *except* for the morphology of the female ear. That alone is the basis of contention.

The female inflorescence of teosinte does not look much like ears of maize. They are small and borne on a small branching structure in the axils of leaves. There are several to many per plant depending on

Weed mimicry in maize, near Amecameca, Mexico. Both weed (teosinte) (*b*) and maize (*a*) have hairy purple sheaths, but the teosinte has thinner stalks. Weed populations are maintained, in part, by the use of animal manures from local dairies contaminated with teosinte fruit cases.

size, growth and tillering of the plant. The ear itself is short and disti-chous, i.e. two-ranked with two rows of paired spikelets embedded deeply in a hard rachis and covered by a hard outer glume. Ears are in clusters and each is enclosed individually by a single husk. The silks protrude through the tip of overlapping husks, much as in maize, except that there is only one husk per ear in teosinte and many in maize. Polli-nation is about the same as in maize. At maturity, abscission layers are produced at the base of each rachis joint and the ear fragments into small, very hard, rather triangular fruit cases, each containing a single caryopsis. The overlapping husks spread and the seed units are dis-persed. Some fall to the ground, some are picked out by birds and some that fall to the ground are also distributed by birds. The natural habitat of the wild races is on steep slopes at mid-elevations in savanna or dry forest vegetation. Again, the long dry season promotes the evolution of annual habit. Some of the weed races thrive in maize fields on relatively flat ground but the wild forms are confined to steep open slopes where the fruit cases easily plant themselves.

The ground plan of a teosinte ear system is shown in Fig. 7.2. The group of grasses to which maize, teosinte and *Tripsacum* (another relative) belong is related to (or a part of, according to some taxonom-ists) the large tribe Andropogoneae. In these grasses, spikelets are borne in pairs, one sessile and the other pedicellate. The sessile one is usually female fertile and the pedicellate one may be male, neuter and reduced to a scale or even wanting. In the subtribe to which sugarcane belongs, both members of the pair are fertile; and there are some small groups in which the sessile spikelet is reduced and the pedicellate one bears the grain. Throughout the tribe, spikelets are basically two-flowered but commonly one of the two is reduced to a scale. In maize and teosinte, the male flowers in the tassel are two-flowered and functional, both producing pollen. In the female flowers of teosinte, the lower floret is reduced to a scale and the spikelets are functionally one-seeded. In maize ears, both members of the spikelet pair are female fertile. All the flower structures of the basic ground plan are found in maize, teosinte and *Tripsacum*. This is an important point, because reduced sterile structures can recover fertility under appropriate genetic control (see Chapter 2, pp. 33–4).

The bone of contention, then, has been centered on the problem of how to get an ear of maize out of an ear of teosinte. Paul Mangels-dorf (1986) maintained throughout his life that the progenitor of

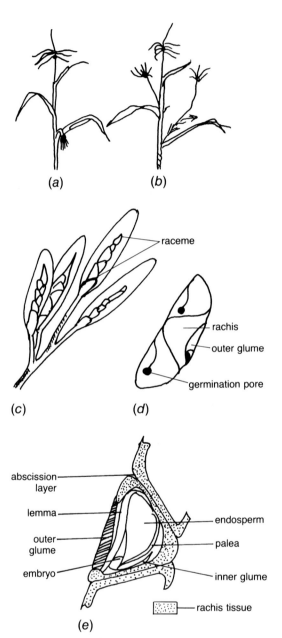

Fig. 7.2. The teosinte ear system: (*a*) short branch; (*b*) long branch; (*c*) lateral inflorescence; (*d*) joints of raceme; (*e*) cross section of fruit case.

maize was a wild maize that later became extinct. Teosinte had little or nothing to do with it and was, in any case, a late derived weed. The problem was solved by avoiding it, but he never did explain the origin of his 'wild maize.' George Beadle crossed maize and teosinte on a massive scale and grew very large F_2 populations. Maize morphology could be recovered in F_2 without backcrossing to maize but at low frequencies. He calculated from the frequency of recovery that about five or six genes were involved. Walt Galinat investigated the contribution of different genes and the correspondence of genes in maize and *Tripsacum* (Beadle, 1980).

Hugh Iltis (1983) proposed that the problem could be resolved by a single 'catastrophic' sexual transmutation. The fact is that there is nothing in the transformation that has not happened repeatedly in the evolution of other cereals. Most of the major figures in the debate were narrowly focused on maize and had little or no experience with other cereals. What are the real differences between the ear of maize and the ear of teosinte?

1. The teosinte ear is fragile and breaks up at the rachis joints. All wild cereals are fragile and all have developed nonshattering races under domestication.
2. In the female spikelet pairs of teosinte, only one is fertile, the other is reduced; in maize, both members of the pair are fertile. Recovery of fertility in the reduced spikelet is also found in cultivated barley and sorghum and in wild *Dichanthium* and *Bothriochloa* (pp. 33–4), and the whole subtribe Saccharininae has female fertile paired spikelets.
3. Teosinte ears are two-ranked. Maize ears have four or more ranks. The recovery of fertility in sterile spikelets produces four-*rowed* ears but are still two-*ranked*. Multiplication of rank is also found in pearl millet but admittedly the genus *Pennisetum* has a tendency in that direction, and so do *Phleum, Alopecuris* and some other grasses.
4. The outer glumes of teosinte are very hard; the glumes of maize are soft. Reduction in glume hardness is also known in wheat, barley, sorghum, rice and in the thin shell of cultivated coix. Furthermore, the male flowers of teosinte itself have soft glumes.
5. In teosinte, the glume covers the seed; in maize the grain is (usually) exposed. The same is found in sorghum, pearl millet and proso millet.

6. In teosinte, the grain is embedded in deep cupules in the rachis; in maize, the grain is borne in shallow cupules. This is a variable character even within maize and the cob conforms to row number and seed size as an integrated unit.
7. Teosinte seeds are small; maize seeds may be small also but are usually several-fold the size of the wild races. Increase in seed size is rather general under domestication.

The transformation of the teosinte ear to the maize ear may appear spectacular, but there are no elements in it that are unique, and the genetic basis does not appear very complex. Actually, the evolution of pearl millet from wild races, with inflorescences 10 cm long or less, to derived landraces, with candles of 2 m plus, is even more striking than evolving a maize ear from tosinte. A clue to the mode of transformation may come from *Tripsacum*. There are several species in the genus; most are tropical. They are perennials and most have either $2n = 36$ (diploid) or $2n = 72$ (tetraploid) chromosomes. Maize and teosinte have $2n = 20$. There are a few triploids in *Tripsacum* with 54 chromosomes and one species, *Tripsacum andersonii* has 64 due to an addition of a *Zea* genome. The Tripsacums are sufficiently closely related that hybrids can be made with maize. The hybrids are not completely sterile and maize morphologies can be recovered after backcrossing to maize. *Tripsacum dactyloides* is the most widespread of the genus and penetrates as far north as Michigan and New England, and the range extends far into South America. It has both diploid and tetraploid races.

Dewald *et al.* (1987) found a mutant of *T. dactyloides* in two well separated wild populations in Kansas. Genetic tests indicate a single gene is involved and it:

1. feminizes many of the male flowers and causes some of them to be perfect;
2. restores female fertility in reduced sterile spikelets;
3. restores female fertility to reduced sterile florets; and
4. induces grain formation in flowers that would be male in the absence of the gene, thus providing grain with soft glumes and grain not embedded in a fruit case.

If a single gene can do all that, the 'mystery of maize' is not so mysterious after all. Part of the Iltis (1983) theory of sexual transmutation is a condensation of the branching structure of the teosinte ear cluster and the feminization of the terminal raceme of the male portion. This at one stroke provides soft glumes and grains free of the fruit case. The *Tripsacum* gene does all that, although some additional modifications and developmental adjustments are needed to make true maize ears. To be sure, we have yet to see such a mutation in teosinte, and perhaps never will, and the fact that something could happen does not mean it did. Still the idea of feminizing male flowers to produce maize ears has much merit.

The question of what constitutes wild maize, however, is independent of time and place of domestication. The known distribution of annual teosinte is shown in Fig. 7.3. Bonavia and Grobman (1989) have presented rather compelling evidence for a separate domestication in the central Andes. We have known for a long time that the maizes of that region are very different in many ways from the maize complexes of Mesoamerica. Considering the remarkable number of vicarious domestications in the Americas, another one would seem to fit the pattern. We do know that the distribution of teosinte was much wider at one time than the present. It was found archaeologically in Tamaulipas where it does not occur today (Mangelsdorf, MacNeish and Galinat, 1967). Specimens have been collected and are on file in herbaria from sites where teosinte no longer occurs (Wilkes, 1967). A tetraploid race has disappeared from Ciudad Guzman since 1910. Was teosinte of some kind once in South America?

We have little evidence to go on, but a diary entry of 7 November 1777 by José Celastino Mutis mentions an inflorescence brought to him by a friend, who had just been for a walk. They both recognized it as some kind of maize but different from the cultivated kind. Mutis called it *maicillo cimarron* and gave it the Latin epithet, *Zea sylvestris*. He was living at the time at Las Minas del Sapo near Ibagué, Colombia. A month later he wrote a brief Latin description, which is on file at the Jardín Botanico in Madrid. The handwriting, spelling and Latin are all difficult; there is no specimen. The fact that the terminal inflorescence had only male flowers would seem to indicate that the plant was indeed a *Zea* and not *Tripsacum*. On two visits to Ibagué, I was unable to find any such plant. I visited the Jardín Botanico to photograph the original description in Mutis' handwriting, but firm conclusions are difficult to reach. Mutis was the most prominent botanist in South America at the time and one is inclined to believe he could tell wild maize from domesticated maize.

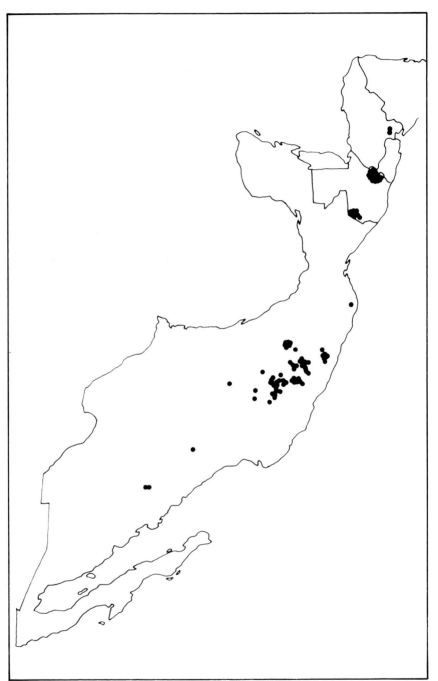

Fig. 7.3. The known distribution of annual teosinte.

What would attract humans to a plant like teosinte with its hard fruit cases and relatively modest yield? Investigators have had a fixation that it must have been a cereal crop because it gave rise to one of the greatest of all cereals. George Beadle ground up fruit cases, seed and all, made tortillas out of the flour and ate them. Several of us have harvested the fruit cases to see what kinds of yields we could get. My personal opinion is that teosinte was first used as a vegetable. Working in a field of teosinte on a hot day, I have many times broken off young succulent ear branches and stuck them in my mouth. They are tender, juicy, sweet and refreshing. Very immature maize cobs have the same quality. Chinese cooks often put them in vegetable dishes. We have even found quids of chewed plant parts in archaeological sites. I believe teosinte was taken into the home garden and there the critical mutation occurred. And, of course, a gene can mutate more than once.

Other cereals

Other cereals domesticated in the Americas were very minor indeed. *Panicum sonorum* was grown on a small scale in Sonora (Nabhan and DeWet, 1984). *Setaria geniculata* was apparently once domesticated in Mexico. The evidence is archaeological. Seed size increased over time and articulation became rough, as if nonshattering races had evolved (Callen, 1967). The crop was quickly abandoned when maize became available. In the southern Andes, a *Bromus mango* was once grown, was described rather hazily by early cronistas and abandoned with the importation of European cereals. Some kinds of grain grass were grown or managed by Indians in the southern California–Mexico border zone (Shipek, 1989). Except for maize, which was a real triumph of plant breeding (or the luckiest of accidents), the American Indian did not do much with the grasses, even though they harvested them sometimes on a considerable scale and sometimes planted them.

Pseudocereals

The American Indians were much more successful with pseudocereals than they were with the minor millet or grass seed crops. The most important at the time of European contact belonged to the genera

Chenopodium and *Amaranthus*. Of the chenopods, the most important was quinoa (*Chenopodium quinoa*). It was a sacred crop to the Incas and a staple of Indians from southern Chile to Colombia. Quinoa grew at elevations higher than maize could be grown. The seeds are very small but highly nutritious. They can be boiled like rice, used to thicken soups, baked, made into beer and some races can be popped. Most of the landraces have saponins in the seed coat which must be leached out. They are water soluble but the traditional process was tedious. Today the seed coat can be removed by milling.

A very closely related form is found in Mexico. The Latin epithet applied is *Chenopodium nuttaliae* and the common name in Mexico is *huauzontle*. It is possible that this is a race of quinoa derived after importation of that crop from South America. However, it is not used much as a grain. The *huauzontle* is a vegetable. The inflorescence is apparently deformed and resembles broccoli or cauliflower in the sense that it becomes a storage organ for starch. It is often fried in batter and is a very acceptable vegetable. The grain kinds used in Mexico were amaranths rather than chenopods (Simmonds, 1976*a*).

Another chenopod important in South America was called kaniwa (*Chenopodium pallidicaule*). It is found at very high elevations where other crops do not do well. Even wheat and rye are unreliable. It is rather weedy and not entirely domesticated; it reseeds itself readily but it yields when all else fails. It, too, is highly nutritious and low in saponins. The seed is toasted and ground to flour; it may be mixed with wheat or used straight, or made into a beverage. It is grown mostly in Peru and Bolivia, in and above the Altiplano.

There were two main species of *Amaranthus* at the time of European contact. Kiwicha (*Amaranthus caudatus*) was the primary one in South America. It is a very attractive, colorful plant with dense full spikes of flowers, usually intensely red, often gracefully pendulous. Perhaps because of the brilliant red inflorescences and upper leaves, it had a sacred ritual function and was suppressed by the Church after the conquest. Seeds are very nutritious as in the other pseudocereals. This amaranth has spread into other parts of the world. It is found in Ethiopia, the Himalayas, the Nilgeris and elsewhere.

The common amaranth of Mexico (*Amaranthus hypochondriacus*) was a truly sacred plant to the Aztecs and other Mexican tribes. Selection was for increased scarlet color, often becoming very intense in the inflorescence and upper leaves of the plant. There was also selection for pale seeds, and this is the most useful character in archaeological material to determine if the plant was wild or cultivated. In due time, it migrated north became a ritual plant of the Pueblo Indians in the American southwest. It has been taken to India where it was adopted by hill tribes in the Nilgeris in the south and along the front of the Himalaya–Karakorum ranges of India and Pakistan. There it has also become a sacred ritual plant. I have often seen scarlet inflorescences hung over doorways, displayed in temples, shrines, in graveyards and other sacred places. In Mexico it was closely associated with the rituals of human sacrifice. The extent of human sacrifice in Mexico shocked officials of the Catholic Church and everything related to it was suppressed where possible. The crop, therefore, went into an eclipse after the conquest and is just now being revived as an important source of nutrition. The Aztecs actually ate popped amaranth soaked in human blood as a sort of communion in their human sacrifice rituals.

A less important pseudocereal in Mexico is chia (*Salvia hispanica*). It never was as important as the amaranths and chenopods, but it is still sold in the markets and one can find barrels full of it. Chia has a very small seed and like other pseudocereals is very nutritious and can be important in the diet.

José de Acosta (1880), a chronicler, who published a natural history of the West Indies in 1604, describes a communion ceremony in which an idol effigy made of maize flour, and amaranth seeds and honey was consumed in reverence and awe. (Amaranth is here translated as beets because of the red color. Most Spanish chroniclers called amaranth, *bledo*.) The ceremony took place in the month of May; they used glass beads for eyes and grains of maize for teeth. The god was Vitzilipuztli and was gaily adorned with fine clothes, feathers and jewelry. In addition to the effigy, there was a great amount of paste made of roasted maize and amaranth grain, which they said were the flesh and bones of the god. All communicants were bound to give one-tenth of their seed to make the idols.

For Christians, familiar words come to mind: '. . . Take and eat; this is my body . . . this is my blood . . .' (Matthew 26: 26 and 28; Mark 14: 23–24.) This is not to equate Aztec ceremony with Christian communion, but the common perceptions are obvious. Gods are consumed ceremonially in order to absorb some godly qualities or to be absolved of perceived guilt. In the Judeo–Christian tradition, the consumption took the form of bread and wine; in Mesoamerica, it was maize and amaranth, the amaranth resembling blood as closely as red wine. The human mind seems to work in analogous ways everywhere. We find parallel behavior in domesticating plants, in developing creation stories, in the sense of the sacred and the holy and in the symbols that emerge from them, in the desire or need to approach the sources of cosmic power, in submission to those powers that cannot be controlled, in abject desire to appease the powers in return for favors or 'salvation.'

Roots and tubers

The American Indians have presented the world with three basic food staples with enormous production, and a suite of lesser roots and tubers not so important on the world scene but very important locally. In fact, Indians of tropical America domesticated a larger assemblage of root and tuber crops than anyone else on earth. The big ones on a global scale are the potato, manioc and the sweet potato.

Most people of European extraction are familiar, at least in a general way, with the romance of the potato. Taken from South America to Europe about 1570 and after some difficulties with tuberization, it became adapted to the long days of the European growing season. The production capacity per hectare is enormous compared to cereals and most other crops. Nutritionally, the potato is high in starch and low in protein but the protein it does yield has an excellent amino acid profile. One can more or less live on potatoes if one eats enough of them. A little supplementation with fish, meat, fresh vegetables or dairy products can make a subsistence diet. The result was a population explosion across northern Europe where this Andean tuber found a cool, congenial climate and rich soils.

The region became overstocked with people who were heavily dependent on the potato. Their vulnerability became apparent with the onset of the potato famines starting in 1841. At that time the population of Ireland was about twice what it is today. Approximately a million died of outright starvation and approximately three million left the country, primarily for the USA. The exodus had profound effects on Boston politics, the New York Police Department, canal construction and the composition of Notre Dame football teams (Salaman, 1949; Hawkes, 1967.)

The cause of the destruction of the potato crop was late blight (*Phytophthora infestans*). It devastated the potato crop on the mainland of Europe as well as Ireland, but the impact was generally less severe because of access to other resources and a lesser imbalance of the human population. The disaster did bring plant pathology into the fold of scientific disciplines and stimulated plant breeders to attack the problem. Resistant genes were found in a tuberous *Solanum* in Mexico and although the fight still goes on, European potatoes are rather well protected. The potato has had profound socio-political impact in areas far removed from its homeland.

The homeland stretches from southern Chile to Colombia and Venezuela at high elevations. It cannot be grown quite as high as a few other Andean crops but it thrives well above zones where maize can be grown. The tuberarium section of *Solanum* is remarkably complex and there have been as many taxonomic treatments as taxonomists who have tackled it. Bukasov (1933) listed over 200 species. Hawkes (1963) reduced these to about half, yet retained 64 species in the tuberosa in which the taxa can be intercrossed and in which there is very little genomic differentiation despite a fairly extensive polyploid series. The main 'species' of interest are diploid $2n = 24$, triploid $2n = 36$ and tetraploid $2n = 48$. The potato of commerce is tetraploid. Diploids and triploids are cultivated in the Andes. The various taxa hybridize readily and have built up swarms of wild, weed and cultivated hybrid derivatives (Hawkes, 1988).

This is of local importance because wild and weed potatoes have toxic quantities of glycoalkaloids. In the cultivated potato, strains have been selected that are relatively safe but even today, in areas far removed from the Andes, certain clones under some conditions can be dangerous. In the Andes, strains selected for low toxicity often cross with wild and weedy races and toxic tubers are produced: the local people must somehow live with the poisons.

Manioc (*Manihot esculenta*) is a lowland root crop of immense value to tropical people around the world. It is of savanna origin where the roots, swollen with starch, help the plant survive through long dry seasons and the fires that are an integral part of the environment. Just where manioc was brought into the *domus* will probably never be known. For a long time it was thought that wild manioc did not exist, but Allem (1987) reported it generally wild in Brazil, Bolivia,

Peru and Venezuela. It could have been domesticated in all of these regions.

There has long been confusion over names for the crop. The Spanish chroniclers who first encountered it on the island of Hispaniola reported the name of the plant to be *mandioca* or *manioc,* and the name of the bread prepared from it, *cassabe. Yuca* is also a common widespread name from Mexico into South America. I shall try to conform to the original usage.

The crop was taken to Africa where it was gratefully received, and today there is more manioc production in Africa than in tropical America. It has also become a staple in parts of Asia and the South Pacific. It is highly variable and has a large ecological amplitude being grown from the dry savannas to tropical rain forests. It is very easily propagated; canes are cut and stuck in the ground during the rainy season and little maintenance is required thereafter. The roots keep well in the ground, and in areas of more or less equitable yearly rainfall can be harvested year around. In the savannas, they are more seasonal.

Manioc is more poisonous than the potato. It contains cyanogenic glycosides which when broken down by enzymes release prussic acid, HCN, one of the most deadly compounds known to man. There are bitter and sweet types. Both contain poisons but the bitter clones have much more than sweet types. Curiously, many of the Indian tribes selected for high toxicity. There are advantages to the bitter types. The glycosides are secondary compounds that give some protection from disease, insects, rodents, etc. But the principal reason for opting for bitter types are yield and the keeping quality of the cassava cakes. In regions where manioc is the primary food, bitter types are preferred; where maize is primary and manioc secondary, sweet types are the clones of choice.

There are two glycosides in the tubers: linamarin and lotaustralin. They can be hydrolyzed by the enzyme linamerase to produce hydrogen cyanide (HCN) that is lethal in small quantities. Detoxification requires rupturing cells to bring the glycosides into contact with the extracellular enzyme. The tuber is peeled and grated and often put into a woven fiber press to express juice and make good contact. The meal must be incubated to allow enzymatic action to convert the glycosides to deadly but heat-labile HCN. An overnight incubation is usually enough. The poison is then driven off in cooking the cake.

There are variations on the theme but the essential steps are: rupturing the cells, enzymatic action and removal of the HCN. This is easily done by baking the cake, but HCN is volatile enough that drying in the sun can be adequate. Various fermentations procedures are also used. Sweet clones are low enough in toxicity that little or no processing is performed. Boiling or baking is considered sufficient. There are cases, however, of low level chronic poisoning that ties up iodine and causes goiter, as well as other health problems. These cases are usually in urban populations where the traditional Indian ways have been forgotten (Siegler and Perera, 1981.)

The fact that the roots must be grated has given archaeologists some evidence about spread and distribution of the crop over time. Some graters were made of many stone flakes embedded in a slab of wood, and batches of flakes can be recovered. Near the coasts, graters may be armed with sharks' teeth and these can sometimes be recovered. The grating tools, like poi pounders in the Pacific, document distribution of a food crop.

The sweet potato (*Ipomoea batatas*) is a third contribution to the world supply in the root/tuber class. Its origin is much more obscure than the others and all evidence is tenuous. It is a hexaploid, $x = 15$, $2n = 90$, and said to be an autohexaploid. The source of the genome is unknown. The wild forms, if there are any, do not seem to tuberize. Several species have been pointed to as possible progenitors, but the cytotaxonomy of section batata to which it belongs has not been adequately investigated (Hawkes, 1989). Nor is archaeological evidence of much help so far. What little evidence we do have to date suggests somewhere in South America and ecologically we would expect it from the savannas. This does not tell us much.

The crop has been taken to many parts of the world and has been well received. There are parts of Africa, Asia and the South Pacific where it is the staff of life. Some cultivars are grown largely for the leaves, used as pot herbs as well as for the sweet roots. The crop is popular in the USA where it thrives in the warm, humid parts of the southeast. There the African word, nyame or yam, was transferred from *Dioscorea* to the sweet potato, and many people are convinced that yam is the appropriate name for the crop.

The other American tubers are generally of local importance only. So I will give here simply an annotated list of the most noteworthy.

Xanthosoma sagittifolium is an aroid, called among other names, yautia, tanier, malanga or ocumo. It is grown extensively around the Caribbean and southward into lowland Amazonia. The crop deserves far more attention than it has received. It is a dooryard and kitchen garden crop, and most of it is consumed by the gardeners or traded to neighbors in the village. It does appear in local markets, but it is impossible to obtain meaningful statistics on production because of its local consumption. It is a food of the poor and little attention is given to food for the poor. Traveling through the wetter parts of the Caribbean islands, Colombia, Venezuela, etc., one cannot help but be impressed by its abundance around houses and in the villages. Weedy races and escapees often line the roadsides and grow along ditches in plantations of other crops. The wild and weedy races are also poisonous due to high levels of oxalic acid, that is often crystallized and deposited as bundles of fine needles. A tiny bite of one unimproved tuber can be very painful. Oxalic acid is somewhat water soluble and can be leached out. However, the better cultivars are relatively low in acid and processing can be rather simple. The leaves of some cultivars, especially the purple ones, are eaten and, as the sagittate leaves are attractive, the plant is often used as an ornamental. Some people think of it as the American taro. It has been introduced to Asia and Africa where it often grows side by side with taro, and it can be used almost interchangeably or even mixed. They are easy to tell apart because almost all taro has peltate leaves. In recent decades, the yautia has been increasing in popularity in the Far East and the taro has become more popular in the Caribbean (Barrau, personal communication).

The American Indian also domesticated a true yam, *Dioscorea trifida*. As we have pointed out, the genus is a large one, pantropical and species have been domesticated in Africa and Asia. The American contribution originated in the dry savannas of northeast Brazil and adjacent Guyana. From there it was probably taken by seafaring Indians to the Caribbean. It has had little impact outside of this zone and it is likely that more African and Asian yams are now grown in the Caribbean than the native American one.

Canna edulis, called achira, belongs to the Cannaceae and is related to the large flowering ornamental canna, commonly found in extensively planted areas or in parks and around railroad stations. It is grown at low to mid-elevations for its starchy rhizomes and probably traces its origins to the valleys of seasonal rainfall in southern Peru,

Bolivia and northwest Argentina. At present it appears to be a declining crop but was once more important. The corms are represented with unmistakable fidelity in the pre-Columbian pottery of Peru.

Pachyrrhizus erosus or jícama, belongs to the legume family, and produces beans in long, slender pods and a handsome white turnip-shaped tuber. The top is a bushy vine. It is a very popular snack food in Mexico where it is native and in South America. Street vendors sell it to passersby. The usual procedure is to cut a fairly thick slice, squeeze some fresh *limon* juice over it and then sprinkle the wet slice with ground hot red pepper. The flesh is crisp, firm with a slight bean-like flavor – if one can taste it under the hot chili pepper. It is a delightful snack, and while jícama is sold in the markets, it is not the kind of tuber one takes home to form the basis of a meal. Jícama was taken early after the conquest to the Philippines and from there was distributed through Indonesia, Malaysia and Indochina where it is also extremely popular. Two other species of *Pachyrrhizus* were domesticated in South America but were never so successful.

Polymnia sonchifolia, called yacon by some, is a member of the composite family and produces sweet juicy tubers up to 20 x 8 cm in size that are eaten raw. It is cultivated at mid-elevations from Colombia to Jujuy in northwest Argentina, and was probably more important at one time than it is now. The yacon stores its food reserves as inulin instead of starch. This is essentially indigestible to humans and it has been suggested that it might be useful for loss-weight diets and diabetics (National Research Council, 1989).

There is a whole suite of high elevation, cold country tubers that include the potato plus ulluco (*Ullucus tuberosus*), oca (*Oxalis tuberosa*), maca (*Lepidium meyenii*) and añu or mashua (*Tropaeolum tuberosum*). The center of the suite seems to be Peru and Bolivia, but some may range to Colombia and to Chile and Argentina. This group was probably not easy to bring into the *domus*; they are all poisonous to some degree. The glycoalkaloids in potato have been mentioned. Wild ulluco contains saponins and is bitter; wild oca and some cultivars are loaded with oxalic acid. Since the acid is only moderately water soluble, some cultivars are leached in running water for a matter of weeks, and then freeze-dried using the cold nights to freeze and pressing them after thawing in daytime. Maca is used both as a food and a medicine. It releases isothiocyanates or mustard oils. Añu is also an isothiocyanate producer. The Indians perceived these two crops as affecting human fertility, positively for women, negatively for men. There is probably some merit in the idea. Except for the potato, none of these crops has contributed much to agriculture outside of the high Andes. There is a noticeable prejudice among urban people of Spanish descent who look down on them as 'Indian foods' and not suitable for westernized civilizations. In their homeland, however, they have been invaluable for survival at elevations higher than the potato can grow. These tubers were, in part, adaptations for plant survival in the bitter cold of high mountains and have permitted humans to live in this difficult environment (Johns, 1989).

Beans

Four species of beans were domesticated within the genus *Phaseolus*, and archaeology tells us that some were among the earliest of American plant domesticates. Wild races of the common bean, *Phaseolus vulgaris*, are found along the eastern slope of the Andes at mid-elevations from Jujuy to Colombia and Venezuela, and continuing on east of the western Cordiliera of Mexico until shut off by arid conditions in Sonora. With a distribution of this kind, one could almost predict more than one, and perhaps several, domestications. Modern biochemical investigations indicate at least two distinct complexes (Gepts *et al.*, 1988) and Brücher (1968) indicates more. As of present information however, the species shows up in archaeological sites in South America some 4000 years before Mexico.

The common bean is the major *Phaseolus* in world production. The Indians used it as dry beans. The green bean, eaten in the pod, seems to have been a European development where the terms *haricot vert* and French bean are commonly used. As with most pulses, the wild and primitive races are rampant vines and the bushy types evolved later. Modern plant breeding has greatly improved local adaptations and yields of both green and dry beans.

The wild lima bean, *Phaseolus lunatus*, has a somewhat similar distribution but a little more restricted. Two separate domestications at least seem sure, the small seeded seiva bean in Mexico and the large seeded lima in South America. Remains of both common and lima beans were found at Guitarrero Cave dating to about 8000 BC.

The scarlet runner bean, *Phaseolus coccineus*, produces a very handsome vine with scarlet flowers and is often used as an ornamental. The seeds are very large and usually mottled red, pink and white. It is hypogeal while the common bean is epigeal, that is on sprouting in the soil, the seed of the runner beans stays underground and sends up a shoot, while the common bean pushes up the seed with its cotyledons above the ground. The two species can be hybridized with some difficulty and the hybrids receive conflicting commands. Wild type runner beans were found in Tamaulipas dating to about 7000 BC. Currently, wild races prefer the more congenial water regimes in southern Mexico.

The tepary bean (*Phaseolus acutifolius*) was domesticated as part of the Sonora complex of northwest Mexico and southwest USA. Understandably, it is drought resistant and adapted to high temperatures. It had declined with the increase in irrigation projects, but interest is increasing for its use on marginal dry land areas in various parts of the world.

There were two species of *Canavalia* domesticated: *Canavalia ensiformis* or sword bean and *Canavalia plagiosperma* or jack bean in South America. Both produce very heavy climbing vines, and very large pods and large seeds. There are toxic properties in both of them. In the highlands of the Andes, a lupine, *Lupinus mutabilis*, was domesticated. It is called chocho and while it is thoroughly domesticated, it has problems of toxicity.

The peanut, *Arachis hypogaea*, is another triumph in plant breeding. The wild forms are found in Jujuy, northwestern Argentina and adjacent areas of Bolivia. They do not look much like the familiar 'jumbo' or circus peanut. In the wild races, two small seeds are separated by a slender, almost threadlike section of pod. Under selection by American Indians, seed size was increased dramatically and the pod condensed to the shape familiar to us. The peanut can be considered either a pulse or an oil-seed crop. It has become a major commercial crop on the world market and important to the economy of several nations in Africa and Asia.

The American Indians did spectacular things with the sunflower. The wild races of *Helianthus annuus* were probably native to the Great Plains and western prairies of what is now the USA, but domestication seems to have been a part of the Eastern Woodland Complex of the lower Ohio Valley and mid-Mississippi watershed. Achenes show up in archaeological sites and become larger with time, reaching a

Fruit of the wild peanut (*a*); plant of the domesticated peanut (*b*).
Courtesy of ICRISAT.

domesticated size of 7 mm or more around 1000 BC in Arkansas and Tennessee. The wild races are not much different from weed races, very common in the Midwest. Kansas is called the sunflower state, not because much sunflower is grown there but because of the enormous abundance of weed sunflower. It is a highly branched annual with many small heads of yellow tube and ray flowers and en masse, can make a brilliant yellow splash on the landscape. Domestication went in the direction of fewer and larger heads, and more and more apical dominance until the ultimate ideotype was achieved with a single, huge terminal head supported by a robust unbranched stem (Fig. 7.4). Increase in achene size was also considerable. Early illustrations of Indian gardens by Europeans depict these fully domesticated races.

Commercially, the sunflower has had more success in eastern Europe and USSR than in its homeland in North America. One reason given is the great abundance of weed sunflower harboring all the diseases and pests known to afflict the crop. In any case, sunflower

Fig. 7.4. Sunflower effect. With apical dominance, the terminal bud releases plant hormones that suppress development of lateral buds found in the axils of each leaf (left). There are degrees of dominance, but complete dominance results in a single, very large inflorescence (right). The effect is observed in the domestication not only of sunflowers but also in maize, sorghum, pearl millet and others. Similar development controls have transformed the viny habit of wild types to bush types in beans, soybean, pigeonpea, etc.

is another major contribution of the American Indian to the world's food supply.

Tomatoes

One of my professors at the University of California (UC) at Berkeley, J. A. Jenkins published a paper in 1948 on the origin of the tomato. I had long escaped with my degree, but dutifully read the paper. I found it curious, if not a little implausible, and filed it away in my memory for future reference. The scenario presented was that the wild races are found in western South America, e.g. Peru and Ecuador, but the tomato was domesticated in Mexico in the Yucatan–Veracruz area. The tomato was taken from there to Europe. It was a quarter of a century later before I could study and collect in southern Mexico, Guatemala and northern South America. My main concern at the time was with relatives of maize, but the tomato story kept running through my mind. As a student of crop evolution, I had to learn what I could.

If the wild races occur in western South America, how did the raw material get to Mexico for domestication? Jenkins proposed that it got there as a weed infesting cultivated fields and other disturbed areas. Sure enough, I found weed tomatoes growing in Maya ruins, along roadsides and in maize fields in Yucatan – the raw materials were there. The wild and weed races have two locules (chambers) per fruit and the more primitive cultivars like cherry and plum tomatoes also have two locules. The larger, more derived kinds have more locules.

The tomato was taken to Europe in the sixteenth century and is illustrated in several herbals of the time. It was a multiloculed, heavily ridged kind still found in Veracruz and Yucatan. All the elements of the Jenkins story were present. I did not have the time, facilities or support to conduct a standard crop evolution study as outlined in Chapter 2, but C. M. Rick of U C–Davis had been doing such studies for years and could do them much better than I. All I had to do was check my observations with him. In general, we agreed that the Jenkins theory could, probably, never be proved, but it was also hard to disprove. The distributions were real: the wild races in western South America, domestication in southern Mexico from weed races.

POMA AMORIS.

The early tomato introduced into Europe in the sixteenth century.
From Matthiolus (1586).

There is no shred of evidence that the South American Indians used or even were aware of the wild races, although they domesticated other Solanaceae for their fruits, e.g. pepino, cocona, lulo. We know of no native name for the wild tomato. In Mexico, however, there are names and the tomato was well established in native cuisine. Our word 'tomato' is derived from the Nahuatl (Aztec) word *tomatle*. But, originally *tomatle* referred to a *Physalis* or husk tomato, still popular in the region. The word *jítomatle* was applied to the tomato, suggesting that tomato was brought into the *domus* later than the *Physalis*. This evidence also fits the Jenkins story.

The introduction into Europe also had some curious features. At least one sample must have been of a yellow variety. Words like *pomme d'or*, *qulden apfel*, *pomodoro* popped up all over Europe. The word *pomodoro* is the common word for tomato in Italy, although it is very hard to find a yellow tomato there. Even more curiously, the name for tomato in Russia is also *pomodoro*. There must be a story behind this, but I do not know what it is – perhaps an Italian chef in the Tsar's palace? Local markets in Italy often feature the heavily ridged pomodoro depicted in sixteenth century herbals. Europeans tried to select and breed for smooth rounded fruits for 400 years when there were such types already available in Mexico. Tomato breeding came into its own in USA in the twentieth century with the development of high-yielding, smooth (non ridged), disease resistant cultivars. These are now the basis of commercial tomato production in Mexico. The circle is now complete: from Mexico to Europe to USA to Mexico, and, of course, much of the Mexican production is sent back to USA, especially for the winter market.

The pattern of domestication is not unique. Another colleague of mine, Th. Hymowitz, used guar (*Cyanopsis tetragonolobus*) as a model for a similar case and coined the term 'transdomestication'. The wild races of guar are African, but no domestic races are found there. Domestication took place in Asia, probably in the Indus Valley, but the crop is now grown primarily in India. It is a legume used as green beans (pods) and the gum extracted from the seeds has industrial uses. The tomato seems to be a clear case of transdomestication.

Heavily ridged tomatoes from Vera Cruze State, Mexico.

Squashes

The genus *Cucurbita* is all New World and five species were domesti-cated by Native Americans, four in Mexico or adjacent regions and one in South America. *Cucurbita ficifolia* is the only perennial of the group and is a highland species. It seems to have been domesticated in southern Mexico, perhaps from *Cucurbita martinezii* and found its way to the Andes in pre-Columbian times. *Cucurbita maxima* is the South American species and probably derived from *Cucurbita andreana* of Argentina and Uruguay. *Cucurbita moschata* and *Cucurbita mixta* were grown from southwestern USA to southern Mexico at the time of European contact. They are connected genetically to wild races in Mexico. The most common and widespread species is *Cucurbita pepo*, contributing the familiar crookneck, patypan, zucchini, pumpkin, acorn and other common table squashes.

Cucurbita pepo is one of the earliest plants domesticated in the New World, and its appearance in early sites is widespread (see Table 7.1). It turned up in Oaxaca about 8000 BC, in Tamaulipos 7000−6000 BC and *c.* 5000 BC at Koster, Illinois. The probability of multiple domest-ications is discussed and described by Heiser (1989).

The wild races have little flesh, are hard and extremely bitter. The seeds, however, are tasty, especially when roasted, and are high in oil and protein. Pumpkin and squash seeds are still sold for snacks. Wild pepos may also have been attractive as rattles and containers. The bitter principle, cucurbaticin, is strongly attractive to adults of the maize rootworm, and can be used as bait for poison control. It has been suggested that this association came about because the Indians grew cucurbits and maize in the same fields for millennia. At any rate, the transformation of a small hard bitter pepo to soft, sweet popular squashes or huge Halloween pumpkins is another gift of Native Americans to the world.

Peppers

The genus *Capsicum* is also entirely New World and five species were, again, involved. Three of the species, however, are enmeshed in a complex difficult to sort out and the conventional taxonomy is suspect. *Capsicum baccatum* and *Capsicum pubescens* are each clearly distinct from each other and from the other three. These two originated from wild progenitors in Bolivia and adjacent regions. *Capsicum baccatum* was the more widespread at the time of European contact, but both were confined to the Andes and southern South America. The complex of *Capsicum annuum*, *Capsicum chinense* and *Capsicum frutescens* was widespread in Amazonia and northward through Central America and most of Mexico at the time of the conquests. The wild *C. annuum* has two distinct chromosome races, each of which shows up in domesticated derivatives, strongly suggesting two independent domestications. The *C. chinense* type is most common in Amazonia and could well have been domesticated independently of the others. The capsicum peppers of commerce, whether sweet bell peppers, paprika or hot chili peppers are almost all of the *C. annuum* type. The popular tabasco hot sauce is of *C. frutescens* origin and probably from South America. It is best known as the McIlhenny Tabasco Pepper Sauce, Avery Island, Louisiana, and is found even in USSR and China (Pickersgill, 1989.)

A pattern of repetitive vicarious domestications, e.g. beans, squash, peppers, cotton, papaya, agave, etc. clearly refutes the idea that domestication is difficult and that a successful agriculture can only rarely be achieved. The American Indians were busy working over the local flora wherever they were and bringing plants into the *domus* with ease and regularity.

Cottons

The cottons exploited by American Indians dominate world production. A diploid cotton was domesticated in the Old World (Africa or India), but current production is probably no more than 1% of the total. The major cotton of commerce is the American upland, *Gossypium hirsutum*, originating primarily in southern Mexico and Guatemala. There are, however, weedy races around the Caribbean that also may have contributed to the germplasm. While upland cotton produces the bulk of the lint for the textile industries, the sea island or Pima cotton, *Gossypium barbadense*, commands premium prices in the market because of its long staple and the high tensile strength of the threads spun from it. Long staple cotton is thought to have been domesticated in Peru, although there are races of it as far away as the Galapagos Islands and lower Amazonia. It also reached the Caribbean islands and the stocks grown by Europeans probably came from there.

The American cottons with spinable lint are tetraploids with the genomic constitution AADD. The A genome corresponds to the diploid cotton of Africa–Asia and the D genome is South American. There is also an AADD tetraploid endemic to some Hawaiian islands but the lint is not spinnable. The presence of an A genome in the Americas has, naturally, raised questions as to its origin and speculation about transoceanic transport by humans. The genus, however, is an old one with species in Africa, Asia, Australia, Hawaii and North and South America. It may well trace back to Gondwanaland (Gerstel, 1976.)

Cotton not only produces lint but enormous amounts of seed that are oil and protein rich. Cottonseed oil is a commodity of commerce and much of it is processed into edible products for human consumption. The residual cake is fed to livestock and the livestock are then consumed. Cotton has become a major source of human nutrition because of the huge production worldwide.

Several species of *Agave* are grown for fibers extracted from the leaves. The most important in commerce are *Agave sisalana* producing sisal and *Agave fourcroydes* or henequen; the others are quite minor. As a group, they come from southern Mexico, especially Yucatan. Sisal is now grown in many tropical countries of Africa, Asia and South America, while henequen is still produced almost exclusively in the Caribbean region.

Plants: a final note

It must be said that Native Americans were superb plant breeders. They domesticated some of the most important food plants in the world: maize, potato, manioc, sweet potato, beans, peanut, squash, pepper, tomato, the cotton of dominance and some of the most delightful fruits, flavors and nuts known anywhere. They delighted in brilliant ornamental flowers and were masters of biochemistry: experts at detoxification and extraction of psychoactive drugs and healing medicines. The American Indian has made enormous contributions to the welfare of mankind.

Ice cream has delighted peoples throughout the world, and many of the flavors, sauces and toppings that accompany our ice creams have orginated from the Americas (Fig. 7.5). We decorate our homes and gardens, shops and restaurants with zinnias, marigolds, fuchsias, dahlias, salvias and others brought into the household by American Indians. Some Europeans might object to our listing of the strawberry as an American native, for they have strawberries too, and much of the early breeding was done in Europe. However, they were working primarily with American octoploid material. The modern, high-yielding strawberry of commerce is the result of synthesis of octoploid races from eastern North America and the coasts of California and Chile. The Chilean Indians had domesticated a large-fruited race before the arrival of Europeans.

The animals

The American Indians, in general, were very fond of capturing young animals and raising them, partly as pets, partly as a mode of communication with the animal world, on which they depended heavily, and partly to eat at the appropriate time. Echoes of this practice persist even where Indian culture has essentially disappeared. Jorge León, a scientist and scholar I admire very much, invited my wife, younger son and me to lunch in a restaurant on the Atlantic shores of Costa Rica. Tepesquintle was on the menu and Jorge indicated he would like some. Always eager to try a new food, I said, 'Sounds good. What is it?' 'It is a kind of rodent they catch in the forest and raise in cages until they are big enough to eat,' he told us. 'What does it look like?' I asked. 'There

```
┌─────────────────────────────────────────────────────────────┐
│                                                               │
│        THE ALL AMERICA ICE CREAM PARLOR                       │
│               🍦 MENU 🍦                                      │
│                                                               │
│                    FLAVORS                                    │
│   Chocolate 🍦 Vanilla 🍦 Pineapple 🍦 Strawberry 🍦 Blueberry 🍦 Cranberry │
│   Papaya 🍦 Guava 🍦 Passion Fruit 🍦 Avocado 🍦 Cherimoya 🍦 Guanábana │
│        Anona 🍦 Zapote 🍦 Pepiño 🍦 Coconá 🍦 Lulo 🍦 Capulín  │
│                                                               │
│                   TOPPINGS                                    │
│   Peanut 🍦 Cashew 🍦 Pecan 🍦 Brazilnut 🍦 Black Walnut       │
│         Piñon Nut 🍦 Hickory Nut 🍦 Beech Nut                 │
│                                                               │
│               TABLE DECORATIONS                               │
│   Zinnias ❀ Marigolds ❀ Fuchsias ❀ Dahlias                   │
│   Salvias ❀ Cosmos ❀ Cannas ❀ Tuberoses                      │
│                                                               │
└─────────────────────────────────────────────────────────────┘
```

Fig. 7.5. One of the world's favourite foods: flavors, toppings and flowers

are some in cages around behind the restaurant. We'll go see them after lunch.' We all ordered tepesquintle (the name means 'mountain dog') and found it delicious. After lunch we went behind the restaurant to see the animals. The cages were empty; we had eaten up the evidence!

Penning animals is a convenient way to preserve meat in the absence of refrigeration especially in the tropics where desiccation is difficult if not impossible. There are ethnographic reports of penned tortoises, iguanas, tapir, monkey, deer, peccary, capybara, paca, tepesquintle and other edible species. Birds were often caught and tamed, whether eaten or not. And of course dogs were widely consumed by the American Indian and considered a special delicacy by some.

Penning animals does not necessarily lead to domestication but provides an intimacy with the animal world that was very important in much of Indian culture. The number of true domesticates was not large. Dogs of various breeds were important as hunting dogs, draft dogs, pack dogs, watch dogs and as food. Each tribal group seems to have had its own kind.

In North and Central America, the turkey was domesticated and often an important part of the provisions. They also served as watch birds; a flock of turkeys can set up an incredible din at the approach of a stranger, a snake or anything unusual. However, they are not of much value for this service at night. In the Caribbean region, the Muscovy duck was domesticated and is important locally as a food supply. This duck is today common around ponds in city parks and in residential districts near the Gulf of Mexico. These populations are mostly feral, not being raised intentionally but being tolerated by the public. Muscovy ducks are easily distinguished from the Eurasian ones by irregular red wattles or warty growths on or around the face. They are usually mostly black with some irregular white patches.

In South America the major domesticates were the llama, the alpaca and the guinea pig. The first two are well-known camelids; both were used for meat and as beasts of burden. The alpaca was a source of fine wool much used in the manufacture of clothing, blankets, etc. The llama is a sturdy animal adapted to the cold high plateaus and the cold high mountain environment. It cannot carry such heavy loads as a horse or donkey but is a very serviceable pack animal. The hide is tanned for leather and made into shoes, belts, carrying cases, tents and other useful articles. Archaeologically, llama bones and teeth have been found in Peru dating to about 3500 BC, and alpaca remains show up some 2000 years later (Wenke, 1984). Earlier dates will probably be found. There may have been some flirtation with domestication of the vicuña, another camelid.

The guinea pig appears archaeologically in the Ayacucho Basin, Peru about 6000 BC. It is an important source of food to this day. The rodent is usually kept in the kitchen where it is fed scraps and green plants taken from the field or bought in the market. Small sheaves or bundles of green wheat or barley are sold in most highland markets for guinea pig fodder. The animals are very territorial and stay in the kitchen area even when doors are open or when the wall of the house is made of sticks through which the guinea pig could easily pass. They move up to the passage and look out but seem to have no desire to escape to the outer world. In Cuzco, I was shown a painting in a church where guinea pig was being served at the Last Supper. The Indian artist apparently felt that any real supper should have guinea pig on the menu.

Of much less importance, but surely worth noting, is the fact that the Aztecs raised a breed of stingless bees both for honey and wax. The yield of this kind is much less than that of the European honeybee but the stingless feature was no doubt appreciated by the Indian beekeepers. The American Indian, like natives of various parts of the Old World, had learned the lost wax process for casting gold or other metals, and beeswax was important to the artists and craftsmen of the times. The New World was also rather short on sugar plants and honey was probably much in demand.

Conclusions

From the evidence assembled so far, it would seem logical to add an Andean center to my centers and noncenters sketch of 1971 (see Fig. 2.2, p. 55). The very early evidence of plant domestication in Peru would indicate something started here. Unfortunately, there are so few sites excavated at this date that the center cannot be defined. Based on the plants brought into the *domus*, one might suggest a sort of elongate center starting at Jujuy and adjacent Bolivia in the south and extending northward to Colombia. At least, the highland complex is very distinct from the lowland system of Amazonia that takes on the characteristics of a noncenter with a mosaic pattern diffuse in time and space.

CHAPTER EIGHT

Some traditional techniques

Bush fallow

Many delayed return hunter–gatherers developed great skill in the use of fire to manage vegetation. These skills were carried over into agricultural pursuits. Fire seems to have been a tool in early agriculture everywhere. Today we think of it as being used primarily in tropical forest regions, but we have evidence that burn rotations were used as far north as Finland and that Neolithic farmers used fire throughout Europe and much of North America. In the Chinese myth of agricultural origins, Shên-nung's element was fire, and burn rotations were important in early Chinese agriculture. Well managed fires are useful and efficient in suppressing woody vegetation almost everywhere.

The classic fire management rotation in the wet tropics is variously called shifting cultivation, bush fallow or slash-and-burn. There are other names but these are the most used in English. The procedure is rather simple in principle but may require great care in execution. A chosen parcel of forest or woody re-growth is more or less clear-cut at the onset of the dry season. The bush and logs are left to dry out and are set afire before the onset of the rainy season. The object at this time is a hot, white ash burn consuming as much of the dry bush and timber as possible. The field is then planted by techniques suited to each crop. I have seen fields in Central America being planted to maize with planting sticks while logs were still smoldering. For crops like manioc, upland rice, pineapple, etc. it may be necessary to wait for the first rains before planting. Crops are often mixed. In West Africa, I have seen fields with manioc, sorghum, sesame, cotton, sometimes upland rice and perhaps other crops, all growing together at rather wide spacing.

The classic slash-and-burn cleared field can be planted for two to four seasons and is then abandoned, although farmers may continue to harvest the manioc for an extra crop or so. The abandoned field grows up to woody vegetation and new fields are cut and burned each year. The bush fallow system rotates slowly year by year around a village. In some cases, the whole village is moved after a rotation is completed. Ideally one need not return to a previous clearing for some 15 to 20 years. By this time a substantial volume of wood has been produced and a good hot white ash fire can be achieved. The system, of course, demands a considerable amount of land for each village or individual farmer, if the farmer is plying his trade independently.

Slash-and-burn has been condemned by many as inefficient, wasteful of land and forest resources and too primitive for a modern world. The fact is that slash-and-burn is probably the most efficient way to manage a tropical forest for agriculture. Those who complain the loudest are politicians with a 'tub to thump' and speeches to make but who know little or nothing of the ecology involved. Slash-and-burn does become a serious problem when population pressures force a reduction in the bush phase of the cycle and prolong or extend the crop phase. A shortened bush period does not permit adequate accumulation of woody material for soil recovery. Soils become more and more impoverished and yields, lower and lower. When the bush cycle falls to some seven years, instead of 15 to 20, the whole system is threatened and will collapse with shorter cycles. But this is a people problem, not a basic fault of the system. The fact is that we have never found a really good substitute for much of the tropical forests of the world.

If shifting cultivation has been practiced for a long time over extensive areas, the nature of the forest begins to change. Most of the rain forest of Amazonia, the largest one on earth, is thought to be derived and modified by these systems. It is not the original forest that the first settlers encountered. In some ways it has become more productive for humans. Some diversity has probably been lost, but useful forest trees are more concentrated than in the primaeval forest. Brazil nuts, cashew, *Paulinia*, *Inga* and other trees with edible fruits are more abundant and accessible than under undisturbed conditions. Some studies have indicated that harvesting the natural products of the Amazonian forest, as they are now constituted, would yield a more economic return than if they were cut down and put into pasture for cattle rearing, a practice now underway on a monstrous scale.

There are a number of modifications of slash-and-burn systems. One in use in East Africa is called *chitemene*. Here the forest is cut over one plot of ground and the logs and brush hauled to another plot nearby, which is then cut. At the end of the dry season, both loads of wood are burned. This gives more ash and better soil restoration on the plot with the double charge.

In sparsely settled forest zones of Southeast Asia (and there are some), a long bush fallow period will provide a very heavy charge of wood, and sometimes more or less virgin forest is cut to be burned. These burns release enormous amounts of energy and burning is serious business. The village elders and the local priests, or shamans, plot the sequence of events. There are ceremonies of divination and prayers of supplication to establish the most auspicious day and time. Chickens are sacrificed to read the entrails, and other animals may be sacrificed to appease the gods. Some practical steps, such as small back fires may be set to help control the conflagration about to ensue. The big event is approached with awe, and for good reason. The amount of energy released approaches that of an atomic bomb and more than one human has been burned to death or at least been scorched by wayward tongues of flame. The heat is so intense that the fire creates its own wind that can be capricious. The local chief or headman is usually given the honors to start the blaze, but he has helpers around the field to get the fire off to an even start. If the burn is a good one, it will be followed by a celebration.

But we must understand the reasons why a substitute for bush fallow is so elusive. The soils under high tropical forests are very fragile. The soil surface may be many meters above parent material below, but the nutrient cycles all take place in a layer only 3–4 dm thick. The giant buttressed trees have extensive but shallow root systems. The nutrient cycles, whether of the elements nitrogen, calcium, phosphorus, iron, silicon, magnesium, potassium or sulfur, are very rapid under tropical conditions. The roots take up nutrients so efficiently that water leaching out of tropical forest soils is almost as pure as distilled water, as far as minerals are concerned. They may, however, contain considerable amounts of tannins and other organic leachates, producing 'black water.' The mineral nutrients are transported upward, reaching leaves and growing tissues. They are returned to the soil in leaf fall, branch fall, rain leachates, fruits and other plant parts, and from the excrement of animals that eat the fruits, pollinate the flowers, prey on each other, etc. Despite many tons of leaf and branch fall per hectare per year, the forest floor is remarkably clear of debris. Organic materials are decomposed rapidly by microorganisms and enter the nutrient cycle. Most forest soils are too low in nitrogen and phosphate for good crop growth and they are poorly buffered. Forest soils can be easily overlimed and this ties up essential nutrients. The soils are tricky and difficult to manage and could, on too much exposure, turn into ironstone.

A good burn from a heavy charge of wood provides a substantial amount of nutrients for crop growth. The very thin layer of high activity, however, poses problems. Inverting it with a plow could be a disaster; exposing it to full sunlight and high temperatures could cause serious losses, especially of nitrogen. Good farming practices would keep the soil covered as much as possible and keep organic content as high as possible. Tropical pastures, including leguminous components, is one practical approach, although tropical pastures are usually more difficult to manage than temperate ones. As of now, the most useful tropical forage grasses come from Africa and the most useful legumes from tropical America. Skillful management is required to blend the two. Well managed tropical pastures can approach the production of forest growth in terms of organic matter and could replace bush fallow, but inputs are considerable and may not be economically possible.

Various other modifications of bush fallow have been proposed. One is the planting of fast-growing trees such as the Australian 'pine', *Casuarina* or *Eucalyptus* in order to get a more rapid production of woody growth. It has been used on a limited scale. Another possibility is to devote more land to commercial tree crops, e.g. cashew, rubber, avocado, Brazilnut, breadfruit, citrus, timber, etc. The produce can be sold and food bought with the proceeds, but someone must raise the food, somewhere. The leaders of Ivory Coast in West Africa have put forth an ecological vision for development in this rather small country. Food crops should be grown in the savanna zone in the north and tree crops, including timber, should be grown in the forest zone. There is merit in such visions, but implementation is always a problem in dealing with socio–economic–political complexities. As usual, the problems are people problems rather than agronomic.

Fire lingers on as a tool in modern mechanized agriculture associ-ated more with Gramineae than with other crops. One of the incen-tives to breed a short strawed wheat in the Palouse country of Washington and Oregon was the enormous amount of wheat straw left after harvest. It used to be burned to get rid of it. With semi-dwarf wheats, this is less of a problem. Rice straw is still burned in California despite bitter complaints of air pollution by smoke. Dry sugarcane leaves are fired in Louisiana and Florida before mechanical harvest. This not only pollutes with smoke but adds bits of charred leaves, which are annoying to some people, to the atmosphere. A large grass seed industry has developed in the Pacific Northwest of the USA and grass is regularly burned after seed harvest. Such practices are repeated in many parts of the world. Matches are cheaper than machines and much cheaper than human labor. Fire will remain part of the agricultural scene.

Soil preparation

The earliest and most primitive tool for loosening soil and preparing a seed bed seems to be the digging stick (Fig. 8.1). It was well known to the hunter–gatherers, and was provided to Aborigines by divine dispensation and used by them so extensively as to approach plowing. I have seen the plain simple stick used in Africa to stir the soil, but modifications are more common. A branched stick may be used with two points or some with three, and I have seen a large four-pointed stick used in Ethiopia, requiring at least two people to operate it. An early modification was to add stone weights. These were sometimes a stone ring attached below the middle of the stick and used in South Africa. I am more familiar with the Ethiopian weighted digging stick and had a fine one that I donated to a museum. This weight is also circular and a hole goes through the stone, but it is rammed onto the top end of the stick that does not go completely through the hole. It weighs some five to six pounds and it takes a lot of work to use it. Mine was tipped by a steel point forged from a truck chassis left over from the Italian invasion of Ethiopia.

It is worth an aside to point out that the village smithies in Ethiopia are worthy of serious study and admiration. After the metal is heated in the forge and placed on the anvil, hammer wielders attack it with grace and precision. Three, four, even five men may be pounding the glowing red metal at once, and the rhythm is so precise, no one pounds his neighbor's thumb or interferes with his stroke. The metal seems to ooze into the desired shape before your eyes. I suppose

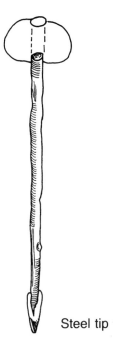

Steel tip

Fig. 8.1. Diagram of an Ethiopian weighted digging stick.

much of this artistry has, by now, given way to machine tools but the traditional techniques were a marvel to watch.

The weighted digging stick in Ethiopia is used not because they do not have plows, which they do, but because in some places, they practice a grass–crop rotation. Fields where crops are grown are plowed by ox-drawn tools, but the grass sod is too tough to handle with the traction usually available to the farmers. As a result thousands and thousands of hectares are turned over with weighted digging sticks or hand plows every year. This is often a communal effort and lines of men may work together, jabbing the implement into the turf and prying out clods that can be inverted to bring the soil back into condition for plowing and harrowing for crop production.

These tools have special meaning for the farmers. In trying to obtain one, I found that I could buy a new one in the market, but found no farmer willing to sell a used one. I later ran into an echo of the same feeling in Chad where I wanted to photograph a sorghum transplanting operation mentioned with décrue agriculture in Chapter 5. The farmer was willing (I think, reluctantly) to let me photograph the heavy transplanting stick rammed into the moist soil but not the actual operation. He did not want to be in the picture. There is something special about the phallic symbolism of the planting stick (and plow) and Mother Earth. Echoes of this lasted at least into the Hellenistic period when ritual sexual intercourse was widely practiced in plowed fields at planting time to increase harvests.

In Konsoland in southern Ethiopia, a sort of multiple digging stick is used that looks something like an Egyptian hoe. Three or even four tines are steel-tipped, equipped with a short handle and used like a hoe to stir the soil. With the narrow terraces and rocky or gravelly

Ethiopian digging stick, close up of the stone ring.

soil, it is an efficient implement but again requires heavy labor. They are made in three sizes, large for men, medium for women and small for children.

The planting stick of the American Indian is another modification. There were short ones and long ones, and their principal use was for planting maize, beans and squash. The skillful planter could punch a hole in the soil, drop a few seeds in it with great precision, step on the hole and move on to the next with ease and grace. If an occasional seed missed the hole, the planter would scuff it into the hole with his foot,

Another modification, not distantly related to the digging stick, was the foot plow used by South American Indians, especially the Incas. This was a stick with a spade-like lower end and a projection above it to place a foot. The implement could be thrust into the soil by foot power and seemed to be rather efficient if the soil was not too hard.

The most primitive of wooden plows is not much different from a large digging stick drawn through the soil by some sort of human or animal traction. I have seen only a few of these. Most wooden plows today are at least metal-tipped, and some are rather sophisticated implements that can be adjusted for depth and may have hard wood sweeps to undercut a narrow strip of soil. In parts of the Near East, wooden plows are sufficiently standardized that one can buy replacement parts from different vendors in the suqs or bazaars, and they will fit. The implement has evolved in the Far East into a graceful and elegant work of art with a torpedo-shaped metal part mounted on a smoothly carved wooden plow.

The single point wooden plow does not turn soil over as modern steel plows do but undercuts the soil, loosens it and usually leaves the soil surface in a cloddy condition and with most of the residues of previous crops on the surface and unburied. This has conservation value in erosion control, but the seed bed may be too rough for use after plowing. A second or third plowing may be necessary, or one or two harrowings may be required to get a usable seed bed. Harrowing may be done by simple bundles of brush or a wooden plank with pegs driven through holes in it. In rice paddy areas of south and east Asia, both plows and harrow-like implements are used for puddling the soil. Puddling of clayey soils makes them more impervious to drainage and leaching so that the paddy fields hold water better.

There are still a few limited areas where plows are drawn by human traction, but animals are in more general use. A single ox, donkey, horse or camel may be attached to the plow but yokes are probably more common. Some yokes are surprising, to say the least. I have actually seen a camel and a donkey yoked together. This could hardly be very efficient but I suppose these were the only animals available. Horse and mule teams are the fastest and most efficient for timely soil preparation. They were the favorites in traditional European and early colonial agriculture in North America. However, more land must be allocated to produce fodder and grain to feed these animals than is required for the slower oxen.

The greatest drawback to animal traction in soil preparation is the time required. It is usually necessary to wait for the first rains of the season to moisten the soil before the first plowing can begin. This is followed by two or three more passes over the land before sowing, and it may be necessary to plow or harrow the seed in. Planting is thus inevitably delayed beyond the optimum. With mechanical traction, the seed bed can be prepared before the rains come and in some cases, seed may be planted before the rains. Tractor-drawn equipment does have the disadvantage of causing plow pan formations and may cause soil deterioration in other ways. The ox-drawn plow does not have enough power to form plow pans in most agricultural soils.

Plow, as used in the Philippines.

Plowing near Noda, Ethiopia.

The hoe, in its many forms, is a widely used tool for soil preparation, planting and weeding. Most of indigenous African agriculture is a hoe agriculture. Millions of hectares are prepared for planting each year and the amount of human labor required is enormous. The typical African hoe has a flat, scoop-shaped metal blade and a short, stout handle. Soil is loosened with a hoe; sorghum, millets, cowpeas and other seed crops are commonly planted by scooping out a small depression with a single motion, dropping a few seeds in it and scuffing some soil over the top with the foot as the planter moves on to the next hill. It can be done with speed and skill. The resulting stands are more or less in evenly spaced rows of hills.

Mounding and ridging are commonly practiced in the tropics and to a lesser extent in temperate climates. Both practices result in better drainage of excess water, better aeration of the soil and a concentration of thin top soil. I have seen pearl millet ridged in Nigeria in areas where rainfall is normally too great for millet to do well. The cultivator takes a scoop of soil from each side of the ridge and puts it in the center, making three layers of top soil in the ridge and small furrows between ridges for drainage. The short handled hoe is the tool of choice. Yams are mounded, and sweet potatoes are grown on raised beds with the same advantages of drainage and top soil concentration. Again, the hoe is the tool that moves the soil. Extensive ridged or mounded fields are found in tropical America and are relics of prehistoric agriculture.

A short handled scoop hoe is also used in Bangladesh to raise and lower elevations of whole fields. Much of the country is so flat and so low-lying that the difference between an 'upland' field and a 'low-land' field is 30–50 cm. To lower one field and raise another, groups of workers scoop up soil into small head trays, carry the cargo to another field and spread it. These lands are subject to yearly inundation and to periodic disastrous floods. Greater disasters are caused by occasional typhoons sweeping in from the Indian Ocean with surges that carry the water far inland to wash over farms and villages alike.

Water management

Décrue agriculture was discussed in some detail in Chapter 5. Along the Nile, the ancient Egyptians augmented use of flood waters by throwing up large dikes to form basins to hold water after the flood waters had drained off down river. This water saturated the silts below and provided more residual moisture for crop growth than there would have been without the dikes. Since the flood came in late summer or early fall, the system was useful only for cool season crops. Warm season crops could be grown only by lifting water from the river.

For garden plots, small low bunds were raised in a checkerboard pattern. In fact, a checkerboard design became a symbol for 'garden.' In spring and early summer when the Nile water was low, these small squares could be irrigated by pot irrigation. There are tomb murals, e.g. Beni Hasan Tomb 3 (Newberry, 1893), showing men filling pots from the river, carrying two pots with a shoulder yoke to a garden and dumping the water into the checkerboard squares. This, of course, is hard work, probably done by slaves and used only for valuable warm season vegetables and ornamentals.

The checkerboard garden system is still in use in Egypt and throughout the Near East. The plan is expanded for field crops in the Indian subcontinent where bunds are put up forming fairly large squares, perhaps 20–30 m on a side. The object here is to hold rains from the monsoon and let the water soak in instead of running off.

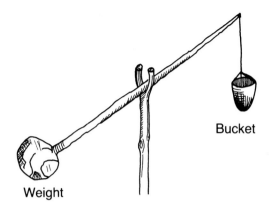

Fig. 8.2. Sketch of a shaduf.

In time, the shaduf (Fig. 8.2) came to Egypt or was invented there. This was simply a sturdy upright pole with a second pole laid across the top with a weight on one end and a bucket with a rope on the other. A man lifted the weight so the bucket could be filled from the river, then let the weight lift up the bucket with water that could be swiveled over a ditch and dumped. This also required a lot of labor but lifted more water per unit of time than the pot system.

The 'screw of Archimedes' (Fig. 8.3) is another water lifting device used until recently. Whether Archimedes was involved or not is a moot question. It is basically a hollow wooden cylinder with a screw device inside. The screw is turned by a man using foot pedals. A full volume of water can be discharged by hard work but the water can be lifted only a short distance. The shaduf has the same problem.

A modification of pot irrigation was developed in which a number of pots are attached to a stout rope or chain and the series of pots lowered and raised through a gear system by animal power. As the animal, usually an ox, but I have seen donkeys, horses, camels at work, walks around and around, the endless belt of pots fill and empty in a continuous water lift. My paternal grandmother had a similar device to lift well water on her small property in Walnut, Kansas. An endless chain had small metal cups and each one had a hole in the bottom, and the water lift was motivated by turning a crank. I used to think the hole was to drain the cups lest water freeze in winter, but the pots used for irrigation also have holes in the bottom in

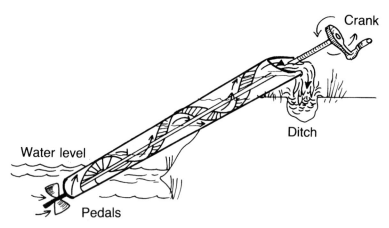

Fig. 8.3. The screw of Archimedes. It is said that this device was
originally designed as a bilge pump for large vessels. The helical
screw can be turned by foot power using the pedals at the lower
end, but the operator must work with his feet in the water
throughout his shift, or it can be turned by a crank at the upper
end, but this requires great upper-body strength. The pump is
usually positioned at *c.* 45° from the vertical or horizontal. Motor
powered screw pumps are in use today to move water in sewage
and storm drains because they are not easily clogged by debris.

climates where it never freezes. They probably have something
to do with filling the pots as they are dipped into the water. Still
another modification is the water wheel, usually quite large and set
out into a stream with at least a fairly strong flow. The current turns
the wheel by pressing against baffles, and pots attached to the rim of
the wheel are lowered into the stream, filled, brought to the top
of the wheel and dumped into a chute as the wheel continues to turn.
The water is carried to an irrigation ditch and the flow is continuous
and requires neither animal nor human labor except for the construction and maintenance of the mechanism.

An animal-powered water lifting device rather common in the
Indian subcontinent consists of a large skin bag attached by a rope to
a yoke of oxen. The oxen are faced away from the source of water
and are backed up to the point that the weighted bag is immersed
and filled with water. Then they are driven forward, hauling the bag
of water up a ramp to a ditch into which the water is dumped.

Aside from Egypt, the other hydraulic civilization in the Near East of ancient times was Mesopotamia. The Tigris and Euphrates flooded because of snowmelt in Turkey but the floods were less regular and less benign. Water was, therefore, exploited by irrigation canals and ditches. The system was very extensive and varied over time through changes influenced by politics, conquests and salinization (Adams, 1965). The rivers carried substantial amounts of silt and the canal system silted up repeatedly. Crews of workmen dug out the silt and deposited it on the canal banks to the point that enormous double ridges were built up. Flying over the region today, these ancient irrigation systems are the most conspicuous features of the landscape.

Ditch irrigation is the most widespread method of distributing water for agriculture and must have been developed at least several times. It is easy to conceive and though ditches and canals may be laborious to construct, the water is delivered by gravity and water lifting devices are not needed. Some of the irrigation ditches in mountainous terrain appear to be masterpieces of engineering but the basics are simple. I well remember my father chatting to a rancher in Idaho. He and his family had dug a canal some five miles long to bring water from one stream over to his meadow hay land on another stream system because the water in his creek was not sufficient. My father asked how he engineered the canal. The old man twinkled. 'You don't have to engineer a ditch,' he said. 'I start at the stream and start digging and as long as the water follows me, I know I'm going downhill. And since I don't dig any more than I have to, I get a nice easy gradient.' 'I can see that,' my father said. 'But how did you know where to start digging?' The old fellow chuckled. 'Well, I didn't know and it didn't come out quite right. You may have noticed I've got a little waterfall near the end.'

So much for engineering. But that is not to belittle the irrigation skills of traditional farmers. Among the most spectacular systems were those constructed by the Incas in Peru. Some of their canals are still in use. In at least one case, the Inca engineer brought a canal to a sharp knife-like rock face and sent the water plunging down to a ditch below. It was not because of a slight miscalculation as in the case of the Idaho rancher. It was obviously deliberate and probably for esthetic reasons. The artificial waterfall is a conspicuous and lovely feature of the valley.

The qanat system of water delivery has been used in arid or semiarid climates where there are mountain ranges to intercept precipitation

not available to the valleys below. It requires rather special conditions
of topography and enormous inputs of labor. Water percolating
through and below an alluvial fan is intercepted by a tunnel system
that may be tens of kilometers long and some hundreds of meters
deep in the upper reaches. There must be an impervious layer
below the alluvium to trap the water. In order to dig the tunnel,
service wells are dug at regular intervals down to the impervious
layer and then connected at the bottom by lateral excavations
(Fig. 8.4).

For maintenance purposes the tunnel is often high enough for at
least a small man to walk through it in an erect position. The tunnel
must be continually serviced to clean up dirt falls from the ceiling or
slumps from the walls. Workmen are lowered into the service wells
for the purpose and soil winched up in buckets to be dumped on the
spoil mounds around each well. From the air, a qanat looks like a
long row of ant hills.

Qanat construction and maintenance is a specialized craft, and there
are guilds of professionals who carry on the tradition from generation
to generation. It was also good employment for blind people, because
lighting deep underground before modern times was so dim and unreliable that sighted people had little advantage. The service wells
were sighted into alignment above ground, but the people digging the
tunnel below had to keep in line, and this was done by sighting on
lamps, torches or lanterns in the part of the tunnel already dug. It is
not an easy system to install or maintain, but many villages and towns
exist only because of the water delivered by qanats for both household
use and irrigation. In general, the water is of good quality and safe
even for foreigners like me to drink.

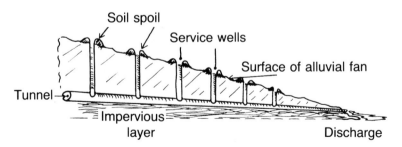

Fig. 8.4. Cross section of a qanat.

Qanats apparently were invented in Iran and are common in Afghanistan. The Arabs adopted the system and spread it with their conquests to suitable regions. It was used to a limited extent in North Africa and taken to Spain by the Moors. The Spaniards in turn introduced it to the New World. Some use of qanats was made in northwest Mexico, and there are some archaeological traces under the city of Pasadena, California.

The rice terraces of the Igorot country of Luzon, Philippines are among the marvels of traditional engineering. Mountain sides are terraced from top to bottom and water for wet rice culture is brought to them all. The mountains are steep and the terraces often very narrow and differences in elevation from one terrace to another striking. The native people have created one of the most remarkable landscapes in the world.

Sowing and reaping

In Europe and Asia the most common method of sowing field crops in traditional agriculture is broadcasting. Even crops we usually think of as row crops like maize, sorghum or cotton may be broadcast. The seeds may be plowed or harrowed in after distribution but under some conditions, this is not necessary. The American Indians were more likely to hill plant with a planting stick or the foot plow in the case of potatoes, manioc, sweet potato, etc. In Africa, broadcasting is most common where fields are prepared with a plow and hoe planting where the hoe is the tool for land preparation.

A variety of tools were developed for harvesting, the cutting ones based on Neolithic flint or obsidian blades. Small hand knives are used for plants harvested individually like sorghum or pearl millet. In some areas, rice is harvested, one or a few panicles at a time, with hand knives. Some are elegant little works of art. I purchased a rice harvesting knife in Indonesia with a beautiful tortoise shell handle and small cutting blade that looked more like a piece of jewelry than a farm implement. Moon-shaped hand knives evolved in the Far East. Multiple bladed sickles were in use in Natufian times in the Near East although we are not at all sure they practiced agriculture. The early sickles were straight but the familiar curved sickle soon emerged. On the plains of Mesopotamia where stone was in short supply, clay sickles were invented. They were heavy but seem to have been serviceable.

In due time metals replaced the stone cutting edges and in some parts of the world, notably Europe and the Mediterranean area, the scythe replaced the sickle for serious large scale harvesting. Some people added a cradle to swath the stalks as they were cut. This is perhaps only a marginal advantage because I have seen people swathing with their legs as they scythe a field, and it seems to work well.

Not all harvesting methods require cutting. In the Caucasus, a simple device using two sticks tied together at one end was used as a sort of stripper at least until recent years. Several ears of grain are pinched between the two sticks and stripped off into a basket. In Roman times, an animal-powered stripper was used in parts of Gaul. This consisted of a two-wheeled cart-like vehicle pushed through the field by oxen and having rows of tines that would strip off heads onto a platform just behind the tines. It was apparently not widely used.

The American Indian had little need for cutting tools for harvesting. Maize ears are twisted out of the husks and brought to the storage/drying area in baskets; pumpkins are twisted off their vines; beans, peppers, tomatoes are hand picked; potatoes are dug with the foot plow and manioc with a digging stick. In Asia, lentils and chickpeas are uprooted and the whole plant brought to the threshing floor.

Materials of cereals and pulses are usually brought to a threshing floor. Roman agricultural writers describe in some detail protocols for making threshing floors, including plastering, wetting with olive oil and other procedures. Most people simply select a convenient spot either among the fields or most often near a village. Bundled sheaves or loose piles of plants are brought in on the backs of people or the backs of any draft animal, e.g. donkeys, horses, cattle, camel, water buffalo, or in animal-drawn carts. Materials are stacked with care because the threshing season may be long. Ethiopians are expert stackers and often take the trouble to make an artistic job of it. In stacking sorghum, for instance, a platform of stover is laid down to keep the panicles off the ground where they might get moldy. Red and white panicles are separated and designs using various patterns are incorporated as the stack is built up. Stacks of emmer and barley are carefully thatched with the same material to shed water. In parts of Africa

Bringing in the sheaves.

and perhaps elsewhere, I found there were taboos about seed on the threshing floor. After the seed is threshed and stored, native farmers are very generous in supplying samples for a plant collector, but no seed should leave the threshing floor until certain rites are performed. I have been run off a farmer's field at the end of a rifle for ignorance of the custom.

In moist climates, some provision for drying may be required. Drying racks used to be common in Europe before the degree of mechanization now in vogue and are still used for rice in Japan, even though Japanese agriculture is well mechanized. In Spain, maize cribs that are very quaint and attractive little structures, allowing free passage of air but protecting the ears from rain, are used. Small scale farmers often dry their harvests on roof tops. I was impressed by Turkish villages that would have been dull gray in the fall except for strings of brilliant red peppers hanging on the walls and bright orange pumpkins and colored maize on roof tops. All are American crops. How dull rural Turkey must have been before Columbus!

Threshing of cereals and pulses at the floor varies according to crop, region and tradition. The simplest method is some sort of flailing; plain, straight sticks will do the job. The hinged flail seems largely European although I have heard of it in Tibet and adjacent high country. I have a photograph of a man in Mali flailing peanuts with a shovel; anything that frees the grains from the plants will do.

Trampling with livestock was common in Europe and still is common in much of Asia and parts of Africa. Cattle are used more than other animals although donkeys with their small hooves are probably more efficient. I have seen mixed droves of cattle and donkeys being driven around and around the same threshing floor. The usual technique is for one to several men, depending on the size of the floor, to spread sheaves of grain or swatches of lentils, chickpeas, bitter vetch, etc. on the floor in front of the animals as they are driven around. When trampling is deemed sufficient, the animals are halted, the floor is cleared to a winnowing pile and recharged with more unthreshed material. Anything not well threshed is returned for further trampling. A common tool for spreading is a sort of pitchfork made of a branched stick. Some compensation for the animal labor is

Stacks of grain awaiting threshing, Ethiopia.

Cattle with donkeys being driven around the threshing floor.

expected as expressed in Deuteronomy 25: 4, 'Do not muzzle an ox while it is treading out the grain.'

The threshing sledge or Roman *tribulum* is considered an advance over simple trampling although recent distribution of the implement seems fairly well confined to the ancient Roman empire The implement in its simplest form was described in Chapter 3. There are some modifications that have evolved: metal teeth have replaced stone blades in some cases, and there is a version with wooden rollers equipped with stout wooden stubs that punch into the material to be threshed as the rollers turn around, simulating the hooves of donkeys or cattle.

When the material is reduced sufficiently by treading or cutting with the sledge, the next step is winnowing. Threshed material is thrown into the air when at least a slight breeze is blowing. The light chaff is blown farther than the heavier grain and the two are separated. With the right breeze, the method is efficient and good separation is obtained. Sometimes the wind does not blow and people have invented an array of fanning devices to produce an artificial breeze for the operation. But of course weed seeds, stones or other contaminants of approximately the same weight as the grain fall into the grain pile. Some can be separated by screening. In Ethiopia, screens are woven of a tough grass (*Eleusine* spp.) and are sold in the markets with a range of mesh sizes. They are artistically made and very attractive; I had one hanging on a wall of my office for many years. But winnowing and screening may not solve all the problems. Stones can be separated by flotation, but it may not be practical to separate out the weeds and they are planted with the crop at the next sowing.

Activities during harvest and at the threshing floor, at least in good years, take on aspects of celebration. Work is often shared by neighbors and accompanied by music and dance. Many people have favorite work chants where a lead voice sings a verse and all join in the chorus. There are areas, of course, where there is some urgency, as in the high mountains where the crops must be gathered and cleaned before the first snows or areas where the dry season is short. But generally the pace is leisurely and the atmosphere festive. A good harvest is something to celebrate.

All of this was commonplace 40 years ago, but on a recent trip to Turkey, driving through the countryside at harvest time for three weeks, I saw only one full blown threshing floor. The institution has been almost entirely replaced by a small, mobile, motor-driven threshing machine that does custom work. The large farms, of course, have combines, but the small farmers who still harvest with a sickle and scythe have their harvests threshed by custom piece work. Narrow mountain roads are virtually clogged at harvest time by piles of sheaves brought by farmers to a road that the custom threshers can reach. This is all called 'progress', of course, but the social aspects must have suffered. I have yet to see anyone beating a drum and singing a traditional song while the thresher devours the sheaves and spits out clean grain.

Seed storage structures take on an astonishing diversity of forms. Some are underground pits of various configurations, some plastered, others not; sometimes they are located under the living or sleeping quarters of the house. There are granaries of clay-like huge pots large enough for a man (or several men) to climb into; there are large wickerware-like bins lined with leaves or a mixture of mud and animal manure; there are wattle and daub structures, plastered and unplastered; stone silos may be built or silos of unbaked brick. The Dogon tribe of Africa is famous for their carved wooden granary doors with ingenious wooden locks. The kafirs of Pakistan and Afghanistan craft storage rooms of wooden planks, beautifully fitted and with handsomely carved wooden handles on the doors. Many people around the world put their storage bins on stilts, sometimes carved in such a way that a ring of wood is left around each leg to keep rats from climbing into the granary. Despite the attention devoted to storage and the evident care and concern, post harvest losses in traditional agriculture are usually high. Moisture, molds, insects, rats and mice, and possibly the neighbors, take their toll.

In seasonal climates, tuber crops require storage also. The most common is some version of a root cellar. The goal is an environment that is cool, dark and moist but with some aeration to reduce spoilage. A pit or storage room dug into the ground or into the side of a hill and equipped with racks for air circulation fits the requirements under most conditions. Yams are often stored above ground on racks protected by thatched roofing. Manioc can be harvested year round when the dry season is not too long and storage is not required. The roots are best left on the plant until needed. The Polynesians who colonized New Zealand found frost-free storage was required for sweet potato as they moved southward. Special pits were designed for the purpose. Potatoes need the same protection in temperate climates.

Preservation of perishables

Preservation by desiccation has been widely practiced for both plant and animal foods. In the high Andes where it is likely to freeze every night, potatoes and sometimes other tubers are spread out on a bed of straw and allowed to freeze at night. After they thaw the next day, they are trampled with the human foot to express what free water was produced and allowed to freeze again that night. The process is repeated until a product of low moisture content is achieved. Materials of 10% moisture or less usually keep well. The dried potatoes are called chuñu and keep well for months or even years.

In the high mountains of the Karakoram in Pakistan, I have seen garden vegetables set out to dry in the sun to be used during the long winters. Tomatoes, cucumbers, bell peppers, squashes, pumpkins, okra, eggplant and others were cut into thin slices and put in the sun on sheets or reed mats. Once dried, they will keep well.

Meat may be preserved in the same way. One American Indian method was described in Chapter 1. Instead of grinding the dried meat, it is often pounded into a sort of pulp. In Turkey, I have seen the process where seeds of fenugreek are added during the pounding. There are a number of variations on the theme.

Salting or covering with brine is another popular way to preserve both plant and animal foods. We do not use the method as much today as formerly. Barrels of salt pork and salt fish were once a common commodity before refrigeration. They were sold in general stores, the markets and were standard for long sea voyages. We still preserve olives in brine. Smoking became something of an art form for processing ham, bacon and salmon. Many traditional farmers had smoke houses of their own, and even today many avid fishermen along the coasts and lakes of USA have small 'smokers' to preserve and add flavor to their catches.

Fermentation, in its various forms, has been the most widely used method for long term preservation around the world. There is a huge dairy industry in Asia functioning without refrigeration. Yoghurt and cheese are the primary stable products. Cheese is often salted in addition to the fungal fermentation. Yoghurt cultures may be a mixture of fauna and flora but they can be kept for years on end. Acid fermentation that brings the pH too low for spoilage microorganisms is widely used. Pickles, sauerkraut and service (pickled fish) are commonplace today but acid fermentation was once more widely used. I once visited a shop in Japan that had some 35 kinds of pickles for sale stored in huge earthenware jars. There were many more in small jars on the shelves. Wines and vinegar derivatives are long keeping, the wine because of the alcohol and the vinegar because of the acid. The alcohol content of beers and ale is too low for long-term preservation without special treatment like pasteurization. Foods can be preserved indefinitely in both alcohol and vinegars. Meiso and soy sauce are both fermentation products of soybean, but preservation is probably due more to high salt content than to the fermentation process.

One of the more interesting fermentations is that of fish pastes in the Far East. The product looks like rotten fish paste and 'smells to high heaven.' Yet it is safe for humans to eat. Microbiologists have not been able to find the microorganisms responsible in nature so it has been suggested that they are the first of all domesticates.

Processing

Cereals are processed the world over by pounding or grinding. The wooden mortar and pestle were widely used in both the Old and New Worlds. It is still a standard tool in Africa, and throughout the continent the most common sound in the villages, morning and evening, is the thunk, thunk, thunk of the women and children pounding grain of some kind. Two or even three people may pound in the same mortar with a rhythm so precise that the pestles do not interfere one with another. Remarkable things can be done in a mortar with skill and experience; the bran can be taken off the caryopses without crushing the grain and winnowed out; grain can be cracked into coarse pieces or pulverized to flour; emmer or spelt can be deglumed without breaking up the grains. Rice can be dehulled the same way. If the mortar is filled fairly deeply, the pestle gives a rubbing action useful for decortication. A lower charge will result in more cracking and pulverizing. Stone mortars and pestles are also used, but the action approaches grinding more than pounding. Small stone mortars and pestles are used to this day to grind fresh spices.

There were elaborations on the theme in Asia where foot-powered pounders were invented. A weighted pole or log is raised by depressing a pedal and let fall by release. The idea was taken a little further in Japan and China by using the weight of water from a bamboo pipe to raise the pounder and let it fall.

Grinding can be as simple as crushing the grain between two stones, one stationary and the other moved by hand; or it can be as sophisticated as mills run by wind or water. The lower stationary stone takes a variety of forms. At some villages in Africa and Asia, a convenient rock outcrop may be used by the whole village. Groups of women take the grain to grind on the bedrock with individual upper stones or 'manos.' The grinding wears depressions in the bedrock and an outcrop ledge may be pockmarked with them. Grinding can be a communal social event in such cases. I have seen a modification of this layout in Africa. A grinding platform is built to a convenient height and the lower stones are fixed on it. In a Muslim household I visited, the head of the house had four wives; so four sleepers were bedded in the grinding platform and all four women could grind at the same time. I watched them work for awhile. They could expertly grind off the bran and separate it by winnowing on the spot. They then could grind the grain into different classes of groats or flour, also by periodic winnowing. The platform has the advantage of not making it necessary for the operators to bend over or kneel.

Kneeling is more common. I remember an Ethiopian woman kneeling and grinding tef with a baby on her back. She said there was an Ethiopian saying that grinding is easier with a baby on the back. It may be that the extra weight helps a little, but the main meaning was that grinding is easier in a happy household and a child makes a household happier.

The lower stone is called by the Indian word, 'metatae,' in Mexico and adjacent regions. It is often nicely crafted of lava or some other coarse-grained stone. It may have legs and the grinding surface may be sloping or concave like a 'saddle quern.' The mano is often shaped like a rolling pin. The ensemble is very artistically attractive. Again the products can be coarse or fine as the operator requires.

Hand-turned rotary querns were devised primarily in Asia and these were probably the prototypes for water and wind mills that came in about Roman times. Grinding was always considered drudgery and usually a menial task. It was assigned to women or slaves (often the same thing). Roman mills were large and heavy, built of stone with the grinding surface conical in outline. The upper stone was turned by slaves or horses. Fine examples were preserved in the ash of Pompeii and the slurry of Herculaneum.

One caveat should be reported about stone-ground flour. The term has become a 'buzz word' in modern advertising. People who eat a lot of stone-ground flour have their teeth worn to the gum line by about 35 years of age as they eat a lot of stone with the flour. Physical anthropologists can detect the arrival of cereal agriculture by tooth wear.

Pulses may be ground also. *Hummis*, a ground chickpea paste, featured primarily in Arab cuisine, is a delightful example and peanut butter is another. Peanuts, chickpea, pigeon pea and others can be roasted, salted and eaten as snacks. Some legume seeds are sprouted, making them soft and metabolizing some of the antidigestive compounds. The most common method of consumption of dried pulses is boiling whole seeds. This also softens them and inactivates antimetabolites. Some of the lupines are toxic and must be boiled in several changes of water. The boil water is sometimes used as an insecticide.

Soybeans may be made into tofu, a nutritious, protein-rich, soft, cheese-like product of many culinary uses. I used to make my own. Basically, the protocol is to soak the beans for some hours, grind them, boil the meal, then strain through a cloth. The milky liquid that goes through the filter is heated and the protein precipitated with either an acid or epsom salts. This is put into a wooden press and excess moisture squeezed out through cheesecloth. The cake remaining in the press is the tofu. The meal remaining in the first straining is called *okara* in Japanese and can be seasoned to make a sort of vegetable sausage. The whey pressed out of the second screening is good for the compost heap.

Whatever the food, methods of processing are basically simple. Material is reduced by pounding, grinding, grating or slicing and is cooked by roasting, frying, boiling or steaming. Using these basic techniques, the most elaborate recipes and menus can be constructed.

CHAPTER NINE

Where we stand

Agricultural origins

We have now completed a brief, sketchy tour around the world looking at times and places and the plants and animals domesticated for
food, fiber and industrial purposes. How did our theorists fare? For
the very earliest traces of plant domestication so far revealed by
archaeology, we find no trace of the sedentary fisherfolk of Carl Sauer
(see Chapter 1, p. 22). The fisherfolk did exist and it may well be that
they domesticated tuberous plants that do not preserve well, and our
evidence is deceiving. In fact, the very earliest traces come from dry
Oaxaca, the arid Jordan Valley and intermontane Peruvian valleys.
These are environments that preserve seeds well. Is the evidence we
have so far real or is it distorted by differences in preservation? Different individuals will probably each have a personal bias in the interpretation of the evidence. Clear evidence of agriculture in the lowland
tropics does emerge in due time, but always later than the seed-based
agriculture of the drier zones.

The archaeological evidence clearly shows that the earliest tentatives of seed agriculture in Peru, Mexico and Palestine were directly
followed by successions of cultures with more and more complex
components of agriculture. These are the strands that fused, coalesced
and evolved into fully functional agricultural systems that laid the
foundations of civilizations around the world. These are the tentatives
that bore fruit and counted most in human history. To be sure, manioc
probably was important in support of the civilizations of Chavín and
Maya, and potato was a fundamental resource of the Inca empire, but
these came later.

Carl Sauer selected sedentary fisherfolk because he thought they
would be secure in their ecology and adaptation to resources and
would have the leisure to conduct the experiments necessary for plant
domestication. One could argue that this very security made it
unnecessary to grow plants for food, while people living in dry and

less secure habitats found it to their advantage to experiment with growing food plants for later harvest. The leisurely pace of agricultural evolution, however, suggests little stress or urgency. The hunter–gatherers of dry climates also had security in their botanical knowledge and survival techniques.

How did the dump-heap theory of Darwin and Anderson (see Chapter 1, pp. 6, 22) come out? Some weeds were domesticated; some domesticates produced weeds. The interactions of wild, weed and domesticated populations are intricate and adaptations move in various directions with ease. As I have pointed out, the progenitor of domesticated sorghum is a climax plant of the tall grass–thornbush savanna. There is no dump-heap implication here. Certainly there is no implication either in emmer wheat, barley, flax, pea, lentil, chick-pea and most Near Eastern crops. Rice and wild maize are not dump-heap plants. On the other hand, the whole early Eastern Woodland complex in USA of sumpweed, sunflower, lambsquarter, ragweed, knotweed, pepos and bottle gourds are all weedy and have a dump-heap look about them. They could have insinuated themselves almost unnoticed into cultivation. The cucurbits are always early in the archaeological record, tend to be dump-heap plants and seem to fit the pattern. On the whole, one can credit the concept with limited applicability. Some of our crops have come from dump-heap weeds, but most clearly did not.

Anderson's (1954) perception of introgressive hybridization in disturbed habitats has great merit and should be taken seriously. The 'strange mongrels' he writes about are indeed material for domestication. Our cultigens are mostly 'monsters' that could not survive in the wild. Some at least were probably derived from hybrids that would not have occurred without human disturbance (Fig. 9.1).

How did Vavilovian theory (see Chapter 2, p. 50) fare? We can credit him with three bull's eyes: Peru, Oaxaca and Palestine are dead center in three of his eight centers. Furthermore, agriculture also evolved independently in China, Southeast Asia and Ethiopia, centers of origin in his scheme. Ethiopia is the only country in sub-Saharan Africa visited by Vavilov and the Russian scientists did not know Africa well until the last two decades. This left some gaps in the theory. There were also other independent origins, but by and large his essay of 1926 was a landmark and still influential. As of that date it was a remarkable perception, but based more on intuition than data.

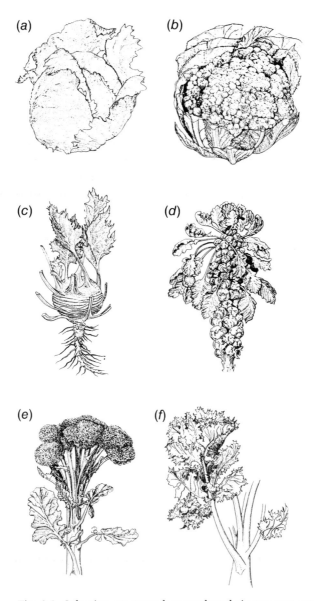

Fig. 9.1. Selection pressure has produced six separate vegetables from a single species, *Brassica oleracea*. Selection for: (*a*) enlarged terminal buds has produced the cabbage; (*b*) inflorescences, the cauliflower; (*c*) stems, kohlrabi; (*d*) lateral buds, Brussels sprouts; (*e*) stems and flowers, broccoli; (*f*) leaves, kale. Kale most closely resembles the wild plant. From Harlan (1976): copyright by Scientific American. Reproduced with permission.

How did Mark Cohen's food crisis (see Chapter 1, p. 23) in pre-history turn out? He assembled all the evidence he could to support it, but some of it seems a bit strained. If one reads only his version, one could be persuaded, but other evidence does not support the concept very well. Growing a few squash plants in Oaxaca could hardly have had much effect on the food supply and the extremely leisurely pace of evolution toward a fully effective agriculture does not fit the conception of crisis. This is not to doubt his archaeological observations. It seems logical to expect some shift in foods hunted or gathered as populations increase and that gatherers might forage far-ther afield. Studies of skeletal remains failed to show nutritional stresses immediately prior to plant domestication. Real evidence of a forcible entry into agriculture is slim.

What does stand out in all the evidence assembled is a synchrony around the world. People everywhere were moving in the direction of food production from the start of the Holocene. This could have been a result of momentum from post Pleistocene adjustments. With the extinction of much of the Pleistocene fauna, humans had to change their way of living. All over the world people turned their attention to smaller game, a greater variety of both plants and animals in the diet, smaller, more refined and more efficient stone tools, a greater emphasis on plant foods, etc. These trends seemed to have pushed on of their own momentum toward the cultivation of plants and the domestication of animals. There was a crisis of sorts at the time, not necessarily due to a shortage of food, but rather a change in the inventory. The shopping list changed because the availability changed.

Why did the Aborigines continue their hunting–gathering way of living when others moved toward agriculture? They did not experi-ence the same crisis. The only placental mammals on the continent were bats and rats, and their game animals did not suffer extinction. This is probably only one of the factors, but the experience of the Aborigines was evidently different from elsewhere in the world.

We may sum up our examination of agricultural origins with two observations. First, we will not and cannot find a time or place where agriculture originated. We will not and cannot because it did not happen that way. Agriculture is not the result of a happening, an idea, an invention, discovery or instruction by a god or goddess. It emerged as a result of long periods of intimate coevolution between plants and man. Animals are not essential; plants supply over 90% of the food consumed by humans. The coevolution took place over millennia and over vast regions measured in terms of thousands of kilometers. There were many independent tentatives in many locations that fused over time to produce effective food production systems. Origins are diffuse in both time and space.

The second observation is that the human species has become so completely dependent for survival on a few plant species that one could well ask which are the domesticated. Did people domesticate plants or did plants domesticate people? Are we not all in the same household? Our domesticated cereals cannot survive without us and we cannot survive without them. The symbiosis is complete; one cannot live without the other. This is where we stand, and the ground is not very firm.

Let us now turn to our present existential condition. Agriculture did evolve in several parts of the world and formed the bases of civilizations in both the Old and New Worlds. Towns and cities arose. Societies became stratified with ruling families, merchants, artisans, standing armies, navies, priestly castes, entertainers, healers, laborers, the poor and the slaves. History tells us of conflicts: slaughters, conquests and defeats, oppression and unrest, plagues and pestilence, crop failures and starvation. Instability of agricultural systems has led to untold misery as populations rise in a series of good years to exceed all possible support in a series of bad years. Many of the conflicts can be traced to the instability of agriculture and most to overpopulation. Now there are more than five billion of us living on the produce of unstable systems. Let us examine the food supply.

What in the world does the World eat?

Actual figures on consumption are erratic, incomplete and sometimes impossible to find. Production figures are readily available, but present some problems. Two main sources are found in most libraries, the FAO Production Yearbooks and the US Department of Agriculture (USDA) Production Statistics. The two seldom agree in detail but figures are at least of the same order of magnitude. *All* figures are estimates and *none* is really correct, but these data are the best approximations we have. The USDA data are stigmatized by quaintly reporting yields and production in bushels (with each commodity a different weight per bushel), barrels, sacks and other obsolete measures. The FAO data are more useful and convertible, and for a few countries are more complete.

But the FAO data have problems too. Rice is reported as 'paddy' or 'rough rice' in American terminology. This means it has the hull attached and must be dehulled to make it equivalent to a naked grain like wheat. This reduces the yield by *c.* 20%. Coconuts and peanuts are reported in the shell. Only *c.* 85% of a manioc root is usable. We do not eat banana and plantain peels. A tiny fraction of orange peels may go into marmalade, but in general we do not eat citrus rinds. In correcting for wastage, I left the skins on potato and sweet potato because we *can* eat them, but for the most part, they are rejected.

After corrections for wastage, the figures are a little better, but there is a major problem with moisture content. It is bad enough to compare apples and oranges, but to compare grapes with wheat is absurd. Reasonable figures for moisture content can be obtained from published tables and this correction is not difficult. In fact, one would not be far wrong by simply assigning moisture contents arbitrarily at 10% for dry seeds like cereals and pulses, 85% for root and tuber crops and 90% for fruits. At least such corrections put the commodities on a somewhat equivalent basis. The figures corrected for wastage and moisture content I have called estimated edible dry matter (EEDM).

There are, of course, fluctuations in production from year to year, plus a general upward trend in most commodities. Wheat production (FAO data) for example has climbed over the decades from some 350 million metric tons (MT) to 400 MT and is over 500 MT in recent years, the only crop in the world at that level of production. The ratios of production, however, have been remarkably stable. Table 9.1 presents figures in EEDM as well as in terms of shares of the whole.

These corrections still do not solve the problem of arriving at world consumption figures. Some seed must, of course, be held back for sowing the next crop, but more importantly a large share of maize, barley, soybean, sorghum, oats and rye is fed to livestock. We eat the animals, the eggs and drink the milk, but this reduces the efficiency over direct consumption. The magnitude of the figures is such that additional corrections would not change the pattern that emerges. More than three-quarters of our food comes from cereals. We are eaters of grass seeds like canaries. Correcting FAO data for moisture

Table 9.1. *World production of major crops* (million metric tonnes)

Crop	EEDM	%
Wheat	468	23.4
Maize	429	21.5
Rice	330	16.5
Barley	160	8.0
Soybeans	88	4.4
Cane sugar	67	3.3
Sorghum	60	3.0
Potato	54	2.7
Oats	43	2.2
Manioc	41	2.1
Sweet potato	35	1.75
Beet sugar	34	1.7
Rye	29	1.45
Millets	26	1.3
Rapeseed	19	0.95
Bean	14	0.70
Peanut	13	0.65
Pea	12	0.60
Banana and plantain	11	0.55
Grape	11	0.55
Sunflower	9.7	0.48
Yams	6.3	0.31
Apple	5.5	0.28
Coconut	5.3	0.26
Cottonseed (oil)	4.8	0.24
Orange	4.4	0.22
Tomato	3.3	0.16
Cabbage	3.0	0.15
Onion	2.6	0.13
Mango	1.8	0.09

and wastage as best I can, production of all meat, milk and eggs in terms of EEDM comes to less than 6% of total plant foods. Meat consumption is high in some countries, but the world as a whole is largely vegetarian, Table 9.2.

Table 9.2. *Food production by kinds and origins*

	% of total
Cereals	72.35
Roots and tubers	6.86
Pulses	6.35
All meat, milk and eggs	6.0
Sugar	5.0
Oil	2.58
From Mediterranean climate (M)	36.75
From tropical savannas (TS)	46.14
M and TS together	82.89
Southwest Asia	39.9
East Asia	26.08
Americas	30.28

The sources of our major crops also present us with overwhelming figures. About 83% of our food resources come from regions of long dry seasons, either Mediterranean or tropical savannas. The geographic sources are about evenly divided among southwest Asia (Mediterranean climate), East Asia and Oceania, and the Americas.

The figures in Table 9.1 should send us serious warnings. Notice how the percentage of edible dry matter falls off very sharply as we scan down the list. It has been asserted by a number of authors that the world depends on a dozen or so crops for survival, but clearly the situation is worse than that. The top five bear the greatest burden of human nutrition. What would happen if one of these should fail? Under present conditions, this would seem unlikely, but we have evidence of severe drought on continental scales. It has happened in the past; it probably will happen in the future. We have called attention to the intermediate periods in Egyptian history due to a succession of low floods of the Nile. An American equivalent would be little or no snow in the western mountains. Life in southern California, especially, depends on snow in the Sierra Nevada. Suppose it did not snow for six years? Who would be left alive? These aberrations do not happen often, but history tells us they do happen.

But there are other hazards to dependence on a few species. Genetic diversity has been dwindling as we have replaced traditional landraces with high yielding varieties (HYV). Our plant breeding programs have always depended on natural diversity of our crops and their wild and weedy relatives. The genetic erosion of recent decades has sent alarm signals through the community of biological scientists. It is not only diversity of crop plants that is eroding but biodiversity in general. Species of plants and animals are becoming extinct at a disastrous rate, and extinction is forever. We are cutting down and burning the rain forests without even knowing what we are destroying. How many plants with healing properties we have extinguished through greed and thoughtlessness we shall never know. Nor do we know the global consequences of this destruction.

I was indoctrinated early in my life with concern for crop genetic resources. The first published expression of concern that I can find was written by my father and his assistant, Mary L. Martini:

> In the great laboratory of Asia, Europe, and Africa, unguided barley breeding has been going on for thousands of years. Types without number have arisen over an enormous area. The better ones have survived. Many of the surviving types are old . . . the progenies of these fields with all their surviving variations constitute the world's priceless reservoir of germplasm. It has waited through long centuries. Unfortunately, from the breeder's standpoint, it is now being imperiled. When new barleys replace those grown by farmers of Ethiopia and Tibet, the world will have lost something irreplaceable.
>
> *H. V. Harlan and Martini, 1936, p. 319*

Both authors died during World War II and could not have predicted the remarkable developments that have taken place since.

Transportation has changed enormously. My father collected in Ethiopia in 1923, four years before Vavilov's expedition. It took him 59 days by muleback to go from Addis Ababa to the Sudan border. This can now be done by car in one day, although one would traverse rather different terrain. But much more important than easier access are the trends toward modernization found everywhere in the world.

In 1923, Ethiopia not only had no vehicular roads but no institutions of higher education whatsoever. Now, it has a network of highways, an Agricultural University and a network of experiment stations. Similar developments took place in Afghanistan and other important areas of crop diversity. It is the success of plant breeding programs located in the centers of diversity that has been most influential in the replacement of ancient landraces with new HYV's. Genetic erosion has been most notable in the very areas where diversity was traditionally the greatest.

Shortly after the end of World War II, the Rockefeller Foundation and the Ministry of Agriculture of Mexico developed a joint program to apply modern agronomic research to the improvement of food crops. It was a modest beginning, but the results were more spectacular than anticipated. Under the direction of Norman Borlaug, HYVs of wheats were developed that could yield 4–6 times as much as traditional landraces, with suitable inputs of fertilizers and weed and pest control (Fig. 9.2) Until then, the usual increment of improvement of a newly released cultivar over the one it replaced was a matter of a few percent. The Borlaug increases were of a different order, and he was awarded a Nobel Prize for his work.

It was decided that an International Rice Research Institute (IRRI) should be established to find out if similar increases could be achieved in that major food crop. More money was needed, so the Ford and Kellog Foundations joined in the initial effort and the IRRI was established at Los Banos in the Philippines. Spectacular results were soon achieved using the same strategies that worked for wheat. Basically, the plan was to change the architecture of the wheat and rice plants to produce short, stiff-strawed cultivars that would not lodge under heavy applications of nitrogen fertilizers. It was a rather simple thing to do, and the 'green revolution' was born. The impact on the world's food supply has been enormous.

These successes brought demands for more institutes to serve more crops and even livestock. A great deal more money was needed for such ambitious developments, so an International Consultative Group for Agricultural Research (ICGAR) was organized to raise the funds to support the network of institutes that came to be established. Funds came from the World Bank, regional banks, national foreign aid programs, private foundations, and direct gifts and grants from a variety of governmental agencies and private sources. IRRI was the first of

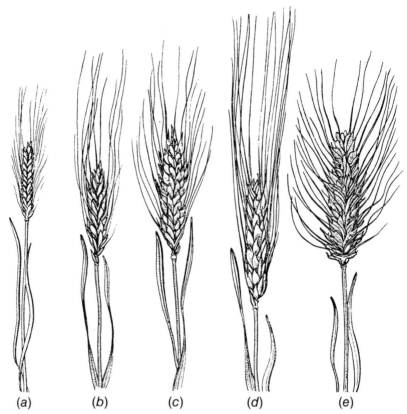

Fig. 9.2. Species of wheat: (*a*) einkorn (*Triticum monococcum*), once grown in Turkey and Europe; (*b*) emmer (*T. dicoccum*), once grown in the Near East, Africa and Europe; (*c*) *T. timopheevii* (no common name); (*d*) and (*e*) principal modern wheats; (*d*) macaroni wheat (*T. durum*), a descendant of a mutated emmer; (*e*) bread wheat (*T. aestivum*), a cross between emmer or macaroni wheat and goat grass. From Harlan (1976): copyright by Scientific American. Reproduced with permission.

the institutes, established in 1960. The joint program in Mexico was upgraded to the Centro Internacional de Mejoramento de Maiz y Trigo (CIMMYT) in 1967. This was followed by the International Institute for Tropical Agriculture (IITA), Ibadan, Nigeria, in 1968 and a similar Centro Internacional de Agricultura Tropical (CIAT), Cali, Colombia, in 1969. A potato center (CIP) was established in Peru in 1972 and the International Crops Research Institute for the Semi-Arid Tropics

(ICRISAT) in Hyderabad, India, the same year. The International Board for Plant Genetic Resources (IBPGR) was established in 1973 and two livestock institutes in Africa in 1974. The last of the group is ICARDA, headquartered at Aleppo, Syria, to service dry areas, primarily of Mediterranean type climates.

Each of the institutes is charged with development of specified, mandated crops and most of the major food crops and some lesser ones are covered. The IBPGR was charged with a broad mandate to collect and preserve, as best it could, germplasm of important crop plants. A good deal of collecting was done, base collections were assigned to various facilities around the world for cold storage and long-term maintenance. Are the collections adequate? Were we too late? Did critical material disappear before the collections were made? Can landraces be preserved *in situ* so that evolutionary processes can continue? These and many other questions can be raised about our management of genetic resources. Who will rejuvenate seed lots when viability wanes? The National Seed Storage Laboratory (NSSL) of USA has no funds, facilities or mandate to do this. What of other facilities? We have put a lot of seed in seed banks, but this is an era of bank failures. How secure is our priceless germplasm? We will not get the answers for many years to come. At present, the larger collections are too large to be used by the present population of plant breeders. A great deal of preliminary work must be done to put the collections into usuable shape before we can do much with them. Meanwhile genetic erosion continues.

Germplasm can be very valuable. As I have pointed out, a few of the accessions I introduced are collectively increasing agricultural income in the USA at well over 100 million dollars annually, and I am just one collector. Many introductions are even more valuable. The enormous value of imported germplasm has raised questions as to who really owns it. Do the peasant farmers of the world who produced or preserved the material over the centuries benefit in any way? Do the countries of origin get anything out of it? These questions have been debated with vigor and sometimes acrimony in FAO (Food and Agriculture Organization of the United Nations) and elsewhere in books, pamphlets and tracts. The charge is made that the developed, industrial countries, in the jargon of the movement called the 'north,' have been robbing the less developed countries called the 'south.' The geography is a bit suspect, but the concept of the rich stealing from the poor is a popular one for politicians who can make speeches that 'play well' at home. Goodness knows the rich have always robbed the poor, but this is not a good example.

For one thing, nothing is stolen. No germplasm is removed from a country or farmer's field that does not also remain. The small samples sent back to the collector's homeland may not even be very representative of the germplasm available and are no loss to either the grower or the nation. Furthermore, little germplasm moves from 'south' to 'north.' Temperate zones have little use for tropical materials as they are. They are very poorly adapted and must undergo radical genetic modification to make them in any way useful, and this is not done cheaply. The 'north' invests the money for conversion, not the 'south.' Similarly, cultivars developed in temperate zones give miserable performances in the 'south.' The major movement of germplasm is east to west or west to east. Africa owes an enormous debt to tropical America for maize, manioc and the sweet potato. What does tropical America get out of it? Well, coffee for one thing, and there is a lot of money in the coffee trade. To be sure the bulk of the money is at the processing and marketing end, and the growers and especially the harvesters get little out of it. The exchange, however, has been beneficial to both regions.

My experience with native cultivators whether in Asia, Africa, Latin America or anywhere is that they are pleased that you are interested in what they are growing. 'You have come all the way from America for my seeds? Here; take them! You are welcome to them, and if I or my neighbors have any other kinds you would like, we will gladly give them to you.' Rarely would a peasant accept money and some felt the offer was an insult. They do not feel abused, and indeed they are not.

Another feature of plant collecting should be mentioned. After my major expedition to Turkey in 1948, when I sent back some 12 000 accessions, I received letters of gratitude from several Turkish agronomists thanking me for the collection of Turkish materials I had assembled, because they had not the resources to make such collections themselves. Sharing the germplasm is part of the process.

Still, the question remains: who owns the germplasm and who should benefit from its use? I take it that the wrangling still goes on by people who otherwise are little involved, but a sort of consensus has emerged that the germplasm is a national resource but that it should be freely shared to all legitimate users. I say 'legitimate' because no seed bank or repository could respond to frivolous requests to 'send me a sample of everything in your inventory.' Requests must be serious and explicit, and must be made by people who could really make use of the accessions. Maintenance and rejuvenation of collections are expensive.

Sharing the germplasm is the way to go, but there are some legal problems with patented materials and advanced breeder's lines or clones developed by private for-profit companies. These companies exist only through the sales of their products that are often very expensive to develop. Breeder's lines evolved by public funds should be freely available, but private companies have proprietary rights to the elite materials they develop. Much of the debates in FAO centered on these problems.

If it can be agreed that germplasm is a common good, the property of all mankind, perhaps some other sharings could serve to ease our divisions. The theme of this book has been centered on food and methods of procurement. Everyone must eat to live; food is a common essential of mankind. We have on occasion shared in the food supply on a global scale. There were some years when the USA sent enormous amounts of grain to India to relieve famine. The shipments were so vast that it modified the demography of India. People migrated to the port cities to bring the mouths closer to the supply. Then the green revolution touched India and relieved the situation at least for the time being. Famine relief has been a feature of the African scene in recent years, but the cause of the shortage is usually attributed to drought and/or war. But drought is normal near a desert. The primary problem is population growth. There are just too many people for sustainable systems. Famine relief is at best a stop gap. The ultimate solution must be stabilization or reduction of the population. The concept does not sit well with politicians or demagogues, but the arithmetic is overwhelming. The developed countries are moving rapidly toward stabilization and eventual reduction, but that is not where the food supply problems are.

But there are other things to share: understanding, respect for other cultures, admiration for the arts, life styles and customs of other lands and other times. The music, dance, poetry, ceramics, weaving, painting, basketry, carvings, costumes, cuisine, the beverages, rites, ceremonies and festivals, if not fully shared can at least be appreciated. I have been so fortunate as to feast in the rich tapestry of human diversity. I was there before the great homogenation set in, before the taped music, the Big Mac and Kentucky Fried Chicken penetrated the Orient. I have seen the great bazaars of the Near East – Istanbul, Damascus, Baghdad, Cairo, Tehran – when they represented cultures now nearly gone. Of them all, the old pazaar of Istanbul before it was burned down was the most romantic and picturesque. People were born, lived out their lives and died in this place. The lofty, vaulted ceilings seemed to disappear in sooty gloom from fires kindled for winter warmth. Camel caravans plodded among the stalls with huge jars, one on each side; olive oil, they told me, but each was large enough to hold a man as in Ali Baba and the 40 thieves. There was an elegant restaurant upstairs with windows looking out on the Golden Horn and heated in winter by great brass braziers of charcoal.

All of this is gone. After the great fire, the pazaar was never replaced and the current markets are lit by neon and modern glitz. One can travel over Turkey today and seldom see a camel or a threshing floor. I appreciated the old ways and was lucky to have seen them, but the homogenization of modern cultures may have value in the long run. Perhaps we can be less divisive; perhaps there can be less conflict, less hatred, less ethnic pride. Current headlines are not encouraging, but, in the end, we may find fewer things to quarrel about and a more universal feeling of brotherhood and commonality. Peace on earth and good will toward men!

References

Acosta, J. de (1880). *The Natural and Moral History of the Indies, Reprinted from the English Translated Edition of Edward Grimston, 1604*. London: The Hakluyt Society, No. 61

Adams, R. Mc. (1965). *The Land Behind Baghdad: a History of Settlement on the Diyala Plain*. Chicago: University of Chicago Press.

Aikens, C. M. and Higuchi, T. (1982). *Prehistory of Japan*. New York: Academic Press.

Akazawa, T. and Aikens, C. M. (1986). *Prehistoric Hunter–Gatherers in Japan*. Tokyo: University of Tokyo Press.

Allard, R. W. (1990). Future direction in plant population genetics, evolution and breeding. In *Plant Population Genetics, Breeding and Genetic Resources*, ed. A. D. H. Brown, M. T. Clegg, A. L. Kahler and B. S. Weir, pp. 1–19. Sunderland, MA: Sinauer Associates Inc.

Allem, A. (1987). *Manihot esculenta* is a native of the neotropics. *Plant Genetic Resources Newsletter*, **71**: 22–4.

Allen, J., Golson, J. and Jones, R. (eds.) (1977). *Sunda and Sahul: Prehistoric Studies in Southeast Asia, Melanesia and Australia*. New York: Academic Press.

Allen, J., and White, J. P. (1989). Human Pleistocene adaptations in the tropical island Pacific: recent evidence from New Ireland, a Greater Australian outlier. *Antiquity*, **63**: 548–61.

Ammerman, A. J. and Cavalli-Sforza, L. L. (1984). *The Neolithic Transition and the Genetics of Populations in Europe*, p. 175. Princeton, NJ: Princeton University Press.

Anderson, E. (1954). *Plants, Man and Life*. London: A. Melrose.

Andrews, A. C. (1964). The genetic origin of spelt and related wheats. *Züchter*, **34**: 17–22.

Angel, T. L. (1984). Health as a crucial factor in the changes from hunting to developed farming in the eastern Mediterranean. In *Paleopathology at the Origins of Agriculture*, ed. M. N. Cohen and G. T. Armelagos, pp. 51–73. New York: Academic Press.

Bailey, R. C., Head, G., Jenike, M., Owen, B., Rechtman, R. and Zechenter, E. (1989). Hunting and gathering in the tropical rain forest: is it possible? *American Anthropology*, **91**: 59–82.

Barker, G. (1985). *Prehistoric Farming in Europe*. Cambridge: Cambridge University Press.

Barrau, J. (1965). L'humide et le sec, an essay on ethnobotanical adaptation to contrastive environments in the Indo-Pacific area. *Journal Polynesian Society*, **74**: 329–46.

Barth, H. (1857). *Travel and Discoveries in North and Central Africa*, 3 vols. New York: Harper and Bros.

Bar-Yosef, O. and Kislev, M. E. (1989). Early farming communities in the Jordan Valley. In *Foraging and Farming: the Evolution of Plant Exploitation*, ed. D. R. Harris and G. C. Hillman, pp. 632–42. London: Unwin Hyman.

Baumhoff, M. A. (1963). Ecological determinants of aboriginal California populations. *University of California Publications of American Archaeology and Ethnology*, **49**: 155–236.

Beadle, G. W. (1980). The ancestry of corn. *Scientific American*, **242**: 112–19.

Bednarik, R. G. (1989). On the Pleistocene settlement of South America. *Antiquity*, **63**: 101–11.

Bell, B. (1971). The dark ages of ancient history I. The first dark age of Egypt. *American Journal of Archaeology*, **75**: 1–26.

Bellwood, P. (1985). *Prehistory of the Indo-Malaysian Archipelago*. Sydney/Orlando: Academic Press.

Berndt, R. M. and Berndt, C. (1970). *Man, Land and Myth in North Australia: the Gunwinggu People*. East Lansing: Michigan State University Press.

Binford, L. R. (1968). Post-Pleistocene adaptations. In *New Perspectives in Archaeology*, ed. S. R. Binford and L. R. Binford. Chicago: Aldine.

Bonavia, D. and Grobman, A. (1989). Andean maize: its origin and domestication. In *Foraging and Farming: the Evolution of Plant Exploitation*, ed. D. R. Harris and G. C. Hillman, pp. 456–70. London: Unwin Hyman.

Bonnichen, R., Stanford, D. and Fastook, J. L. (1987). Environmental changes and developmental history of human adaptive patterns. The Palestinian case. In *North America and Adjacent Oceans During the Last Deglaciation*, ed. W. F. Ruddiman and H. E. Wright, pp. 403–24. Boulder, CO: Geological Society America.

Boserup, E. (1965). *The Conditions of Agricultural Growth*. London: Allen and Unwin.

Brücher, H. (1968). Die Evolution der Gartenbohne *Phaseolus vulgaris* L. aus der sudamerikanishen Wildbohne *Ph. aborigineus* Buck. *Angewante Botanik*, **42**: 119–28.

Brunken, J. M., deWet, J. M. J. and Harlan, J. R. (1977). The morphology and domestication of pearl millet. *Economic Botany*, **31**: 163–74.

Bryan, A. L. (1983). South America. In *Early Man in the New World*, ed. R. Shutler, pp. 136–46. Beverly Hills, CA: Sage Publications.

Bukasov, S. M. (1933). The potatoes of South America and their breeding possibilities. *Bulletin of Applied Botany, Genetics and Plant Breeding* (Leningrad), Supplement 58.

Callen, E. O. (1967). The first New World cereal. *American Antiquity*, **32**: 535–8.

Campbell, A. H. (1965). Elementary food production by the Australian aborigines. *Mankind*, **6**: 206–11.

Campbell, J. (1988). *Historical Atlas of World Mythology*. Vol. II, *The Way of the Seeded Earth*, Part I: The Sacrifice. New York: Harper and Row.

Candolle, A. de (1959). *Origin of Cultivated Plants*, a reprint of the 2nd edn of 1886. New York: Hafner.

Carter, G. F. (1971). Pre-Columbian chickens in America. In *Man Across the Sea*, ed. C. L Riley *et al.*, pp. 178–218. Austin: University of Texas Press.

Carter, G. F. (1980). *Earlier Than You Think; a Personal View of Man in America*. College Station: Texas A. & M. University Press.

Chadwick, J. (1973). *Documents in Mycenaean Greek*, 2nd edn. Cambridge: Cambridge University Press.

Chang, K.-C. (1986). The Archaeology of Ancient China, 4th edn. New Haven, CT: Yale University Press.

Chang, T. T. (1989). Domestication and spread of the cultivated rices. In *Foraging and Farming: the Evolution of Plant Exploitation*, ed. D. R. Harris and G. C. Hillman, pp. 408–17. London: Unwin Hyman.

Chase, A. K. (1989). Domestication and domiculture in northern Australia: a social perspective. In *Foraging and Farming: the Evolution of Plant Exploitation*, ed. D. R. Harris and G. C. Hillman; pp. 42–54. London: Unwin Hyman.

Chavannes, E. (1967). *Les Mémoires Historiques de Se-Ma Ts'ien* (transl. and annotated), Vol. I. Paris: Adrien–Maisonneuve.

Childe, V. G. (1925). *The Dawn of European Civilization*. New York: Alfred Knopf.

Childe, V. G. (1952). *New Light on the Most Ancient East*. London: Routledge and Paul.

Christie. A. (1983). *Chinese Mythology*. Feltham, Middlesex, UK: Hamlyn Publishing Group.

Clark, J. D. and Brandt, S. A. (eds.) (1984). *From Hunters to Farmers: The Causes and Consequences of Food Production in Africa*. Berkeley: University of California Press.

Cohen, M. N. (1977). *The Food Crisis in Prehistory*. New Haven, CT: Yale University Press.

Cohen, M. N. and Armelagos, G. J. (eds.) (1984). *Paleopathology at the Origin of Agriculture*. New York: Academic Press.

Cook, O. F. (1939). *A New Palm from Cocos Island Collected on the Presidential Cruise of 1938*. Washington, DC: Smithsonian Miscellaneous Publication, No. 98.

Coon, C. S. (1971). *The Hunting People*. Boston: Little, Brown and Co.

Coursey, D. G. (1976). Yams. In *Evolution of Crop Plants*, ed. N. W. Simmonds, pp. 70–4. London: Longman.

Dahlberg, F. (ed.) (1981). *Woman the Gatherer*. New Haven CT: Yale University Press.

Dancette, C. and Poulain, J. F. (1968). Influence de l'*Acacia albida* sur les facteurs pedoclimatiques et les rendements des cultures. *Sols Africains*, **13**: 197–239

Darwin, C. (1896). *The Variation of Animals and Plants Under Domestication*, 2nd edn, 2 vols. New York: D. Appleton and Co.

Darwin, C. (1909). *The Descent of Man and Selection in Relation to Sex*, 2nd edn. New York: D. Appleton and Co.

Davis, J. M. (1987). *The Archaeology of Animals*. New Haven, CT: Yale University Press.

De Jonghe, E. (1905). Historyie de Méchique: Manuscrit français inedit du XVI siécle. *Journal de la Société des Americanistes de Paris*, NS Vol. 2, no. 1.

Dennell, R. (1983) *European Economic Prehistory: A New Approach*. New York: Academic Press.

Dewald, C. L., Burson, B. L., deWet, J. M. J. and Harlan, J. R. (1987). Morphology, inheritance and evolutionary significance of sex reversal in *Tripsacum dactyloides* (Poaceae). *American Journal of Botany*, **74**: 1055–9.

deWet, J. M. J., Harlan, J. R. and Price, E. G. (1976). Variability in *Sorghum bicolor*. In *Origins of African Plant Domestication*, ed. J. R. Harlan, J. M. J. deWet and A. B. L. Stemler, pp. 453–64. The Hague: Mouton Press.

Dincauze, D. F. (1984). An archaeo-logical evaluation of the case for pre-Clovis occupations. *Advances in World Archaeology*, **3**: 275–323.

Drucker, P. (1963). *Indians of the Northwest Coast*. Garden City, NY: Natural History Press.

Eberhard, W. (1965). *Folktales of China*. London: Routledge and Kegan Paul.

Erman, A. (1927). *The Literature of the Ancient Egyptians*. New York: E. P. Dutton.

Evans, L. T. (1975). The physiological basis of crop yield. In *Crop Physiology: Some Case Histories*, ed. L. T. Evans, pp. 327–55. Cambridge: Cambridge University Press.

Fiore, S. (1965). *Voices from the Clay*. Norman: University of Oklahoma Press.

Fitzgerald, C. P. (1950). *China, a Short Cultural History*. New York: D. Appleton–Century Co.

Flannery, K. V. (1965). Archaeological systems theory and early Mesoamerica. In *Anthropological Archaeology in the Americas*, ed. B. J. Meggers, pp. 67–87. Washington, DC: The Anthropological Society.

Flannery, K. V. (ed.) (1986) *Guilá Naquitz: Archaic Foraging and Early Agriculture in Oaxaca, Mexico*. New York: Academic Press.

Fox, W. S. (1916). *Greek and Roman*, Vol. I. In *Mythology of All Races*, 13 vols., ed. L. H. Gray. Boston, MA: Marshall Jones Co.

Gepts, P., Kmiecik, K., Pereira, A. and Bliss, F. A. (1988). Dissemination pathways of common bean (*Phaseolus vulgaris*, Fabaceae) deduced from phaseolin electrophoresis variability. I. The Americas. *Economic Botany*, **42**: 73–95.

Gerstel, D. U. (1976). Tobacco. In *Evolution of Crop Plants*, ed. N. W. Simmonds, pp. 273–77. London: Longman.

Glover, I. (1986). *Archaeology in Eastern Timor*. Canberra: Department of Prehistory, Research School of Pacific Studies, Australian National University.

Golson, J. (1984). New Guinea agricultural history: a case study. In *A Time to Plant and a Time to Uproot: a History of Agriculture in Papua, New Guinea*, ed. D. Denoon and C. Snowden, pp. 55–64. Boroko: Institute of Papua, New Guinea.

Gowlett, J. A. J. and Hedges, R. E. M. (1987). Radiocarbon dating by accelerator mass spectrometry: applications to archaeology in the Near East. In *Chronologies in the Near East. Relative Chronologies and Absolute Chronology, 16 000–4 000 B.P.*, ed. O. Aurenche, J. Evin and F. Hours, pp. 121–44. Oxford: BAR International Series, No. 379, i and ii.

Gowlett, J. A. J., Hedges, R. E. M., Law, I. R. and Perry, C. (1987). Radiocarbon dates from the Oxford AMS system: datelist 5. *Achaeometry* **29**: 125–55.

Gradmann, R. (1909). *Der Getreidebau im Deutschen und Römischen Alterum*, p. 111. Jena: Hermann Costanoble.

Gregg, S. A. (1988). *Foragers and Farmers: Population Interaction and Agricultural Expansion in Prehistoric Europe*, p. 275. Chicago: University of Chicago Press.

Gregory, A. C. (1886). Memoranda on the Aborigines of Australia. *Journal of the Anthropological Institute of Great Britain and Ireland*, **16**: 131–3.

Grey, G. (1841). *Journals of Two Expeditions of Discovery in Northwest and Western Australia During the Years 1837, 38 and 39 . . .* 2 vols. London: T. and W. Boone.

Groube, L. (1989). The taming of a rain forest: a model for late Pleistocene forest exploitation in New Guinea. In *Foraging and Farming: the Evolution of Plant Exploitation*, ed. D. R. Harris and G. C. Hillman, pp. 292–304. London: Unwin Hyman.

Haffer, J. (1969). Speciation in Amazonian forest birds. *Science*, **165**: 131–7.

Hahn, E. (1896). *Die Haustiere und Ihre Beziehungen zür Wirtschaft des Menschen*. Leipzig: Duncker and Humbolt.

Hahn, E. (1909). *Die Entstehung der Pflugkültur*. Heidelberg: C. Winter.

Hallam, S. J. (1975). *Fire and Hearth: A Study of Aboriginal Usage and European Usurpation in Southwestern Australia*. Canberra: Australian Institute of Aboriginal Studies, No. 58.

Hammond, G. P. and Rey, A. (1940). *Narratives of the Coronado Expedition 1540–1542*. Albuquerque: University of New Mexico Press.

Harlan, H. V. and Martini, M. L. (1936). Problems and results of barley breeding. In *USDA Yearbook of Agriculture*, pp. 303–46. Washington, DC: US Government Print Office.

Harlan, J. R. (1971). Agricultural origins: centers and noncenters. *Science*, **174**: 468–74.

Harlan, J. R. (1976). The plants and animals that nourish man. *Scientific American*, **235**: 89–97.

Harlan, J. R. (1981*a*) Who's in charge here? *Canadian Journal of Fisheries and Aquatic Science*, **38**: 1459–63.

Harlan, J. R. (1981*b*) The early history of wheat: earliest traces to the sack of Rome. In *Wheat Science – Today and Tomorrow*, ed. L. T. Evans and W. J. Peacock, pp. 1–19. Cambridge: Cambridge University Press.

Harlan, J. R. (1982*a*). Relationships between weeds and crops. In *Biology* *and Ecology of Weeds*, ed. W. Holzner and M. Numata, pp. 91–6. The Hague: W. Junk.

Harlan, J. R. (1982*b*). Human interference with grass systematics. In *Grasses and Grasslands: Systematics and Ecology*, ed. J. R. Estes, R. J. Tyrl and J. N. Brunken, pp. 37–50. Norman: University of Oklahoma Press.

Harlan, J. R. (1989*a*) Wild grass-seed harvesting in the Sahara and sub-Sahara of Africa. In *Foraging and Farming: the Evolution of Plant Exploitation*, ed. D. R. Harris and G. I. Hillman, pp. 79–98. London: Unwin Hyman.

Harlan, J. R. (1989*b*). Wild grass seeds as food sources in the Sahara and sub-Sahara. In *Sahara*, **2**: 69–74.

Harlan, J. R. and deWet, J. M. J. (1965). Some thoughts about weeds. *Economic Botany*, **19**: 16–24.

Harlan, J. R. and deWet, J. M. J. (1972). A simplified classification of cultivated sorghum. *Crop Science*, **12**: 172–6.

Harlan, J. R. and deWet, J. M. J. (1974). Sympatric evolution in sorghum. *Genetics*, **78**: 473–4.

Harlan, J. R., deWet, J. M. J. and Price, E. G. (1973). Comparative evolution of cereals. *Evolution*: **27**: 311–25.

Harlan, J. R. and Pasquéreau, J. (1969). Décrue agriculture in Mali. *Economic Botany*, **23**: 70–4.

Harlan, J. R. and Stemler, A. B. L. (1976). The races of sorghum in Africa. In *The Origins of African Plant Domestication*, ed. J. R. Harlan, J. M. J. deWet and A. B. L. Stemler, pp. 465–78. The Hague: Mouton Press.

Harlan, J. R. and Zohary, D. (1966). Distribution of wild wheats and barley. *Science*, **153**: 1074–80.

Harrington, J. P. (1932). *Tobacco among the Karuk Indians of California*. Smithsonian Institution Bureau of American Ethnology Bulletin, **94**.

Harris, D. and Hillman, G. C. (eds.) (1989) *Foraging and Farming: the Evolution of Plant Exploitation*. London: Unwin Hyman.

Hawkes, J. G. (1963). *A revision of the tuber-bearing Solanums*, 2nd edn. Edinburgh: Scottish Plant Breeding Station Records.

Hawkes. J. G. (1967). The history of the potato. *Journal of the Royal Horticultural Society*, **92**: 207–24, 249–62, 288–302, 364–5.

Hawkes, J. G. (1988). The evolution of cultivated potatoes and their tuber bearing wild relatives. *Külturpflanze*, **36**: 189–200.

Hawkes, J. G. (1989). The domestication of roots and tubers in the American tropics. In *Foraging and Farming: the Evolution of Plant Exploitation*, ed. D. Harris and G. C. Hillman, pp. 481–503. London: Unwin Hyman.

Healey, C. J. (1988). Culture as transformed disorder: cosmological evocation among the Maring. *Oceania*, **59**: 106–22.

Heiser, C. B. Jr (1989). Domestication of Cucurbitaceae: *Cucurbita* and *Lagenaria*. In *Foraging and Farming: the Evolution of Plant Exploitation*, ed. D. Harris and G. C. Hillman, pp. 471–80. London: Unwin Hyman.

Herodotus (1928). *The History of Herodotus*. Transl. by G. Rawlinson, ed. M. Komroff. New York: Tudor Publishing Co.

Higgs, E. S. (1967). The domestic animals. In *The Hawa Fteah (Cyrenaica)*, ed. C. B. M. McBurney, pp. 313–19. Cambridge: Cambridge University Press.

Higham, C. F. W. (1976). Reply to K. L. Hutterer. *Current Anthropology*, **17**: 221–42

Higham, C. F. W. and Maloney, B. (1989). Coastal adaptation, sedentism and intensification in prehistoric Southeast Asia. In *Foraging and Farming: the Evolution of Plant Exploitation*, ed. D. R. Harris and G. C. Hillman, pp. 650–66. London: Unwin Hyman.

Hillman, G., Colledge, S. M. and Harris, D. R. (1989). Plant-food economy during the epipalaeolithic period at Tell Abu Hureyra, Syria: dietary diversity, seasonality and modes of exploitation. In *Foraging and Farming: the Evolution of Plant Exploitation*, ed. D. R. Harris and G. C. Hillman, pp. 240–68. London: Unwin Hyman.

Ho, P.-T. (1969). The loess and the origin of Chinese agriculture. *American Historical Review*, **75**: 1–36.

Ho, P.-T. (1974). *The Cradle of the East: an Inquiry into the Indigenous Origins of Techniques and Ideas of Neolithic and Early Historic China 5,000–1,000 B.C.* Chicago: University of Chicago Press.

Hrozny, F. (1913). Das Getreide in alten Babylonien. *Sitzungsberichte der Kaiserliche Akademie der Wissenschaft*, Wien, **173**: 1–218.

Hutterer, K. L. (1983). The natural and cultural history of southeast Asian agricultural, ecological and evolutionary considerations. *Anthropos*, **78**: 169–212.

Iltis, H. (1983). From teosinte to maize: the catastrophic sexual transmutation. *Science*, **222**: 886–94.

Ingold, T., Riches, D. and Woodburn, J. (eds.) (1988). *Hunters and Gatherers*, 2 vols., Vol. I, *History, Evolution and Social Changes*, New York: Berg Publishers Inc.

Isaac, E. (1970). *Geography of Domestication*. Englewood Cliffs, NJ: Prentice Hall.

Jacobsen, T. and Adams, R. Mc. (1958). Salt and silt in ancient Mesopotamian agriculture. *Science*, **128**: 1251–8.

Janushevich, Z. V. (1978). Prehistoric food plants in south-west of the Soviet Union. *Berichte der Deutsche Botanische Geselschaft*, **91**: 59–66.

Jenkins, J. A. (1948). The origin of the cultivated tomato. *Economic Botany*, **2**: 379–92.

Johns, T. (1989). A chemical-ecological model of root and tuber domestication in the Andes. In *Foraging and Farming: the Evolution of Plant Exploitation*, ed. D. R. Harris and G. C. Hillman, pp. 504–22. London: Unwin Hyman.

Jones, R. (1969). Firestick farming. *Australian Natural History*, **16**: 224–28.

Jones, R. and Meehan, B. (1989). Plant foods of the Gidjingali: ethnographic and archaeological perspectives from northern Australia on tuber and seed exploitation. In *Foraging and Farming: the Evolution of Plant Exploitation*, ed. D. R. Harris and G. C. Hillman, pp. 120–35. London: Unwin Hyman.

Keatinge, R. W. (ed.) (1988). *Peruvian Prehistory*. Cambridge: Cambridge University Press.

Kirch, P. (1982). Advances in Polynesian prehistory: three decades in review. In *Advances in World Archaeology*, Vol. 1, pp. 51–97. New York: Academic Press.

Kislev M. (1973). Hiṭṭa and Kussamet. Notes on their interpretation. *Lesonenu*, **37**(2–3): 83–95.

Klimek, S. (1935). Culture element distributions: I. The structure of California Indian culture. *University of California Publications of American Archaeology and Ethnology*, **37**: 1–70.

Koyama, S. and D. H. Thomas (eds.) (1982). *Affluent Foragers Pacific Coasts, East and West*. Osaka, Japan: National Museum of Ethnology.

Ladizinsky, G. (1975). Collection of wild cereals in the upper Jordan Valley. *Economic Botany*, **29**: 264–7.

Lathrap, D. W. (1968). The 'hunting' economies of the tropical forest zone of South America: an attempt at historical perspective. In *Man the Hunter*, ed. R. B. Lee and I. DeVore, pp. 23–9. Chicago: Aldine.

Lathrap, D. W. (1977). Our father the cayman, our mother the gourd: Spinden revisited or a unitary model for the emergence of agriculture in the New World. In *Origins of Agriculture*, ed. C. A. Reed, pp. 713–51. The Hague: Mouton.

Latourette, K. S. (1941). *The Chinese, Their History and Culture*. New York: The Macmillan Co.

Laufer, B. (1919). *Sino–Iranica*. Chicago: Field Museum Publication, 201, Anthropology Series, Vol. 15.

Lee, R. B. (1968). What hunters do for a living, or how to make out on scarce resources. In *Man the Hunter*, ed. R. B. Lee and I. DeVore, pp. 30–48. Chicago: Aldine.

Lee, R. B. (1984). *The Dobe !Kung*. New York: Holt, Rinehart and Winston.

Lee, R. B. and DeVore, I. (1968*a*). *Man the Hunter*. Chicago: Aldine.

Lee, R. B. and DeVore, I. (1968*b*). Problems in the study of hunters and gatherers. In *Man the Hunter*, ed. R. B. Lee and I. DeVore, pp. 3–12. Chicago: Aldine.

Lévi-Strauss, C. (1950). The use of wild plants in tropical South America. In *Handbook of South American Indians*, Vol. 6, ed. J. H. Steward, pp. 465–86. Smithsonian Institution Bureau of American Ethnology Bulletin, **143**.

Lewis, H. T. (1989). Ecological and technological knowledge of fire: Aborigines versus park rangers in northern Australia. *American Anthropology*, **91**: 940–61.

Li, H.-L. (1970). The origin of cultivated plants in southeast Asia. *Economic Botany*, **24**: 3–19.

Logvinenko, N. S., Krass, P. M., Trut, L. N., Ivanova, L. N. and Belyaev, D. K. (1978). Genetics and phenogenetics of animal hormonal characteristics. IV. Effect of domestication on ontogenesis of androgen-secreting foxes. *Genetics*, **14**: 2177–83.

Lourandos, H. (1980). Changes or stability? Hydraulics, hunter–gatherers and population in temperate Australia. *World Archaeology*, **1**: 245–64.

Loy, T. H. and Wood, A. R. (1989). Blood residue analysis at Çayönü Tepesi. *Journal of Field Archaeology*, **16**: 451–60.

Lucas, A. (1962). *Ancient Egyptian Materials and Industries*, 4th edn. Revised and enlarged by J. R. Harris. London: Edward Arnold.

Lynch, T. F. (1980). *Guitarrero Cave: Early Man in the Andes*. New York: Academic Press.

Mabuchi, T. (1964). Tales concerning the origin of grains in the insular areas of Eastern and Southeastern Asia. *Asian Folklore Studies* **23**: 1–92.

MacDonald, B. (1988). *The Wadi el Hasa Archaeological Survey 1979–1983, West-Central Jordan*. Waterloo, Ontario: Wilfred Lauries University Press.

MacNeish, R. S. (1983). Mesoamerica. In *Early Man in The New World*, ed. R. Shutler, pp. 125–35. Beverly Hills, CA: Sage Publications.

Mangelsdorf, P. C. (1986). The origin of corn. *Scientific American*, **255**: 72–8.

Mangelsdorf, P. C., MacNeish, R. S. and Galinat. W. C. (1967). Prehistoric maize, teosinte and *Tripsacum* from Tamaulipas, Mexico. *Botany Museum Leaflets, Harvard University*, **22**(2): 33–63.

Masson, V. M. (1968). The urban revolution in South Turkmenia. *Antiquity*, **42**: 178–87.

Maurice, T. (1795). *The History of Hindoostan*, 2 vols. New Delhi, Novrang.

Mayer, F. H. (transl. and ed.) (1986). *The Yanagita Kunio Guide to the Japanese Folktale*. Bloomington: Indiana University Press.

Meadow, R. H. (1984). Animal domestication in the Middle East: view from the eastern margin. In *Animals and Archaeology*, Vol. 3, *Early Herders and Their Flocks*, ed. J. Clutton-Brock and C. Grigson, pp. 309–37. Oxford: BAR International Series No. 202.

Meggers, B. J., Ayensu, E. S. and Duckworth, W. D. (eds.) (1973). *Tropical Forest Ecosystems in Africa and South America Comparative Review*. Washington, DC: Smithsonian Institution Press.

Moore, D. R. (1976). Reply to Hutterer. *American Anthropology*, **17**: 221–42.

Muzzolini, A. (1987). Les premiers moutons sahariens d'aprés les figurations repustres. *Archaeozoologia*, **I92**: 129–48.

Muzzolini, A. (1988). Une ébauche de scénario pour le peuplement ovin ancient dans le Basin méditérranien. In *Populations Traditionélles et Premières Races Standardisées d'Ovicaprinae dans le Basin méditérranien*, ed. J. J. Lauvergne, pp. 289–98. Paris: Les Colloques d'INRA No. 47, Editions INRR.

Muzzolini, A. (1989*a*). La 'Néolithisation' du nord de d'Afrique et ses causes. In *Néolithisations*, ed. D. Aurenche and S. Cauvin, pp. 145–86. Oxford: BAR International Series, No. 516.

Muzzolini, A. (1989*b*). Les débuts de la doméstication des animaux en Afrique: faits et problèmes, In *Ethnozootechnie No. 42. État Sauvage Apprivoisement, état domestique*, pp. 7–22. Paris: Journée d'étude du 26-10-88.

Nabhan, G. and DeWet, J. M. J. (1984). *Panicum sonorum* in Sonoran desert agriculture. *Economic Botany*, **38**: 65–82.

National Research Council (1989). *Lost Crops of the Incas.* Washington: National Academy Press.

Newberry, P. E. (1893). *Beni Hasan,* Part I. London: Kegan Paul, Trench Trübner & Co.

Nicholaisen, J. (1963). *Ecology and Culture of the Pastoral Tuareg.* Copenhagen: Copenhagen National Museum.

Nordenskiöld, E. (1922). Deductions suggested by the geographical distribution of some pre-Columbian words used by the Indians of S. America. *Comparative Ethnographic Studies*, **5**. Göteborg: Elanders Boktryckeri Aktiebolag.

Noy, T., Legge, A. J. and Higgs, E. S. (1973). Recent excavations at Nahal Oren Israel. *Proceedings of the Prehistoric Society*, **39**: 75–99.

O'Connell, J. F., Hawkes, K. and Blurton Jones, N. (1988). Hadza scavenging: implications for Plio/Pleistocene homonid subsistence. *Current Anthropology*, **29**: 356–63.

Oka, H. I. (1988). *Origin of Cultivated Rice.* New York, Japan Scientific Societies; for USA and Canada: Elsevier.

Oldfather, C. H. (transl.) (1946). *Diodorus of Sicily*, 10 vols. Cambridge, MA: Harvard University Press.

Oviedo, y. Valdes, G. V. de (1944). *Historia General y Natural de las Indias.* Asunción, Paraguay: Guaranía.

Peeters, J. P. (1988). The emergence of new centers of diversity: evidence from barley. *Theoretical and Applied Genetics*, **76**: 17–24.

Pickersgill, B. (1989). Cytological and genetical evidence on the domestication and diffusion of crops within the Americas. In *Foraging and Farming: the Evolution of Plant Exploitation*, ed. D. R. Harris and G. C. Hillman, pp. 426–39. London: Unwin Hyman.

Pimentel, D. (1974). *Energy Use in World Food Production.* Environmental Biology Report 74–1. Ithaca, NY: Cornell University.

Pimentel, D. and Hall, C. W. (eds.) (1989). *Food and Natural Resources.* New York: Academic Press.

Piperno, D. R. (1989). Non-affluent foragers: resource availability, seasonal shortages, and the emergence of agriculture in Panamanian tropical forests. In *Foraging and Farming: the Evolution of Plant Exploitation*, ed. D. R. Harris and G. C. Hillman, pp. 538–54. London: Unwin Hyman.

Pliny (1950). *Natural History.* Transl. by H. Rackham. Cambridge, MA: Harvard University Press.

Pope, G. G. (1989). Bamboo and human evolution. *Natural History*, **10**/89: 48–57.

Prescot, W. H. (1936). *History of the Conquest of Mexico and History of the Conquest of Peru.* New York: Modern Library.

Price, T. D. and Brown, J. A. (1985). *Prehistoric Hunter–Gatherers: the Emergence of Cultural Complexity.* New York: Academic Press.

Pyramarn, K. (1989). New evidence on plant exploitation and environment during the Hoabinhian (late stone age) from Ban Kao caves, Thailand. In *Foraging and Farming: the Evolution of Plant Exploitation*, ed. D. R. Harris and G. C. Hillman, pp. 282–91. London: Unwin Hyman.

Ray, V. P. (1963). *Primitive Pragmatists: the Modoc Indians of Northern California*, Seattle: American Ethnological Society, University of Washington Press.

Recinos, A. (1947). *Popol Vuh, Las Antiguas Historias del Quiché*. Mexico, DF: Fondo de Cultura Economica.

Renfrew, C. (1975). *Before Civilization: the Radiocarbon Revolution and Prehistoric Europe*. New York: Alfred A. Knopf.

Renfrew, J. M. (1969). The archaeological evidence for the domestication of plants: methods and problems. In *The Domestication and Exploitation of Plants and Animals*, ed. P. J. Ucko and G. W. Dimbleby, pp. 149–72. Chicago: Aldine.

Riches, D. (1982). *Northern Nomadic Hunter–Gatherers a Humanistic Approach*, p. 242. London: Academic Press.

Rick, J. W. (1980). *Prehistoric Hunters of the High Andes*. New York: Academic Press.

Ruddiman, W. F. and Wright, H. E. (eds.) (1987). *North America and Adjacent Oceans During the Last Deglaciation. The Geology of North America*, Vol. K-3. Boulder, CO: Geological Society of America.

Sahlins, M. (1968). Notes on the original affluent society. In *Man the Hunter*, ed. R. B. Lee and I. DeVore, pp. 85–9. Chicago: Aldine.

Salaman, R. N. (1949). *The History and Social Influence of the Potato*. Cambridge: Cambridge University Press.

Sauer, C. O. (1952). *Agricultural Origins and Dispersals*. Cambridge, MA: MIT Press.

Schmitz, P. I. (1987). Prehistoric hunters and gatherers of Brazil. *Journal of World Prehistory*, **1**: 53–126.

Shipek, F. C. (1989). An example of intensive plant husbandry: the Kumeyaay of southern California. In *Foraging and Farming: the Evolution of Plant Exploitation*, ed. D. R. Harris and G. C. Hillman, pp. 159–70. London: Unwin Hyman.

Shutler, R. Jr. (ed.) (1983). *Early Man in the New World*. Beverly Hills, CA: Sage Publications.

Siegler, D. S. and Perera, J. F. (1981). Modernized preparation of cassava in the Llanos Orientales of Venezuela. *Economic Botany*, **35**: 356–62.

Silberbauer, G. B. (1981). *Hunter and Habitat in the Central Kalahari Desert*. Cambridge: Cambridge University Press.

Simmonds, N. W. (1976a) Quinoa and relatives. In *Evolution of Crop Plants*, ed. N. W. Simmonds, pp. 29–30. London: Longman.

Simmonds, N. W. (1976b). Sugarcanes. In *Evolution of Crop Plants*, ed. N. W. Simmonds, pp. 104–8. London: Longman.

Simmonds, N. W. (1976c). Bananas. In *Evolution of Crop Plants*, ed. N. W. Simmonds, pp. 211–15. London: Longman.

Simoons, F. J. (1970). The traditional limits of milking and milk use in Southern Asia. *Anthropos*, **65**: 547–93.

Snowden, J. D. (1936). *The Cultivated Races of Sorghum*. London: Allard and Son.

Spriggs, M. (1989). The dating of the Island Southeast Asian Neolithic: an attempt at chronometric hygiene and linguistic correlation. *Antiquity*, **63**: 587–613.

Stanford, D. (1983). Pre-Clovis occupation south of the ice sheets. In *Early Man in the New World*, ed. R. Shutler, pp. 65–72. Beverly Hills, CA: Sage Publications.

Steward, J. M. (1934). Ethnography of the Owens Valley Paiute. *University of California Publications of American Archaeology and Ethnology*, **33**: 233–40.

Vanderplank, J. E. (1968). *Disease Resistance in Plants*. New York: Academic Press.

Vanzolini, P. E. (1973). Paleoclimates, relief and species multiplication in equatorial forests. In *Tropical Forest Ecosystems in Africa and South America: a Comparative Review*, ed. B. J. Meggers, E. S. Ayensu and W. D. Duckworth. Washington, DC: Smithsonian Institution.

Vavilov, N. I. (1926). *Studies on the Origin of Cultivated Plants*. Leningrad: State Press. (Russian and English).

Vega, G. de la (1961). *The Royal Commentaries of the Inca Garcilaso de la Vega*. New York: Orion.

Wafer, L. (1903). *A New Voyage and Description of the Isthmus of America*. Cleveland, OH: G. P. Winship, The Burrows Bros.

Walters, I. (1989). Intensified fishery production at Morton Bay, southeast Queensland, in the late Holocene. *Antiquity*, **63**: 215–24.

Wendorf, F., Schild, R., El Hadidi, N., Close, A., Kobusiewicz, M., Wieckowska, H., Issawi, B. and Haas, H. (1979). Use of barley in the Egyptian late paleolithic. *Science*, **205**: 1341–7.

Wenke, R. J. (1984). *Patterns in Prehistory*, 2nd ed. Oxford: Oxford University Press.

West, B. and Zhou, B.-X. (1988). Did chickens go north? New evidence for domestication. *Journal of Archaeological Science* **15**: 515–33.

White, P. and Connell, J. F. (1982). *A Prehistory of Australia, New Guinea and Sahul*. Sydney: Academic Press.

Wilbert, J. (1987). *Tobacco and Shamanism in South America. Psychoactive Plants of the World*. New Haven, CT: Yale University Press.

Wilke, P. J. Bettinger, R., King, T. F. and O'Connell, J. F. (1972). Harvest selection and domestication in seed plants. *Antiquity*, **46**: 203–8.

Wilkes, H. G. (1967). *Teosinte: The Closest Relative of Maize*. Cambridge, MA: Bussey Institute, Harvard University

Williams, N. and Hunn, E. (eds.) (1982). *Resource Managers North American and Australian Hunter–Gatherers*. Boulder, CO: Westview Press.

Winterhalder, B. and Smith, E. A. (eds.) (1981). *Hunter–Gatherer Foraging Strategies: Ethnographic and Archaeological Analysis*. Chicago: University of Chicago Press.

Woodburn, J. (1988). African hunter–gatherer social organization: is it best understood as a product of encapsulation? In *Hunters and Gatherers, Vol. I, History Evolution and Social Change*, ed. T. Ingold, D. Riches and J. Woodburn, pp. 31–64. New York: Berg Publishers Inc.

Yen, D. E. (1989). The domestication of environment. In *Foraging and Farming: the Evolution of Plant Exploitation*, ed. D. R. Harris and G. C. Hillman, pp. 55–75. London: Unwin Hyman.

Zohary, D. (1989). Domestication of the southwest Asian Neolithic crop assemblage of cereals, pulses and flax: the evidence from the living plants. In *Foraging and Farming: the Evolution of Plant Exploitation*, ed. D. R. Harris and G. C. Hillman, pp. 358–73. London: Unwin Hyman.

Zohary, D. and Hopf, M. (1988). *Domestication of Plants in the Old World*. Oxford: Clarendon Press.

Index

Numbers in italic denote illustrations or tables.